Globalizing Afghanistan

American Encounters/Global Interactions

A series edited by Gilbert M. Joseph and Emily S. Rosenberg

GLOBALIZING AFGHANISTAN

Terrorism, War, and the Rhetoric of Nation Building

EDITED BY ZUBEDA JALALZAI & DAVID JEFFERESS

Duke University Press *Durham & London 2011*

© 2011 Duke University Press
All rights reserved

Printed in the United States of America
on acid-free paper ∞

Designed by Jennifer Hill
Typeset in Arno Pro and Chestnut
by Keystone Typesetting, Inc.

Library of Congress
Cataloging-in-Publication Data
appear on the last printed page
of this book.

For my parents
Abdur Raheem & Amina Jalalzai

— ZJ

American Encounters/Global Interactions

A series edited by Gilbert M. Joseph and Emily S. Rosenberg

This series aims to stimulate critical perspectives and fresh interpretive frameworks for scholarship on the history of the imposing global presence of the United States. Its primary concerns include the deployment and contestation of power, the construction and deconstruction of cultural and political borders, the fluid meanings of intercultural encounters, and the complex interplay between the global and the local. *American Encounters* seeks to strengthen dialogue and collaboration between historians of U.S. international relations and area studies specialists.

The series encourages scholarship based on multiarchival historical research. At the same time, it supports a recognition of the representational character of all stories about the past and promotes critical inquiry into issues of subjectivity and narrative. In the process, *American Encounters* strives to understand the context in which meanings related to nations, cultures, and political economy are continually produced, challenged, and reshaped.

Contents

❦

Acknowledgments

We first conceptualized *Globalizing Afghanistan* in 2002 as the theme for Rhode Island College's October Series, an annual art, film, and lecture series of the Faculty of Arts and Sciences. We would like to thank all of those who helped to bring issues of globalization and Afghanistan to the fore at that critical historical moment. For this opportunity I thank Rhode Island College and in particular the Rhode Island College Foundation, the School of Arts and Sciences, the College Lectures Committee, the Committee on General Education, the Bannister Gallery, the Artists' Co-op, the Departments of Anthropology, Art, English, History, Political Science, and Sociology, and the Film Studies Program for financial as well as creative support. I thank my colleagues Paola Ferrario, Carolyn Fluehr-Lobban, Richard Lobban, Spencer Hall, Claus Hofhansel, Donna Kelly, Laura Khoury, Marlene Lopes, Eung-Jun Min, Dan Moos, Dennis O'Malley, Katherine Rudolph-Larrea, Robert Shein, Amritjit Singh, Claudia Springer, Bryan Steinberg, and Dave Thomas for helping to bring the series into being. For her administrative support I am greatly indebted to Bernadette Doyle. Most of all I would like to thank the dean of arts and sciences at that time, Richard Weiner, for not only supporting this October Series but for establishing the series in the first place. His tenure as dean did much to encourage faculty research and enhance the intellectual community of Rhode Island College. In this capacity, we will sorely miss his caring and enthusiastic leadership.

We would like to thank the reviewers and editors at Duke University Press for helping us to refine these essays and our project overall and helping us to integrate these essays into a cohesive manuscript. In particular we thank Reynolds Smith, Valerie Millholland, and Sharon Torian.

We also thank Naomi Pauls, who provided the index for the book, and the Okanagan campus of the University of British Columbia for providing a Publication Grant.

Thanks to Dan Moos for his insightful and valuable readings of the manuscript throughout its various incarnations, and for his love and support throughout the entire process. With great affection I also thank my children, Kazim, Zaid, and Imani, for sharing me with the project.

— ZJ

Introduction

Globalizing Afghanistan

Zubeda Jalalzai & David Jefferess

Globalizing Afghanistan: Terrorism, War, and the Rhetoric of Nation Building
brings together the work of distinguished international scholars and activists in various disciplines and proximities to the region, those who have
worked actively on the ground and those with more long-term political or
philosophical perspectives, in order to situate Afghanistan within global
networks of power and influence. Studying Afghanistan offers key insights
into globalization as both a theoretical concept and a political, economic,
and cultural process. Likewise engaging globalization in this study raises
critical questions about Afghanistan's current positioning in the world as a
sovereign nation-state as well as contemporary international politics and
the project of nation building more generally. Contested spaces like Iraq,
Palestine, Guantánamo Bay, and Afghanistan have played vital roles in
contemporary politics as sites of war, resistance, and detention in the U.S.-
led war on terror. These spaces are variously nonnational or neonational
and as such are difficult to define within traditional understandings of the
nation and even within typical perceptions of internationalism, particularly international law. Further, Iraq and Afghanistan, as transitional states
under UN mandate, have been recuperated within emerging discourses of
human security and international responsibility as sites of contemporary

nation-building projects, following those (continuing) in Bosnia, Kosovo, Cambodia, and Timor-Leste. The invasion and occupation of Afghanistan and the international project of Afghanistan's national reconstitution illustrate the complicated workings of global power, capital, citizenship, and justice. As such the essays in this collection reveal how Afghanistan is being globalized and how the ongoing conflict there requires an engagement with the framework of globalization.

Globalization, in our understanding, rearranges certain national and ideological boundaries and redirects international movements of capital, people, and ideas in a world driven by information, expansive economic change, and a general compression of both time and space that in some instances contracts the world and at others creates even greater distances. Globalization accounts in part for the permeability of national and regional boundaries in the current Euro-American presence in Afghanistan, a site of contemporary warfare and resistance that likewise cross and redefine national boundaries. We understand globalization as a political, economic, and cultural process heavily reliant on technology to effect global transfers of information, money, culture, and people, manifested in varied and often paradoxical ways. Critics have seen at least two major trends in globalization. On the one hand, globalization moves to standardize the world in terms of language, currency, value, lifestyle, and the like— what has been called the Coca-Colonization and McDonaldization of the globe.[1] On the other, globalization hybridizes cultures through an amalgamation of previously distant or distinct products and citizens. Between these two poles emerges a variety of permutations of and responses to those possibilities. For instance, in the wake of the cold war's polarization of the global order, the emergence of ethnically or religiously based "nationalisms" can be both a reaction against the globalization of consumer capital and a function of this very same process. While the prevailing logic of globalization and unregulated capitalism is to eliminate political and symbolic borders, the conflict in Afghanistan reveals the continued significance of borders. For instance, the ambiguous space of the Afghan-Pakistani border created by the infamous Durand Line, drawn by the British foreign secretary Mortimer Durand in the late nineteenth century, was not recognized by those on either side who maintained ethnic identification with one another. This porous border problematized the construction of distinct national identities and frustrated U.S. and NATO military forces' attempts to stem the Taliban insurgency. The fluidity of the Afghan border, transgressed by the very act of invasion and international nation building, ironically illuminates the stability of the borders of the intervening nations, who attempt to maintain highly fortified barriers against objectionable immigrants and economically threatening products.

The essays in *Globalizing Afghanistan* provide an important intervention in both the ongoing analysis of the conflict and the nation-building project in Afghanistan and in current theories of globalization. Much of the analysis of the ongoing war in Afghanistan focuses on the politics and rationale of the U.S.-led military intervention, and our introduction is no exception. The essays, however, examine the conflict's influences and effects on the fluidity of the Afghan-Pakistan border, global routes of the opium trade, the role of Afghanistan as a site for evolving articulations of transnationalism (particularly feminist transnationalism), and Afghanistan's place in the imaginary of Iranian film. As the conflict continues these essays necessarily become historical themselves, shaped by the contexts of Afghan economic and political agency, the social position of women, the ongoing politics of gender, and Afghanistan as a signifier of the "failed state" or the resurgent nation. These essays provide important engagements with the theoretical concerns of globalization studies, particularly the post–cold war politics of war and the hegemonic project of nation building, democratization, human rights, and global integration.

As we suggest in our discussion of Michael Hardt's and Antonio Negri's *Empire* and *Multitude*, a stable political and cultural—though not singular or totalizing—theory of globalization is continually troubled by its events. While economic and cultural globalization after the cold war seemed to dismantle the center-periphery dichotomy and require a radically new understanding of global relations of power, the war on terror, and specifically its battlefields of Afghanistan and Iraq, has restored the need for a critique of imperial politics. Indeed Afghanistan has become an ideological battleground, at times an example of the emergence of a postnational cosmopolitan political ethic and at other times an example of the nation-state's reestablished preeminence through the ongoing NATO intervention, justified in terms of national security and international order. The course of the conflict has foiled attempts to understand it: from the seeming end of military hostilities in 2003 to the restoration of nation building and human, particularly gender rights as the dominant frames for understanding Afghanistan, to the resurgence of the Taliban throughout the country in the middle of the decade, and, at the time of this collection's publication, a significantly increased U.S. military engagement not only in Afghanistan but, under the Obama administration, also in Pakistan's border regions. This collection does not seek to provide a definitive retheorizing of globalization. The various close engagements with the politics of women's rights, the production and export of opium, the ambivalent position of Pukhtoon journalists, and the role of the intellectual in contending with specific globalized conflicts all transcend the historical moment of their writing.

One could argue that from its location on the legendary Silk Road and its long history of invaders and imperial rulers (Aryans, Persians, Greeks, Arabs, Mongols, Mughals, English, and Soviets) Afghanistan is no stranger to internationalization.[2] Ironically Afghanistan's exposure to outside forces and influences sits alongside its apparent separation and isolation from the rest of the world. Travelers ranging from adventurers, explorers, and soldiers even into the contemporary era speak of Afghanistan as a forgotten place and perceive themselves as part of a select group who see, firsthand, what most of their countrymen could never access.[3] After the Soviet defeat and the subsequent withdrawal of both the Soviets and the U.S. in the late 1980s, Afghanistan during the period of civil war and under the Taliban seemed particularly shut out from global consciousness. From the beginning of the current conflict, however, globalization has played a significant role in framing Afghanistan. Refusing the unidirectionality of border crossings and violent foreign strikes and expropriating America's own technologies of travel, the hijackers on September 11, 2001, targeted centers of U.S. commercial and political power. In a very immediate way the logic of globalization accounted for the possibility of such attacks, for once networks of travel and political influence were established those pathways became available for variable and unintended uses. Furthermore the concerted efforts of the U.S. at the time to limit the direction of global exchanges (adopting protectionist and isolationist policies while insisting on its own ubiquity in the international arena) narrowed the pathways available for international exchange such that the most efficacious avenue for confrontation led right to the heart of U.S. political, cultural, and economic centers. The attacks also underscored another global force: a concentrated Islamist reaction against the United States.[4] This basic conflict between the forces of empire, as defined by Hardt and Negri, and Islamism—both global in perspective—vied for dominance in Central Asia before and after the September 11 attacks.[5]

Nonetheless journalists, politicians, and many academics represented the attacks as marking a fundamental change in global politics and the role of the United States and Europe in the world. Alternatively the attacks provided another example of the failure of international bodies, such as the United Nations, to provide global security and to avoid the predictable consequences of U.S. foreign policy in the Middle East since the Second World War. Coming a year after the publication of Hardt's and Negri's *Empire*, which posited a new global "bio-power" without center and margins, these attacks reinscribed the notion of an imperial center at odds with a disorderly "barbarian" periphery. To that point the emergent field of globalization theory appeared to distinguish itself from postcolonialism by, for instance, disrupting the "tendency to see globalization as little more than a form of intensified neo-imperialism headquartered in the United States," albeit as primarily a cultural project of shaping a global hegemony based on consumerism, capitalism, and modernity.[6] Yet in the late 1990s theories of globalization also imagined, from a cultural studies perspective, the emergence of a cosmopolitan or hybrid global culture,[7] or, from an international relations perspective, the emergence of a post–cold war order that would be marked not by a politics of national interest but by an ethical politics of human security that privileged the needs of the individual over the sovereignty of the state. From a variety of perspectives globalization marked a renewed commitment to the universality of humanity, at least rhetorically. After September 11 these ideals of a universal order marked by cosmopolitanism and an emergent international community seem to have been much too hopeful. These same narratives have been recuperated to justify and explain the ongoing Euro-American intervention in Afghanistan, at times seeming to replace and provide an antithesis to the rhetoric of a war on terror—and its seemingly overt neo-imperial designs. At other moments they are recuperated within a rhetoric of justice as vengeance and humanitarian uplift.

Dismissing such a narrative, commentators such as Noam Chomsky, among many others, criticized the initial military action by the U.S. and the U.K. in Afghanistan as a bold act of colonial conquest. While the United States claimed war as an act of retribution for the September 11 attacks— President Bush boasting, "We will find those who did it; we will smoke them out of their holes; we will get them running and we'll bring them to justice"—Chomsky observed that the war in Afghanistan "left the U.S. with military bases in Afghanistan and Central Asia, helping to position U.S. corporations more favorably in the current phase of the great game to control Central Asian resources, and also to extend the encirclement of the far more important Persian Gulf."[8] (Chomsky's use of the past tense here indicates the belief, widely held at the time, that the military aspect of the intervention in Afghanistan had been completed by early 2003.) The very words of key figures in these interventions reinforce the thesis that the U.S.-led invasions and occupations of Afghanistan and Iraq constitute a project of expanding and solidifying America's global dominance. The Project for a New American Century's "Statement of Principles"—which Dick Cheney, Donald Rumsfeld, and Paul Wolfowitz all signed—claimed in 1997 that for the United States to maintain its post–cold war position as the world's "preeminent power," it had to "accept responsibility for America's unique role in preserving and extending an international order friendly to [American] security, [American] prosperity, and [American] principles."[9] The Bush administration's rhetoric justifying the wars in Afghanistan and Iraq vacillated from representations of the United States acting alone to wield justice to engaging in a humanitarian project of bringing democracy and freedom to the rest of the world. However, President Obama's speech in December 2009 outlining "the way forward in Afghanistan and Pakistan" frames the military "push" much more narrowly in terms of the national security of the United States and its NATO allies: "Our overarching goal remains the same: to disrupt, dismantle, and defeat al Qaeda in Afghanistan and Pakistan, and to prevent its capacity to threaten America and our allies in the future."[10] Following an extensive review process Obama announced in March 2009 and reasserted in December of that year a rapid deployment of more than thirty thousand

additional U.S. troops, who will "target the insurgency, break its momentum, and better secure population centers," as well as train Afghan security
forces, with the aim of beginning to reduce combat troops by July 2011.[11]
This policy marks the return to a war-fighting stance for the United States,
a project of defeating the Taliban and al Qaeda, at the same time that
President Karzai of Afghanistan seeks negotiations with the Taliban.

Traditional understandings of neocolonialism do not account for the
new global right, as theorized by Hardt and Negri, that not only provides a
rhetoric for the foreign policy of the U.S. and its allies, but also informs
how the West and North understand and imagine a globalized world. The
complex way notions of terrorism, war, security, and the rhetoric of nation
building are at play in the international community's intervention in Afghanistan provides insight into the evolving idea of globalization. The
ongoing NATO military and international administrative presence in Afghanistan reflects both the rupture in thinking about globalization following September 11 as well as the recuperation, with modifications, of post–
cold war political theories of globalization. For instance, while the role of
UN peace operations provided a relatively minor and prefatory point of
discussion in Hardt's and Negri's *Empire* (2000), in *Multitude* (2004),
published after the invasions of Afghanistan and Iraq, Hardt and Negri
characterize war as the regime of biopower and as the primary organizing
principle of the global order.[12] This new global right is premised on inter-
dependence, connectedness, and commonality but requires surveillance,
coercion, and enforcement. David Chandler writes, "Today the language of
'interests' has been superseded by that 'Other-regarding' ethics which appears to have taken the politics of power and interests out of foreign
policy."[13] In *Empire in Denial* Chandler argues that through the discourses
of capacity building, empowerment, needs, and the apparent universality
of democracy and national sovereignty, Western states deny their specific
political interests and influence in shaping a global order. The United
States, Great Britain, and Canada, to name but three of the primary external state players in Afghanistan's nation-building process, exercise the
seemingly contradictory fear *for* the other (using the discourse of rescue
and humanitarian assistance) and fear *of* the other (using the discourse
of national security) in a way that denies the imperial designs or consequences of their intervention. Indeed President Obama's justification for

the military push scheduled for 2010 to July 2011 repeatedly disavowed
any imperial framework for the American presence in Afghanistan, asserting that the United States seeks to be Afghanistan's "partner, and never
[its] patron."[14]

Representations of Canada's role in the conflict provide an example of
the way these distinct and paradoxical discourses can function simultaneously to justify the military presence in Afghanistan and, more importantly,
the complex and contradictory demarcations of the "nation" within a context of globalization and cosmopolitanism. Canada's representation of this
intervention and the mainstream media's coverage of Canadian military
operations in Afghanistan have served to reinforce the Canadian state,
both as political entity and cultural imaginary. For instance, Canada's policy toward Afghanistan, as articulated in 2007, was shaped by a 3-D framework (diplomacy, defense, and development) titled "Protecting Canadians
—Rebuilding Afghanistan." Hence Canada's role in Afghanistan is constructed by a rhetoric of both benevolence and national self-preservation;
on the one hand, Canadian forces are protecting Canadians by battling
"terrorists" overseas, while on the other, Canadian soldiers are dying in
order to facilitate the development of Afghanistan and its people. These
discourses mask political interests that conform neither to fear *of* nor fear
for the Other, but reflect Canada's integration in a global system; as critics
of Canada's role in Afghanistan from both the left and the right of the
political spectrum have noted, with its role in Afghanistan, Canada gains a
voice among the Western powers disproportional to its size and maintains
positive diplomatic relations with the United States, upon which the Canadian economy depends.[15]

While earlier analyses of globalization were preoccupied with explicat-
ing and critiquing forms of cultural imperialism—American media, for
instance—or the spread of consumer capitalism through the neoliberal
policies of international financial institutions, the UN-sanctioned intervention in Afghanistan marks the way democracy has become the central
conceptual principle of the global order after September 11. Economic and
cultural formulations of globalization may be seen as folded into and
therefore necessary to the ideal of a standardized democratic form of
governance. In both Afghanistan and Iraq the initial U.S.-led invasion and
destruction of the political order became elided from historical memory
and replaced with the notion that the international project of democracy

promotion results from these states having failed. The rhetoric of the "failed" or "fragile" state, which has become central to the foreign policies of countries in the Organization for Economic Cooperation and Development, constructs the functioning state as necessarily democratic, as defined by the West.[16] They may have been antidemocratic, but the Baath and Taliban regimes in Iraq and Afghanistan, respectively, constituted a political order; indeed the Taliban's establishment of order ending Afghanistan's civil war won it acceptance by many Afghans and the tacit support of the United States, among other countries.[17] In the context of these various, and sometimes contrasting, discourses of nation building, democracy promotion, and international security, Afghanistan emerged as an important site for investigating globalization in part because of how the invasion and occupation of Iraq had marginalized the Afghanistan conflict and normalized the presence of the multinational force in Afghanistan as a humanitarian project.

Globalizing Afghanistan focuses on Afghanistan as a paradigmatic example of a globalized national space. In fact many of the components of the war in Iraq had their counterparts in the Afghan case, such as violent internal opposition, the abuse of prisoners, rampant crime and political corruption, and the use of contractors rather than soldiers and other official personnel. Most significant are the steps taken by the international community to establish ostensibly democratic nations in both spaces by strategically supporting local leaders who are subsequently legitimized by national elections. Despite the continued violence and ethnic divisions that threaten national unity, the United States had positioned Afghanistan as a success story and, as George W. Bush remarked in 2004 in the final presidential campaign debate against Senator John Kerry, as evidence of "freedom on the march." U.S. Secretary of State Colin Powell described the Afghan elections as representative of the universal nature of the human desire for democracy:

The people of Afghanistan showed us . . . that democracy applies anywhere in the world where people are given the opportunity to practice it. . . . I think it is illustrative of what is possible in other parts of the world, certainly illustrative of what can happen in Iraq. . . . I believe the people of Iraq want the same thing the people in Afghanistan and the people in so many nations want: the opportunities to step forward to decide who will be their future leaders.[18]

At the time, the apparent successes in Afghanistan, its seemingly smooth transition to democracy and a new nationalism initiated by the Afghan war, justified the invasion of Iraq. If forces could quell terrorist uprisings and insurgencies, the people's universal desire for democracy would surface.

Powell's understanding that people desire to choose their own leaders may seem paradoxical since Afghans and Iraqis did not select their incumbents, and the Afghan government had only limited influence outside of Kabul, responding more to the policies of international NGOs than to the electorate. Geoff T. Harris, writing generally of NGOs, suggests that while their long-term effectiveness has certainly been one issue, "a more serious danger is that NGO projects may disrupt local markets and traditions, thereby inadvertently fostering a dependency syndrome within communities."[19] Tariq Ali reflects on this dynamic in the Afghan case seven years after the first engagement:

The problem was not lack of funds but the Western state-building project itself, by its nature an exogenous process—aiming to construct an army able to suppress its own population but incapable of defending the nation from outside powers; a civil administration with no control over planning or social infrastructure, which are in the hands of Western NGOs; and a government whose foreign policy marches in step with Washington's. It bore no relation to the realities on the ground.[20]

Furthermore, as has become increasingly clear, the Afghan case is far from the success story anticipated by the Bush administration even after a second round of presidential elections in 2009, which were intended to more authentically legitimize the Afghan government by countering the perception that outside powers were engineering Afghans' choice of leaders. Widespread charges of corruption and vote tampering further complicated this supposed culmination of Western-style democracy. In justifying the military push in 2010, President Obama distanced the United States from the Afghan nation-building project, placing responsibility for its success—and by implication its failures since 2003—squarely on Afghans themselves. Paradoxically the globalization of the war on terror and concurrent, and often consequent, humanitarian assistance in Afghanistan necessitated nation building, because, according to Christopher Freeman, "the laws that protect human rights cannot be enforced without government . . . nor can public services be sustained or poverty eradicated without social and economic development. . . . Similarly, the containment and persecution of terrorist groups cannot be assured without the rule of law."[21] These goals require the construction of a national entity to effect them. Quite directly, therefore, internationalism constitutes a key element in the very structure of such nations.

Global politics in fact explains the degree of correlation between the wars in Iraq and Afghanistan, which began very much in dialogue with one another.[22] Key exchanges between these countries on both the nationalizing and the insurgent fronts had been in play throughout. For example, the exchange of resistance tactics such as the kidnapping of foreigners, a repeated occurrence in the Iraqi insurgency, were taken up initially in Afghanistan with the kidnapping of three international United Nations election workers in October 2004.[23] Their abduction cast a pall on the first Afghan elections that were otherwise hailed as a great success. The Karzai administration denied claims that they agreed to release twenty-four Taliban prisoners in exchange for the UN workers but did acknowledge that their release impacted Afghanistan's reputation and "national pride."[24] An example of rhetorical correspondence between Iraq and Afghanistan is evident in the use in both nations of the term *mujahideen*, an Arabic word meaning "ones who struggle." Earlier the term referred to Afghan resistance to the Soviet invasion starting in 1979; those mujahideen were backed by the United States, and President Reagan introduced their leaders on the White House lawn as "the moral equivalents of America's founding fathers."[25] Later, however, *mujahideen* also came to refer to the guerrilla fighters in Iraq now set squarely against the international forces.

Issues regarding detention and justice have also circulated among the neo- or nonnational spaces of Guantánamo Bay, Afghanistan, and Iraq. The connection between Guantánamo Bay and Afghanistan rested on the fact that the U.S. naval station is under U.S. jurisdiction yet outside the bounds of the United States, a situation that allowed the United States to detain prisoners there without according them the due process generally available to prisoners in the United States or to POWs under the Geneva Convention.[26] The treatment of Taliban prisoners of war in Afghanistan links Afghan and Iraqi prisoners, according to Seymour M. Hersh, because the mishandling of Taliban POWs set the stage for the abuses at Abu

Ghraib, the Iraqi prison run by the U.S. military. Referring to the report on the Abu Ghraib abuses written by Provost Marshal Donald Ryder, Hersh says, "There was evidence dating back to the Afghanistan war . . . that M.P.s had worked with intelligence operatives to 'set favorable conditions for subsequent interviews'—a euphemism for breaking the will of prisoners."[27] Alexander Cockburn contends that the abuses in Afghanistan were tantamount to war crimes, as with the hundreds of Taliban prisoners of war who suffocated in container trucks or those executed without any legal mandate.[28] According to Jameel Jaffer and Amrit Singh, records now indicate that these were not isolated incidents conducted by sadistic individuals: "Senior officials endorsed the abuse of prisoners as a matter of policy— sometimes by tolerating it, sometimes by encouraging it, and sometimes by expressly authorizing it."[29]

In these nonnational or neonational spaces (where the infrastructure and conventions of modern nationhood do not exist or where these have been laid on top of existing communal and political structures), decisions to employ the rules of the Geneva Convention rest in fact on the issue of nationality. The Bush administration, for example, did not consider *Taliban* to be equivalent to *Afghan*, an assessment that does have grounding in Taliban operations and ideology. The Taliban could, theoretically, be a multinational force organized by a particular religious and cultural mission rather than national affiliation. But the association of Pashtun ethnicity with the Taliban also undercut its national scope by underrepresenting other Afghans (Tajiks, Turkmen, Uzbeks, Hazaras).[30] This perspective has played a significant role in the war on terror in Afghanistan. According to the *New York Times*, John C. Yoo, the Justice Department lawyer who was the major architect of the USA PATRIOT Act, claimed that since Afghanistan was a " 'failed state' . . . its fighters should not be considered a real army but a 'militant, terrorist-like group.' " The *Times* also cited Alberto F. Gonzales, the White House counsel at the time, who identified the war on terror as a new kind of war that "could hardly be reconciled with the 'quaint' privileges that the Geneva Conventions gave to prisoners of war, or the 'strict limitations' they imposed on interrogations."[31] Since Taliban and al Qaeda fighters are not legally allied with a particular nation (or, it seems, a successful nation), they do not fall under the laws designed for traditional international relationships, including war. Afghanistan under the Taliban was recognized only by Pakistan, Saudi Arabia, and the United Arab Emirates. Although the war with Iraq is acknowledged as truly international, supposed terrorists inside Iraq fall outside previously codified relationships. While captured Iraqi fighters were generally considered prisoners of war, those non-Iraqi fighters taken prisoner in Iraq during the insurgency were identified with the more global (nonnational) terrorist networks and therefore as participants in the murkier workings of a new warfare to which the Geneva Convention seemingly did not apply.[32]

As a site of ongoing military action and as a nation-building project of the international community, Afghanistan continues to shape the kind of justice and resistance taking place in the war on terror. Though political administrations may have changed in the United States and there seems to be significant movement regarding Iraq and Guantánamo Bay, President Obama's strategy for Afghanistan replicates in large measure what it had been under President Bush. In fact Afghanistan has been redefined as the primary site of the war on terror, which threatens to pull in Pakistan and other regions that have played a significant role in Afghanistan's perilous situation. American political pressure on Pakistan to intensify strikes against al Qaeda and Taliban insurgents in South Waziristan, controversial U.S. military air strikes in Pakistan territory, and indeed the inclusion of Pakistan in the very name of the Obama policy for the conflict reveal the expanded scope of the conflict. Also, if we are to see Afghanistan as an exemplary, though problematic, reconstructed nation, we must understand the material and philosophical complications it raises in international relations, democracy, and the nation. The process Afghanistan has gone through (the Bonn Agreement, an interim government, a constitutional *loya jirga*, a transitional government, national elections) accorded it a more structural though still problematic legitimacy.

Questions about Afghan democracy and nation building include the degree to which Afghanistan can regulate relations inside its borders, such as security and law, as well as achieve sovereignty in international relations. In addition to development projects and the establishment of a strong central government viewed as legitimate by its own citizens and the international community, some of Afghanistan's particular goals for establishing national cohesion include developing a national infrastructure that will provide healthcare, education, and human rights to all Afghan citizens;

reducing the role of ethnicity in politics; constructing a strong central army (while disarming local leaders and the general populace); and eliminating opium production. Complications have restricted each of these goals. Specifically in terms of opium production (and its links to Afghan insurgents), Afghanistan does not yet have an alternative agricultural crop that can produce the revenues of the poppy fields.[33] Jan Koehler's and Christoph Zuercher's fieldwork in 2005 regarding rural attitudes about poppy cultivation found that citizens in Nangarhar and Laghman provinces identified opium poppy production as routine and economically necessary.[34] In an assessment of Canadian involvement in Afghanistan published in May 2007, the Senlis Council, an independent international think tank, recommended that the international community help the Afghanistan government regulate and license poppy production for the legal production of medicines such as morphine and codeine. Such a policy, which has been successful in managing the production and trade of opium in other countries, has not been embraced.[35] In addition to the cultural problems of disarming the Afghan citizenry, some critics claim that U.S. policy during the 1980s on warlords and opium production encouraged both during the Soviet war, and continues to undermine the centralized power of the Afghan National Army.[36] Furthermore tensions between Afghanistan and the international community have surfaced in the fight against opium producers. Undercutting Afghanistan's sovereign status, for example, in November 2004 a "mystery aircraft" treated opium crops with an herbicide that was not authorized by the Karzai government and in fact went against the nation's antidrug policy.[37]

In terms of the broader issues of democracy and sovereignty, the Afghan case is profoundly problematic. For example, while the possibility of democratic principles taking root in Afghanistan seems progressive, we need to ask how far this exchange still participates in a neocolonial reconstruction of Afghan politics and culture. For Michael Ignatieff, one of the most prominent theorists of a new global Right, the so-called international community's project of nation building in Afghanistan needs to be recognized alongside similar projects in Bosnia and Kosovo. In Afghanistan, he writes, the international community seeks to "bring order to the barbarian zones." Ignatieff also contends that nation building "is the kind of imperialism you get in a human rights era, a time when the great powers believe simultaneously in the right of small nations to govern themselves and their own right to rule the world." He argues that self-interest drives the United States and its allies, which prevents their fostering this new global right of democracy, human rights, good governance, and equality before the law, and renders hypocritical their claims for the humanitarian nature of their presence. While criticizing the international community's presence in Afghanistan as rushing the process or financing Western relief organizations rather than Afghans, Ignatieff nonetheless contends that though "nobody likes empires . . . there are some problems for which there are only imperial solutions."[38] Afghanistan reveals the paradox of a universal global Right that must be continually policed. This discourse silences the voices of organizations like the Revolutionary Association of the Women of Afghanistan, who have argued that only the people of Afghanistan themselves can create "freedom and democracy";[39] the right of democracy and the rhetoric of benevolence disempower those who seek to imagine and assert their own freedom. Rashid Khalidi argues that the Western influence in the Middle East since the First World War has actually undermined the development of local democracies and parliamentary systems.[40] A greater focus on local efforts to appropriate democracy, freedom, and the nation might also better engage issues particular to the Afghan situation.[41]

In addition to the disastrous state of affairs after the retreat of the Soviets and the Americans in the 1980s, ethnicity has continued to disrupt cohesive action and general unity. Ironically the nation-building process has had to consider ethnicity in selecting members to particular posts in the new government in order to ward off charges of favoritism.[42] Sven Gunnar Simonsen claims that ethnic affiliation has actually become a greater force in postwar and post-Bonn Afghanistan, precisely because ethnicity had to be accounted for in new political and institutional structures.[43] Foreign Minister Abdullah Abdullah, however, saw the role of ethnicity in Afghan politics as generally overblown and called the attention to ethnicity divisive and unrepresentative: "There were lots of attempts and efforts to divide Afghanistan into the ethnic lines, which have not succeeded and will not succeed."[44] Abdullah's renunciation of ethnic distinctions as a basis for political organization is consistent with the ideals of modern nationhood as the imagined constitution of "the people." As has been the case in other attempts by the international community to build nations, the question is whether this nation-building exercise from outside and above will reconcile diversity or exacerbate divisions.

Contemporary Afghanistan raises significant questions regarding the nature of democracy in a globalized world. Although Hamid Karzai won a major victory as the nation's first elected president, as an appointee of the international community his victory only partially represents Colin Powell's understanding of a people's desire to choose their own leaders.[45] While perhaps gesturing toward self-government, the globalized nature of nation building in Afghanistan calls into question national sovereignty as previously defined. On this point the irony of Karzai's following statement is not lost: "You want us to stand on our own feet; you want us to defend our own sovereignty and provide security to our people, and you're helping us do that."[46] Without the international community Afghanistan will continue to suffer internal unrest and scarcity of resources. Certainly the world's role in Afghanistan's economic and political hardships, including the most recent Afghan war, has been profound and well documented. But the money as well as the physical and ideological space provided by the international community that allows groups in Afghanistan to move out of established ethnic, gendered, and political discourses is of no small benefit. Still, with so much of the resources and power coming from outside Afghanistan, the continued violence and instability, and the recognition that the international community will continue to facilitate this process through NATO stabilization forces, the diplomatic corps, and international aid agencies for at least another decade, the nature of Afghan sovereignty will likewise continue to remain uncertain.

Judith Butler has studied how the concept of sovereignty significantly shaped the U.S. war on terror. From its claim that Guantánamo Bay was sovereign, to its offensive war strategy that justified preemptive strikes to protect its own sovereignty, the United States has understood sovereignty as "produced through the suspension (or fabrication) of the rule of law, [and one that] seeks to establish a rival form of political legitimacy, one with no structures of accountability built in."[47] Sovereignty in the context of democracy and elections also allowed the U.S. to elide contradictions in its foreign policy. In 2004, when asked about the Saudi elections, in which women are not allowed to run for office or to vote, Secretary of State Powell employed the concept of sovereignty to indicate the Saudi government's right to set the terms for its own elections: "This is the choice that the Saudi Government has to make. I think women should be allowed. As you know, we have universal suffrage in our country. These things have to come in due course." In quelling the violence to allow for Iraqi elections, Powell also downplayed the role of the U.S. in Iraqi sovereignty: "It's not for the U.S. to oppose or impose. It's for the Iraqi Interim Government. This is a sovereign nation. They have a government led by Prime Minister Allawi and President Sheikh Ghazi."[48]

Even after the elections of 30 January 2005 questions of Iraqi sovereignty remained. Because of the major role the United States played in the construction of the Iraqi government and its continued presence in the country as a military and economic force, many in Iraq as well as Iraqis in the international community did not recognize the new government as a sovereign entity. While planning the initial handover in June 2004, Paul Bremer, the Coalition Provisional Authority administrator, explained the role of the U.S. after Iraqi independence:

At that moment the occupation ends, we have a sovereign Iraqi government in place. It is clear that no matter how well we do in building up the Iraqi security forces . . . they will not be able to deal with the security threat that will still exist after June 3. So the coalition that we have now will transform itself from being an occupation to being a partnership. We will be invited guests by the Iraqi government to help them assure their security.[49]

The subsequent violence attested to the difficulty in changing perceptions of the United States from occupiers to guests. As a gruesome statement against this U.S.-led internationalism, in 2004 insurgents wrapped the decapitated body of a Japanese national in a U.S. flag, illustrating their view that all international forces in Iraq represent the United States.[50] The refusal of the U.S. to hand over Saddam Hussein to the Iraqi government also reveals the notion at that time of Iraqi dependence.[51] With President Obama's major troop withdrawal from Iraq the political codependence asserted by the Bush administration clearly shifted at least in terms of the presence of combat troops versus non-combat, counter-terrorism troops and Americans' physical presence as guarantors of Iraqi freedom. The rights of women in Iraq and Afghanistan have played an especially problematic role in tracing national sovereignty and have highlighted the distinction between global and local interests as well as between national and international power relations. Iraq's constitution, adopted by referendum in October 2005, emphasized the legal equality of the sexes (article 14), but at the same time refused to recognize any laws that contradict Islamic law. Many critics see this provision as actually limiting the rights women had under previous Iraqi law. Article 19 of the Iraqi Provisional Constitution of 1970, for example, also specified sexual equality before the law, but without appealing to Sharia law.

Isobel Coleman examines the nature of this criticism, which aptly links Iraq back to Afghanistan under the Taliban. She cites the head of the Organization of Women's Freedom in Iraq, Yanar Muhammad, who believes this centralizing of Islamic law will turn Iraq "into an Afghanistan under the Taliban, where oppression and discrimination of women is institutionalized."[52] In fact the Afghan elections of 2005 and the construction of the Afghan constitution in 2004 raise the identical issues of Sharia law, gender equality, and national sovereignty. For example, both the Afghan and Iraqi constitutions assert gender equality (a provision not specified in the U.S. constitution) but defer to Sharia law. Since there can be no law directly contradicting Sharia law, codified gender inequality may take precedence, as for example when the testimony of two female witnesses equals that of one male, as specified by Islamic law. Negotiating these sometimes contradictory legal codes and emphasizing local over global interests has put the Afghan government in a particular bind. Karzai's government had to walk carefully between the interests of Western governments and those who called for underscoring Afghanistan's identity as an Islamic republic.

Women's roles and rights in Afghanistan need not simply be a project of international feminists or other Western agents, nor have they been absent in Afghan history and culture. Arline Lederman reminds us that prior to Taliban rule Afghan women played active and significant roles in politics as well as social life: "In 1977 women comprised over 15 percent of Afghanistan's highest legislative body and . . . by the early 1990s, 70 percent of schoolteachers, 50 percent of government workers, and 40 percent of doctors in Kabul were women. In addition, women throughout the Afghan society were social and economic agents, valued helpmates, and revered leaders." She cites the legal equity that women had under King Amanullah in the 1920s and King Mohammad Zahir Shah until 1973, including the assertion of his loya jirga in 1964 that men and women were legally equal.[53] The Revolutionary Association of the Women of Afghanistan was organized in 1977 and after the Soviet invasion in 1979 actively worked for women's rights and resisted foreign and antidemocratic forces.[54] The anti-woman policies of the Taliban and the mujahideen leaders sharply set back women's legal position in Afghanistan.

Starting with the loya jirga in 2003, women in Afghanistan were afforded greater legal representation and more direct involvement in politics. Mahbooba Hoqooqmal, minister for women's affairs, affirmed that about 40 percent of the voters in the presidential elections of 2004 were women; that year, for the first time, a female candidate, Massouda Jalal, ran for president.[55] Also that year women won a greater percentage of seats in the lower house of the Afghan Parliament than was specified in the constitution.[56] Women's issues have also received significantly greater political attention, as evidenced by the creation of the Ministry of Women's Affairs to advance women's legal representation and institutional concerns (education, healthcare, employment).[57] To some degree these apparent successes reflect the paradox of nation building in a globalized Afghanistan; at present these initiatives reflect the expectations of Western democracy more than an Afghan democratic will, and the state has neither the capacity to implement these policies nor the commitment of the populace to fulfill them.

The presidential elections of 2009 saw the number of female voters significantly decrease, primarily due to intimidation, violence, and the failure of many female polling stations to open. While voter turnout in general decreased dramatically, women seem to have been disproportionately affected. According to the Associated Press, 650 female polling stations did not open. While there were more female candidates (two for president and over three hundred vying for provincial council seats) than in any previous election, Noor Khan and Nahal Toosi cited the prediction of Haround Mir, the director of Afghanistan's Center for Research and Policy Studies, who said that "the low female turnout [was] one reason the next government [would be] likely to do little for women beyond appointing a handful of token positions."[58]

Outside of Kabul women continue to live in dire conditions, and in some places are further marginalized and disenfranchised as a result of a conservative backlash that is not confined to the Taliban, which the government sometimes had to placate. According to a UN report from 2006, widespread poverty and illiteracy and high maternal mortality rates continue to threaten Afghan women.[59] Afghanistan's Independent Human Rights Commission documented more than fifteen hundred cases of male violence against women in 2006, including beatings and forcible marriage, followed by attempted suicide.[60] There had long been organized resistance to female education and representation in politics. Dating back to 2005, citizens in Bamiyan province demonstrated against the government's decision to appoint a female governor, Habiba Sorabi.[61] More problematic, however, were the threats against Sima Samar as minister for women's affairs after fundamentalists accused her of blasphemy for speaking out on the offenses of both the Taliban and the mujahideen and the continuing violence against women and girls. According to Soutik Biswas, the lives of many women representatives in the Afghan government are threatened regularly, but the government cannot ensure their protection.[62] In a troublesome amalgamation of global and local interests Karzai established the Department of Islamic Teaching under the Ministry of Religious Affairs, reminiscent in some sense of the Taliban's Department of Vice and Virtue.[63] The Karzai government also passed the Shia Family Law, which allowed a husband to refuse to support his wife if she failed to have regular sexual intercourse (except in cases of illness). The law also restricted Shia women from traveling without a male escort (exactly identical to the law restricting female movement under the Taliban). Though Karzai promised to change the law after massive international and local criticism, the key provisions of the law were passed expeditiously and without the possibility of debate.[64] While structures for redress are in place, Sippi Azarbaijani-Moghaddam argues that entities like the Ministry for Women's Affairs lack real power and support. She cites the parliamentary debate in 2006 that engaged the issue of "whether women parliamentarians required *mahrams* or chaperones on public trips."[65]

In light of these persistent problems and threats, the move in February 2007 to offer political amnesty to former fighters accused of war crimes in Afghanistan seemed particularly problematic. Many of these former fighters ran for political positions in the Afghan National Assembly and were not held legally accountable for their earlier actions.[66] The offer of amnesty, which attempted to mend fences from an international perspective, appeared to others to further cement Afghanistan in violence and its anti-democratic history. Malalai Joya, a member of the Afghan Parliament who was suspended in 2007 amid accusations of insulting her fellow parliamentarians, believed the decision ignored international law, destabilized Afghan reconstruction, and demonstrated the West's marginalizing of local interests: "The U.S. government removed the ultra-reactionary and brutal regime of the Taliban, but instead of relying on Afghan people, pushed us from the frying pan into the fire and selected its friends from among the most dirty and infamous criminals of the 'Northern Alliance,' which is made up of the sworn enemies of democracy, human rights, and are as dark-minded, evil, and cruel as the Taliban." She recalled that the United States claimed in 2001 that it would not support fundamentalism, but in Afghanistan, she said, "the agonizing truth is that the U.S. is committing the same mistakes."[67] The Afghan Parliament's rejection of seventeen out of twenty-three of Karzai's nominees for cabinet posts in January 2010, however, did redress some stark injustices (most evident in their rejection of Ismail Khan, a former warlord, as a second-term minister of energy).

However it is done, facilitating local supporters of democracy and women's rights is the most effective way to ensure those rights. As writers in this collection notice very keenly, the impetus for women's rights must come from Afghans themselves in order to build a lasting, representative, and legitimate government. These Afghans and those helping to effect democracy in the country must be put into productive dialogue with one another. Contesting the image of the Afghan woman as passive and victimized should therefore be a key component in this exchange. Outsiders (including Afghan expatriates) need to acknowledge their position as outsiders and allow space for local strategies for resistance and building equality. Witness the rise of the Pink Sari Gang of Uttar Pradesh in India, led by the charismatic Sampat Pal, who challenges official corruption and defends the rights of women by teaming up with scores of women dressed in pink and wielding pink batons. In addition to the threat of violence, they verbally challenge men by calling out their abusive practices and their failure to adhere to their traditional roles.[68] International feminism could not anticipate this kind of grassroots resistance, nor could it predict the power of shaming afforded to forceful women who take up leadership positions in their villages. Along with the equality promised by such challenges, we must also be prepared to accept traditions that do not necessarily correspond to our own local, cultural values but that speak to the identities and values of the people most directly affected.

The essays collected in *Globalizing Afghanistan* address the war on terror as a significant historical shift in the foreign policy of the U.S. and its allies, as well as international understandings of national sovereignty and democracy. In Afghanistan the initial U.S. invasion was followed by a stabilization force managed by NATO and an assistance mission mandated by the United Nations which sought to violently root out terrorism and engage in nation building within the rhetoric of human rights and democracy, ostensibly through Afghan (local) leadership. The writers collected here look at the complications in that process and provide important contexts for the world's struggle against terrorism as well as the roles played by international Islam, international aid, news and entertainment media, and international feminism in globalizing Afghanistan. *Globalizing Afghanistan* begins by introducing globalization and the international wars on terror, then discusses the country's cultural, political, and economic globalization historically and more recently, and ends with a theoretical look at globalization, the media, and the role of academics. The issues raised by international intervention in Afghanistan include the ways both the structure of the nation and the ideology of nationalism have been recently defined in the Afghan context.

Economic matters have clearly been fundamental in the globalization of Afghanistan and have illustrated the tensions between local and international interests as well as ideological agendas. The opium trade has been particularly significant in highlighting Afghanistan's problematic economy. Nigel C. Gibson ("It's the Opium, Stupid: Afghanistan, Globalization, and Drugs") examines the role of the drug economy in Afghan nationalism. Gibson underscores the globalizing of both the nation-building project and the existing opium trade. In the current context of internal and international warfare, he illustrates how opium permeates not only the Afghan economy and politics, but also the "the economy of war" and the arming of local leaders.

Central Asia has historically been an important passageway between Asia and the West and an important variable in the early integration of the world, but in more recent times Afghanistan figured prominently in the continuing development and confrontation of empire and Islamic fundamentalism. With the Soviet invasion in 1979 and the subsequent backing by the U.S. of the Afghan mujahideen, Afghanistan played a crucial role in the cold war between the Soviet Union and the United States. Later, after the withdrawal of both the Soviets and the Americans, Afghanistan became an important actor in a Saudi-based Islamist reaction against the United States. Consequently this militant response shared some (but not all) of its ideological and material interests with the Taliban. Rodney J. Steward ("Afghanistan in a Globalized World: A Longer View") provides a valuable historical context regarding the rise of the Taliban, going as far back as the nineteenth century, to the struggle between Britain and Russia over Afghanistan during the Crimean War. Steward juxtaposes the global forces at play in Afghanistan historically with a local insistence on place.

In Afghanistan international interests are also reflected in seemingly internal phenomena such as ethnicity, a factor that plays critical local and international roles. Altaf Ullah Khan ("The 'Afghan Beat': Pukhtoon Journalism and the Afghan War") illustrates the relationship of Pukhtoon ethnic ties between Pakistan and Afghanistan in the border region formerly known as the North West Frontier Province, recently renamed Khyber-Pakhtoonkhwa. Khan, a Pukhtoon journalist based in Peshawar, presents his findings from personal interviews he conducted of Pukhtoon journalists at the beginning of the Afghan-U.S. war. Because of the limited number of Pukhtoon journalists and the possibility of threats to their lives, Khan maintains these journalists' anonymity. Both their voices and Khan's own are unique in this collection for the personal nature of their connection to and presentation of the issues at hand. Cross-purposes are also evident in Pakistan's role in Afghanistan. Pakistan's intelligence service played a key role in supporting the Taliban while it claimed to be supporting the fight against the Taliban. Khan illustrates the ways that journalists in Peshawar (the province's major city) only partially identify with their national and media center in Pakistan (the predominantly ethnic Punjabi Islamabad) and negotiate Pakistani state-driven imperatives in covering Afghanistan and their own personal investment in Afghan politics.

Globalizing Afghanistan sees Afghanistan emerging as a seemingly contradictory "globalized nation," one that tries to consolidate various international and local interests. Ironically the diversity of international and
local influences may compromise certain conceptions of the modern, albeit
globalized, nation. Nonstate actors such as the international NGOs Human
Rights Watch and Amnesty International played a significant part in bringing Taliban-controlled Afghanistan into public consciousness. The international feminist movement in particular justified intervention into Afghanistan under the Taliban. The essays by Maliha Chishti and Cheshmak
Farhoumand-Sims ("Transnational Feminism and the Women's Rights
Agenda in Afghanistan") and Gwen Bergner ("Veiled Motives: Women's
Liberation and the War in Afghanistan") address the role that international feminism has played in contemporary Afghan politics. Chishti and
Farhoumand-Sims engage the apparent liberation of Afghan women in
international feminism that nonetheless "others" and pacifies them. They
argue that with other national and class disparities the international feminist movement easily conflates Western donor agendas and Western cultural norms onto the issues facing Afghan women. Bergner illustrates how
Western cultural norms operated in Western media coverage of the literal
unveiling of Afghan women after the fall of Kabul. She writes, "The representation of Afghan women in post-9/11 American media and politics
serves as a textbook case of the gendering of nationalism in a global frame."

Karman Rastegar's essay ("Global Frames on Afghanistan: The Iranian
Mediation of Afghanistan in International Art House Cinema after September 11, 2001") extends the issue of representing Afghanistan to the
artistic and cultural production of Iranian films that garnered significant
international attention. Rastegar centralizes the issues involved in channeling images of Afghanistan through Iranian interlocutors, who on some level
are seen by attendees of international film festivals as more trustworthy
than Western filmmakers. But identifying these images as unproblematic
representations downplays the role that Irani politics plays in the depic-
tions of Afghanistan as well as the power differentials between the two
nations themselves. Rastegar follows his analysis of the "global spectacle" of
9/11 with the continued insistence on presenting the Afghan spectacle. He
writes, "After September 11 the need to produce not only images of but also
representations for Afghanistan would be intimately related to the cause of

reintegrating the nation into a globalized world, whether by military or humanitarian endeavor." In this way Iran is key in the cultural globalization of Afghanistan that has direct political causes and reverberations.

We conclude the book with Imre Szeman's essay ("The Current Amazement: Afghanistan, Terror, and Theory") that sees September 11, 2001, as an important historical and linguistic moment in defining new national and criminal subjectivities circulating on a global scale. Szeman connects globalization through the discourses of war with the exporting of an economic rationality that is less a historical inevitability than an economic and political project. Both Afghanistan and Iraq have become primary sites for this economic rationality (to varying degrees of success) through war and reconstruction. Szeman also examines the role that academics may play in understanding and challenging these economic and political rationalities.

Globalizing Afghanistan investigates the unfolding of international events both in the specifics of the Afghan case and also in more general trends in the politics and culture of globalization. Along with Iraq, Afghanistan has emerged as one of the most politically and ideologically significant areas in the world. *Globalizing Afghanistan* contributes to the broad question of how Afghanistan will come through this long process of nationalizing and globalizing. Our intention is to scrutinize not only the details of this particular place and time but to imagine the larger implications of culture, politics, and economics in a world quite clearly enmeshed.

Notes

A much earlier version of this introduction appeared in the newsletter of the *Faculty of Arts and Sciences, Rhode Island College*, no. 26 (October 2002), 5–9.

1 Pieterse, "Globalization as Hybridization," 99.

2 See Ahmed Rashid's *Descent into Chaos*.

3 Colonial British writers of the nineteenth century as well as later English and American writers have produced numerous books about trekking through Afghanistan, precursors to bestsellers like Jason Elliot's *An Unexpected Light* and Rory Stewart's *The Places in Between*. While this is not the space for an exhaustive list, some notable early travel writers include George Foster (*A Journey from Bengal to England*, 1798), Mountstuart Elphinstone (*An Account of the Kingdom of Caubul*, 1815), Henry Pottinger (*Travels in Beloochistan and Sinde*, 1816), Alex-

ander Burnes (*Travels into Bokhara*, 1834; *Cabool: Being a Personal Narrative of a Journey*, 1836), and Charles Masson (*Narrative of Various Journeys in Balochistan, Afghanistan, the Panjab, and Kalat*, 1842–3).

4 Islamism, though charged with various meanings, here signifies a pan-Islamic militant movement that adheres to, among other tenets, an anti-Western political and cultural agenda.

5 *Empire* is Michael Hardt's and Antonio Negri's term for a "new form of global sovereignty," held for the moment by the United States. While Hardt and Negri do not conflate the United States and empire, they do concede that though the U.S. may be currently playing the role of empire, empire is a concept open to a host of international actors who can change over time (*Empire*, xii). See also Barber, *Jihad vs. McWorld*.

6 O'Brien and Szeman, "Introduction: The Globalization of Fiction / The Fiction of Globalization."

7 According to the recent work of Kwame Anthony Appiah, *cosmopolitanism* signifies shared values and similarities between apparently diverse contexts or peoples. See his *Cosmopolitanism: Ethics in a World of Strangers*.

8 White House, "President Urges Readiness and Patience"; Chomsky, *Hegemony or Global Survival*.

9 Project for a New American Century, "Statement of Principles."

10 Obama, "Remarks by the President in Address to the Nation on the Way Forward in Afghanistan and Pakistan."

11 White House, Office of the Press Secretary, "Fact Sheet: The Way Forward in Afghanistan and Pakistan."

12 Hardt and Negri, *Multitude*, 12.

13 Chandler, *Empire in Denial*, 71.

14 Obama, "Remarks by the President in Address to the Nation on the Way Forward in Afghanistan and Pakistan."

15 See Maloney, "Soldiers Not Peacekeepers"; McQuaig, *Holding the Bully's Coat*.

16 In June 2007 the magazine *Foreign Policy* and the U.S. Fund for Peace think tank ranked Afghanistan the eighth most unstable country in the world in their annual ranking of "failed states."

17 As Mahmood Mamdani reminds us, the Taliban regime received acceptance, if not support, from the Clinton administration in the late 1990s (*Good Muslim, Bad Muslim*, 160).

18 Harb, "Powell Sees Afghan Election as Illustration of Iraq's Potential."

19 Harris, *Recovery from Armed Conflict in Developing Countries*, 241.

20 Ali, "Afghanistan."

21 Freeman, "Introduction: Security, Governance and Statebuilding in Afghanistan," 4.

22 Haqqani, "Think Again"; Vanessa Williams, "Fighting in the Shadows of Iraq: Some Fear Afghanistan Has Become a Forgotten War," *Washington Post*, 2 June

2004, A1. Ahmed Rashid writes that Afghanistan's perilous situation is the direct result of the U.S. invasion of Iraq and "Washington's refusal to take state-building in Afghanistan seriously": "For Afghanistan the results have been too few Western troops, too little money, and a lack of coherent strategy and sustained policy initiatives on the part of Western and Afghan leaders" ("Afghanistan on the Brink," 24).

23 Keith B. Richburg, "Karzai Officially Declared Winner," *Washington Post*, 4 November 2004, A8.

24 Associated Press, "Freed U.N. Workers Visit Afghan President," 28 November 2004, MSNBC website (accessed 30 November 2004).

25 Quoted in Mamdani, *Good Muslim, Bad Muslim*, 119.

26 The legal jurisdiction regarding Guantánamo Bay at the time of this writing is in flux. The U.S. Supreme Court is to hear a challenge to the war crimes trials system (2006), and military judges have dismissed cases against Salim Ahmed Hamdan and Omar Khadr (2007).

27 Hersh, "Torture at Abu Ghraib."

28 Cockburn, "Green Lights for Torture." Cockburn cites the documentary *Massacre at Mazar* by Jamie Doran for his source on Taliban dead.

29 Jaffer and Singh, *Administration of Torture*, 2. See also Finely, *The Torture and Prisoner Abuse Debate*, which discusses a number of cases of abuse at both Guantánamo Bay and Bagram predating the exposure of abuse at Abu Ghraib.

30 The terms *Pashtun*, *Pakhtoon*, and *Pathan* (and their variants) refer to the same Pashto-speaking ethnic group. In his essay in this book Altaf Ullah Khan refers to his ethnic group as "Pukhtoon." This group constitutes the majority in Afghanistan and Pakistan's Khyber-Pakhtoonkhwa as well as significant portions of Baluchistan. There is one major dialect division of Pashtu, an Indo-European language, between a northern Pukhtu (prevalent among Pashtuns in Kabul and Khyber-Pakhtoonkhwa) and southern Pashtu (prevalent among Pashtuns in Kandahar and Baluchistan, Pakistan). See M. Hassan Kakar's first note in his introduction to *A Political and Diplomatic History of Afghanistan* for a detailed discussion of the names, history, and broad genealogy of the Pashtuns.

31 Tim Golden and Jack Begg, "Threats and Responses: Tough Justice; After the Terror Attacks, a Secret and Speedy Rewriting of Military Law," *New York Times*, 24 October 2004, International sec., 13.

32 According to Douglas Jehl, the CIA returned two Iraqi prisoners whom they had initially taken out of the country. Jehl believes this action links Iraq, Afghanistan, and al Qaeda: "The opinion would essentially allow the military and the C.I.A. to treat at least a small number of non-Iraqi prisoners captured in Iraq in the same way as members of Al Qa'ida and the Taliban captured in Afghanistan, Pakistan or elsewhere." Douglas Jehl, "U.S. Action Bars Rights of Some Captured in Iraq," *New York Times*, 26 October 2004, A1, A18.

33 Bagley, "Afghanistan: Opium Cultivation and Its Impact on Reconstruction."

Bagley notes the U.S. government's support of Gulbuddin Hekmatyar, a warlord and the leader of the Hezb-e-Islami Party, who relied on the opium trade for resources. Ahmed Rashid writes that the "drug trade has undermined everything from security to development, while increasing public frustration with the government" ("Afghanistan on the Brink," 25).

34 Koehler and Zuercher, "Statebuilding, Conflict, and Narcotics in Afghanistan," 71.

35 See Senlis Council, "Prime Minister Harper Must Dramatically Overhaul Canada's Strategy Development, Aid and Counter Narcotics Policy in Afghanistan."

36 Baker, "Winning the Peace?"

37 Associated Press, "Afghan Government Condemns Spraying of Opium Crops by Mystery Aircraft." *Malaysia Star,* 30 November 2004, online (accessed 30 November 2004).

38 Ignatieff, *Empire Lite,* 21, 106, 11.

39 Ravishankar, "Afghanistan: The Liberation That Isn't."

40 Khalidi, *Resurrecting Empire,* 58. Khalidi, for example, points to the West's role in Iran after the Second World War when Britain—with the help of the United States—challenged the democratic and parliamentary government of Mohammed Mosaddeq.

41 The emergency loya jirga and the constitutional loya jirga were intriguing gestures to indigenous democratic structures. *Loya jirga* is a Pashtu term meaning "great council or meeting." The jirga system has been the traditional governmental structure of the Pashtun tribes in Afghanistan and Pakistan and is based on tribal elders meeting to settle disputes, consult about issues, and select leaders. Critics have indicated that greater attention to redefining this kind of local political structure in the context of Afghan nationalism might have more success and legitimacy than structures imported from the West.

42 On controversies involved in such decisions, see Rashid, "New Afghan Cabinet Configuration Source of Discontent for Many Pashtuns."

43 Sven Gunnar Simonsen. "Ethnicizing Afghanistan? Inclusion and Exclusion in Post-Bonn Institution Building." *Third World Quarterly* 5, no. 4 (2004), 707–29.

44 Carnegie Endowment for International Peace, transcript from briefing of Dr. Abdullah, foreign minister of Afghanistan. Abdullah's statement was in response to Stanley Kober's question: "How do you create national identities, for example, in Pakistan, in Afghanistan that supersede the Pashtun identity of people on both sides of the border?"

45 The international influence on the Afghan elections was also illustrated in the unprecedented number of refugee ballots cast in the neighboring countries of Pakistan and Iran. See United Nations Office for the Coordination of Humanitarian Affairs, "Afghanistan-Iran-Pakistan: Largest Refugee Election Participation in History." According to Peter Erben, the director of the International Organization for Migration's Out of Country Registration and Voting Program, 850,000 Afghan refugees in Iran and Pakistan voted in the presidential elections (Piñeiro, "Afghanistan Out of Country Election Turnout in Pakistan and Iran").

46 White House, Office of the Press Secretary, "President Bush Meets with President Karzai of Afghanistan."

47 Butler, *Precarious Life*, 66.

48 Harb, "Powell Sees Afghan Election as Illustration of Iraq's Potential." President Bush spoke similarly of Iraq when questioned about the threat of Muqtada al-Sadr: "The interim Iraqi government will deal with al-Sadr in the way they see fit. That's they're sovereign. When we say we transfer full sovereignty, we mean we transfer full sovereignty. And they will deal with him appropriately" (White House, Office of the Press Secretary, "President Bush Meets with President Karzai of Afghanistan").

49 U.S. Department of Defense, "Bremer Says Transition to Iraqi Sovereignty Gaining Momentum."

50 Associated Press, "Video Shows Beheading of Japanese Hostage: Al-Zarqawi Group Warns Tokyo to Withdraw Forces from Iraq," MSNBC website, 2 November 2004 (accessed 19 November 2004). The perception of American responsibility extends to the rulers of Iraq, as seen in Allawi's sharp words to the United States after the killing of forty-nine newly trained Iraqi soldiers. See Edward Wong, "Allawi Blames 'Negligence' by U.S.-Led Force for Ambush Deaths of 49," *New York Times*, 27 October 2004, A10.

51 White House, Office of the Press Secretary, "President Bush Meets with President Karzai of Afghanistan." The Bush administration claimed that, though sovereign, Iraq was too insecure to hold such a high-profile prisoner. Bush commented:

> I fully agree that it's a sovereign country. That's why we're working with them to make sure that there is good security. Look, nobody wants Saddam Hussein to leave, and when there's a transfer of responsibility, we want to make sure that he is secure. He's a killer. He is a thug. He needs to be brought to trial. We want to make sure that the transfer to a sovereign government is done in a timely way and in a secure way.

Binoy Kampmark has linked the multiple ways that the United States shaped the entire legal context of Saddam Hussein's trial and execution:

> The Iraqi body that is trying Saddam is largely an American creature, despite international contributions towards legal training. (The International Bar Association has also provided assistance to training prosecutors and the five judges trying Saddam.) The Americans fund the Special Tribunal overseeing the trial; jurists from Iraq have received crash courses in legal training from lawyers specially appointed by the U.S. Justice Department, rich in the rhetoric of constitutional ethic and habeas corpus, despite being initially selected by Iraqi authorities. The Regime Crimes Liaison Office, a body of legal experts created by the U.S. Government in May 2004, provides advice to the High Tribunal in Baghdad. ("The Trial of Saddam Hussein," 196)

Despite the continued instability of Iraq after the legal transfer of power with the election of the Iraqi National Assembly in 2005, Saddam Hussein remained ostensibly in Iraqi custody. His subsequent trial and execution were effected through the Iraqi Special Tribunal (a product of the Iraqi Governing Council in 2003), which brings to trial cases of war crimes and crimes against humanity. In late 2006 Hussein was tried and executed for crimes against humanity. Through this specifically Iraqi legal system, bolstered by an elected Iraqi government, the issue of national sovereignty regarding the trial of Saddam Hussein appeared legitimate. However, none can deny the continuing role the United States played in Hussein's captivity and his prosecution as well as in postelection Iraq more generally. Hussein's trial and execution illustrated the tenuous sovereignty that is installed from without and compromised by continuing connections to the United States due to the supposed lack of know-how, stability, or security.

52 Coleman, "Women, Islam, and the New Iraq."

53 Lederman, "The *Zan* of Afghanistan," 47, 48.

54 Mansoor, "The Mission of RAWA," 76–78.

55 Afghanistan Online, "The Plight of the Afghan Woman." Other sources indicate that 41 percent of voters were women.

56 Women were guaranteed 25 percent (sixty-eight) of the seats in the lower house of Parliament but in the 2005 elections actually took 28 percent, according to the Joint Electoral Management Body of the Islamic Republic of Afghanistan and the website Afghanistan Peace Building.

57 United Nations, "Secretary-General on the Situation of Women and Children in Afghanistan."

58 Noor Khan and Nahal Toosi, "Afghan Elections Seen as a Setback for Women," Associated Press, Google website, 24 August 2009 (accessed 3 September 2009).

59 United Nations Development Fund for Women, "Women in Afghanistan."

60 Biswas, "Women Under Siege in Afghanistan."

61 Afghanistan Online, "Getting More Women into Politics." See also IRIN Humanitarian.

62 Biswas, "Women Under Siege in Afghanistan."

63 Curphey, "Women in Afghanistan Fear New Taliban-Like Rule."

64 Associated Press, "Afghanistan's Contentious Family Law Quietly Enacted," CBC website, 17 August 2009 (accessed 8 September 2009).

65 Azarbaijani-Moghaddam, "On Living with Negative Peace and a Half-Built State," 134.

66 Afghanistan Justice Project, "Amnesty Would Jeopardize National Reconciliation and Security."

67 Joya, "The U.S. Has Returned Fundamentalism to Afghanistan."

68 See Akshay Mahajan, "Rebels in Hot Pink," *Hindustan Times*, 21 August 2009, online at http://www.hindustantimes.com/Rebels-in-hot-pink/Article1-445695 .aspx; Philip Reeves, "Female Gang In India Operates Dressed In Pink," *NPR: Morning Edition* online, 24 November 2008 (accessed 8 September 2009).

It's the Opium, Stupid

Afghanistan, Globalization, and Drugs

Nigel C. Gibson

An account of fighting in Afghanistan from the spring of 2007 says almost everything that needs to be said about the seemingly never-ending Afghan war:

> The patrol was stuck, enveloped in a poppy field in a Taliban ambush. Automatic rifle fire came toward them from a tree line about 175 yards to the west and from a row of mud-walled Afghan houses to the east and north.[1]

Being stuck in a red poppy field evokes the popular image of death worn on the lapel every 11 November in Britain and Canada. The red poppy is a symbol that comes not only from the killing fields of the First World War but from earlier disastrous British imperial adventures into Afghanistan in the 1840s and 1860s.[2] This period also saw the beginning of war photography and governments' attempts to control such images.[3] In a familiar pattern, the bodies pile up in the present Afghanistan war, though we do not see them in the media (see Imre Szeman's essay in this book). Five years into the war NATO forces in southern Afghanistan faced a "resurgent" Taliban, who killed an average of five coalition soldiers every week between 1 May and 12 August 2006.[4] Military leaders warned the coalition governments that victory in Afghanistan was far from certain.[5] After intense fighting in 2006 which inflicted high casualties on the Taliban and a Taliban offensive in spring 2007, these commanders once again pressured their governments for more troops and supplies.

Until the election of President Obama in 2008, America's commitment to the occupation of Afghanistan played second fiddle to the Iraq war, which had been named (by those who supported the occupation of Afghanistan but opposed the occupation of Iraq) as a reason why the Afghan war dragged on and will drag on well past the withdrawal of troops from Iraq. One reason for the continuing violence is that Afghanistan is "enveloped in poppies"—red gold—which despite eradication attempts continues to post record-breaking crops.[6] Afghanistan, the opium capital of the world, is the source of cheap heroin. The opium industry represents at least 50 percent of Afghanistan's gross domestic product, which dwarfs its "formal economy," backed by the EU and NATO.[7]

Opium has been a major driver of Afghanistan's economy since 2001 and permeates political life. It dominates the economy, particularly the economy of war, and thus contributes to making it a war without end.[8] Since the opium trade is essential to funding local leaders and the Taliban insurgency, President Karzai has insisted, "Either Afghanistan destroys opium or opium destroys Afghanistan."[9] But the destruction of the poppies would also herald the destruction of "Afghanistan." Poppy production (employing nearly three million people) gives most farmers a means of survival. Additionally the apparatus of a (narco) state—as much as one can speak about such an institution—is probably most efficient (and equally brutal) in the areas controlled by the Taliban and the opium warlords. Ironically the opium industry creates state-like structure.

Much more than the invasion of Iraq by the United States and Great Britain, the overthrow of the Taliban is still considered a "just war," for two reasons: first, it ousted a "rogue regime" that gave refuge to Osama bin Laden and al Qaeda; second, it was considered a humanitarian intervention to "liberate" the people, especially women, from the "feudal" Taliban regime (see the essays in this book by Gwen Bergner and Maliha Chishti and Cheshmak Farhoumand-Sims).[10] More than seven years after the invasion, however, NATO is losing the war on both counts. The Taliban controls significant areas of the country, and despite tactical defeats in 2006 (mainly based on fighting a conventional war rather than an insurgency) it still controls vast areas in the south. The mountainous areas between Afghanistan and Pakistan which provided refuge to al Qaeda remain beyond the control of NATO as well as Pakistani forces (who had been seen as supporting the Taliban). The Karzai government's lack of capacity to control vast areas of the country, bemoaned by many,[11] is echoed by the Pakistani government's inability to police the Khyber-Pakhtoonkhwa (formerly North West Frontier Province) and by NATO's inability to control the south. President Musharraf's attempted compromise with "Islamic militants" in the semiautonomous North Waziristan led to accusations of turning a blind eye to the consolidation of the Taliban in the area. NATO's inability to deal with the Taliban in the south led to aerial bombings in 2006, with the consequent death of many innocent people. The strategy continued into 2007.[12] The sum of these conditions points to a failure to maintain security by the world and regional powers (NATO, Pakistan). Meanwhile suicide bombings have rocked Kabul, indicating the absence of security in the heart of the most secure zones.[13] Despite the rhetoric to justify the invasion, the humanitarian situation in the country as a whole has not improved, as evidenced by constant warnings of impending food shortages and other crises. Significantly the situation for women has not really changed much at all and may in fact have taken some steps back.[14]

A Prisoner of Kabul: Karzai, the Media, and the Mayor

The scene of Hamid Karzai's first presidential inauguration, with newly laid blacktop, whitewashed buildings, and scrubbed streets, may well have been set in a back lot in Burbank, California. The dapper, young, English-speaking president-elect, surrounded by foreign press, foreign dignitaries, and foreign troops, was hailed as the new democratic president of Afghanistan. Karzai is actually an old hand in Afghanistan politics. He served as deputy foreign minister in the post-Soviet government of Burhanuddin Rabbani, which was overthrown by the Taliban in 1996. He originally supported the Taliban but then declined their offer to serve in their government. Pragmatically pro-West and a close ally of the former king, he is a Kandahar Pashtun still favored by some former Taliban supporters but increasingly isolated from any real basis of support in the country.

Some months after Karzai's election in 2004, when a new cabinet was announced, the old war-criminal warlords were excluded (with the exception of perhaps the most powerful one, Ismail Khan, who commanded fifteen thousand men, the largest semiautonomous force, and who was made minister of energy). According to the new Afghan constitution, a member's degree of education determined his or her cabinet position. Thus new members of the cabinet had impressive résumés. They had variously worked for the World Bank, taught in the United States, and spoke the language the donors wished to hear. Overall the cabinet list read like a public relations press kit for Western consumption. There was also one female member, a first in the nation's history. Since the first election the veneer has rubbed off, and the real power, with intimate connections to the narco economy, has emerged. The warlord Ismail Kahn was appointed minister of water and energy, and Qasim Fahim, an advisor to Karzai, was accused of war crimes, as was the chief of staff to the commander in chief of the army, Rashid Dostum. Izzatullah Wasifi, convicted of selling heroin in Las Vegas, was appointed anticorruption chief. On the other hand, one of the elected women, Malalai Joya, survived four assassination attempts and said that her "voice [was] always being silenced even inside the parliament."[15]

President Karzai was known as the "mayor of Kabul," a city which, on the surface, and especially in contrast to the way it looked in 2002, is prospering.[16] It is an artery for international aid, bustling with thousands of governmental and international and national nongovernmental organizations, as well as secret government organizations with connections to the narco economy.[17] Kabul's existence and security is based on an aid economy—official and semiofficial—backed by U.S. and European troops.

The Pitfalls of Humanitarian Aid

A wide range of liberal opinion in the United States supported the war against the Taliban. They argued that U.S. military intervention would lift the burqa off the women and bring enlightenment to a nation that had suffered under the Taliban regime (see Gwen Bergner's essay in this collection). Newspaper articles heralded the "liberation" of women, yet for the majority little has changed. Given current developments, the Americans' commitment to democracy and human rights seems primarily rhetorical.

In fact after September 11, 2001, according to Antonio Donini, chief of the Lessons Learned Unit at the United Nations Department of Humanitarian Affairs, the human rights effort in Afghanistan, which has always been subject to political instrumentalization, has been "wiped off the UN agenda."[18] Just as the U.S. had bankrolled local leaders, aid and aid workers are sucked into the politics of taking sides. The uncritical support for the Karzai government by the UN Mission in Afghanistan made it difficult to raise human rights concerns; abuses of human rights in warlord-controlled areas were overlooked, with reprisals inflicted against communities who were thought to be pro-Taliban.

The splendor of the pomp and ceremony of Karzai's first presidency differed starkly from the poverty of the common people's lives in the rest of the country, particularly in the rural areas where Western military occupation has brought neither human rights nor economic change. The Kabul government had neither the capacity nor perhaps the will to create a functioning legal system.[19] In common political science parlance, Afghanistan is a "failed" state, a collapsed state, or at least a weak state, which is to say the central administration does not have a monopoly on the means of violence over the territory. The government is simply not in control. Thus Karzai's claim in November 2004 at the Kabul narcotics conference that "terrorism as a force has gone" was taken with some skepticism since armed groups control vast areas of the country; the violence that has continued, even in Kabul, bears this out. Yet that grandiose statement represents Karzai's attempt to shift the discourse. By declaring a "holy war" on the opium trade he indicated that the interconnection between drugs, Islamism, and political power is very real and undercuts "nation building."[20]

The fundamental problematic of this nation-building exercise, and more specifically the humanitarian aid regime in Afghanistan, however, is that it operates within the context of a narco economy. Afghanistan's political economy is based on a relationship between international aid and the drug economy. The issue is not only to what extent international aid will "aid violence" by privileging certain regional areas and the political figures who opened up areas for assistance,[21] but how it will interface with the opium trade. Ironically, by opening up the economy to commodity production, the drug trade has played a role similar to the World Bank's neoliberal economic policies that have been forced on Third World economies.

Poppy Growing and Nation Building

Violence continues in the south and the east of Afghanistan, where U.S. forces engage the insurgents and the rebels.[22] Yet at the same time the American concern with terrorists, that is, the Taliban and al Qaeda, rather than with the government's drug and warlord allies, indicates that whatever nation building will finally look like, it already includes the latter in some form; the Karzai administration, despite efforts to rise above the fragmented and regional (often considered "tribal," "ethnic," or "cultural") politics, should be considered another regional player, albeit with powerful military backers.[23] At the time of this writing, Kabul's rule is bolstered by forty-two thousand U.S. and NATO troops and a combined Afghanistan force, including paramilitary organizations with allegiance to individuals rather than the state, estimated at fifty thousand. Consequently neither the central administration nor its powerful backers has the capacity to impose its rules or laws across the whole country.

With the U.S. military stretched and taking increasing casualties in Iraq in 2005 and 2006, the Western media reported the transition to democracy in Afghanistan as a limited success. At the same time, because U.S. foreign policy was for so long focused almost entirely on Iraq, until the Obama administration, the occupation of Afghanistan could not be allowed to consume too many soldiers. Thus from the point of view of American empire, Afghanistan's nation building has long been required to be done "lite" and on the cheap.[24] Rather than further involvement, U.S. policy before Obama preferred further disengagement with a pro-U.S. government backed by the UN in place as soon as possible. Yet the weakness of Karzai's government and the Afghan nation continues to cause some concern; it is much easier to back a proxy force than to build a national government.

Ironically the only way for Afghanistan to pay for its development as a state is the same way the warlords paid for arms over the past twenty-five years: drug money. The great paradox for the American presence in Afghanistan is that the regional and fragmented narco mini-states are partly its own making (see the conclusions of Alfred McCoy).[25] The issue here is how the establishment of a Kabul state, with a limited electoral democracy based on an elite pact among the warlords and regional leaders and with little authority outside the city, will articulate with the opium economy. In other words, rather than thinking in terms of a binary—a clean state on one side and a narco state on the other—the question is to what degree a legitimate state can be based on narcotics. The Taliban understood that international recognition constituted one aspect of legitimacy. After the Taliban's suppression of poppy farming in 2000, they found no necessary correlation between narcotics control and international recognition, especially evident since the Taliban was criticized (rightly) for other abuses while the Northern Alliance of drug lords became legitimate overnight after 9/11.[26] Yet in the context of the political economy of opium, the possibility that the Taliban could become legitimate seemed slim. They certainly hedged their bets by banning the cultivation of opium poppies but not the distribution of opium stockpiles.[27]

The Center of the Drug World

Often described as being on the periphery of the world (or indeed, from another world), Afghanistan has played a major role in the three great empires of the past two hundred years: the British, the Russian, and the American. Indeed two were defeated on its soil, and there is little reason to doubt that the third may be defeated there as well. All three have engaged in opium wars. Rather than premodern and backward, contemporary Afghanistan plays a critical role in the modern world. Indeed Afghanistan is a product of modern globalization (sometimes called its dark side), as the integration of political (fundamentalist) Islamism and its opium bear witness.[28] As Barnett Rubin points out, Afghanistan's economic networks are transnational, not national or subnational.[29] The transnational opium trade connects Afghanistan with Iran, Dubai, and Pakistan. Furthermore global supply and demand also affect the opium trade.

The heroin economy remains an important determinant for Afghanistan's future, and while many authors have argued that opium was a by-product of the war against Soviet occupation (Griffin, McCoy, Cooley), some argue that the global opium and heroin industrial complex might have helped induce that war.[30] Only after a two-year failure of the monsoon rains in the Burma-Laos area (the heroin capital in the 1970s) did heroin production in South Asia became significant. At the same time, the CIA, working with the Pakistani Inter Services Intelligence Directorate (ISI), already heavily involved in the drug trade, began to fund Islamist warlords.[31] By the 1980s Pakistan was the world's biggest supplier of heroin. Yet the political economy of illegal and illicit commodities (drugs and arms) thrives on armed conflict, which includes the disruption of legitimate state and border controls. Nothing is better for the production of opium than a war that leads, hothouse fashion, with the force of arms, to the destruction of indigenous and often self-sufficient food production and to the introduction of the money economy, or more precisely the cash-cropping opium economy.

A Note on Gulbuddin Hekmatyar

In retrospect the CIA's decade-long Afghan war during the 1980s upset a delicate political balance in Central Asia, devastating Afghanistan, destabilizing Pakistan, and mobilizing radical Islamism. Today's warlords are in many cases the same resistance leaders the U.S. backed in the war against the Soviets and who became the Northern Alliance allies against the Taliban in 2001. Today they represent a significant political problem, but their links to the drug trade are secondary. Though Gulbuddin Hekmatyar was not part of the Northern Alliance and opposed the U.S. invasion, he was perhaps the greatest recipient of CIA aid in the 1980s. Created by the Pakistani ISI, backed by the U.S., a "freedom fighter" against the Soviets, he served as Afghanistan's prime minister in the early to mid-1990s and represented part of the Northern Alliance. In 2004 *Time* magazine claimed the CIA tried to assassinate him that year because he was considered "a dangerous enemy of Karzai and the U.S."[32] The U.S. government's quibble with Hekmatyar is not about his links to narcotics. In fact according to Alfred McCoy, when he became a CIA asset in the 1980s the CIA protected him against investigation and removed restraints on his trafficking: "Once the CIA had invested its prestige in an opium warlord, it could not allow one of its covert-action assets to be compromised by a drug investigation."[33] When Hekmatyar was designated an enemy, the protection was lifted. Excluded from the central administration, he remains a serious opponent with a significant power base. Though he has been allied with the Taliban, he now denies any association, and though he is on the U.S. Most Wanted list,[34] his name surfaced in 2008 as a possible future prime minister.[35]

Afghanistan's Real Political Economy: A Potted History

Opium, the thriving, global, multibillion-dollar industry, drives Afghanistan's economy. In a most profound way Afghanistan is integrated into the global economy as the center of narcotics networks and also expresses an important aspect of contemporary world politics: the legacy of "late cold war" U.S. proxy wars and their connection to drugs, gun running, and money laundering.[36] The process of becoming a narcopolitical economy has been in process since the late 1970s, when the U.S. used drug money to fund Afghan freedom fighters against the Soviet invasion. These same warlords took over power in Kabul after the Soviet army withdrew, plunged the national economy further into the opium trade, sunk the country deeper into civil war, and fought alongside U.S. special units in the war on terror against the Taliban and al Qaeda in 2001.

Opium exports surpass the sum of all Afghanistan's other exports combined. For example, they far outstrip the projected value of the heralded Pakistan, Turkmenistan, and Afghanistan gas pipeline. Most of the opium is shipped to laboratories in Pakistan and consumed in South Asia or exported through Central Asia to Russia and Europe. The opium economy spans an arc from poor farmers reliant on it for survival on one end to the millionaire warlords integrated into transnational and global networks of production and distribution of heroin on the other. Since the fall of the Taliban poppy cultivation had increased a massive 1,500 percent, from 8,000 hectares to 131,000 hectares in 2004 and nearly 200,000 hectares in 2007. Afghanistan is the opium capital of the world, producing over 90 percent of the world's opium for heroin production and supplying Europe with 95 percent of its heroin.[37] Yet because only about 5 percent of the heroin on the streets of the U.S. came from Afghanistan, the U.S. government first viewed the problem as something that European governments should devote resources to fighting. Nevertheless while increasing its drug testing on military personnel in Afghanistan (aware of the devastation that opium wrought on the Soviet military), the U.S. has been critical of the British drug enforcement that funds programs to compensate local governors who are deeply involved in the opium trade. The local governors had been paid to eradicate a percentage of the poppies grown in their provinces and, according to one reporter, "want to pocket the 'eradication' money while making some semblance of eradication to keep Kabul happy."[38]

Though this program has been abandoned there is no reason to think that new eradication programs will have significantly different results.

The U.S. government's counternarcotics strategy is based on "five pillars," including the development of alternative livelihoods and legal reform, which, according to its own accounting office, has failed.[39] Like the earlier "five pillars of security sector reform,"[40] the five pillars of the counternarcotics strategy fly in the face of local realities, where poppies provide livelihood. In addition Afghan farmers have not seen any of the $180 million of government incentives allocated to develop alternative livelihoods.[41]

Much of the $780 million earmarked to eradicating opium production will go to American security firms, who will also work with local warlords. But even a massive increase in the U.S. budget for its war on drugs, as the experience in Colombia suggests, is likely to be woefully inadequate. Such eradication strategies may actually be counterproductive, falling heavily on poor Afghan farmers and leading to the brutalization of local opium-cultivating communities, the devastation of local agricultural economies, and, in the context of the opium economy, actually increasing drug production.[42] War encourages heroin production; thus a war on drugs, understood as a military operation (spraying crops, destroying laboratories, disrupting drug distribution), only affects the economics of demand and supply. On the other hand, the amount of nonmilitary aid needed to shift Afghanistan, especially its rural areas, out of its present state (the culmination of twenty-five years of war) is not only a massive financial commitment but requires a serious paradigm shift.

President Karzai understood that becoming more than the mayor of Kabul depends on controlling the opium business. His financial minister argued in the *New York Times* that the new war on opium would require $40 billion and a ten-year commitment. In contrast, the total aid—and not just for opium eradication—pledged to Afghanistan at the Tokyo conference in 2002 and the Berlin conference in 2004 was $13.4 billion. By February 2005 donors had implemented only $3.3 billion in reconstruction projects.[43] Farmers would have to shift from poppy cultivation to less lucrative crops. This adaptation would require a long-term structural commitment to Afghanistan's rural areas because at the village level opium is integrated into the local economy, including its taxation and lending structures, as well as in its social relations. Indeed the war and the opium economy have helped change social relations, including creating new lines of patronage, with young men now controlling trade. Cash-crop poppy cultivation has encouraged the privatization of previously common grazing land. The erosion of self-sufficient farming has meant increasing inequality, the possibility of future food shortages, and the end of traditional rules about redistribution to the poor.[44] Addressing these issues requires a long-term commitment that is not on the agenda. Moreover opium is a global commodity which runs through the veins of powerful international networks. Like other global commodities, it has an international market and a recognized exchange value. (In fact it also acts as a medium of exchange.) A large part of its value issues not from cultivation but from processing in laboratories, refinement into heroin, and distribution into the global drug market. In practice Karzai understands that it is less about controlling the opium business than about resisting being swallowed up by it.

What's Needed: Trees, Not Buildings

Afghanistan's shift from a system of diverse agriculture to a monocrop opium culture has been aided by the nearly thirty years of war. The poppy economy blossomed with the breakup of the Soviet Union and the collapse of the Afghan state.[45] As Jonathan Goodhand points out, the collapse of the communist government in Kabul saw the decline of external patronage, which forced the warring parties to pursue "wide alternative networks in the regional or global markets."[46] The increasingly porous post-Soviet Central Asian borders, along with liberalization and market deregulation in the 1990s, helped lubricate these networks. Heavy weaponry, land mines, and political policy destroyed herds, orchards, and the delicate ecological balance that had survived previous conflicts. For example, the Taliban cut down trees to undermine the ethnic Tajik areas north of Kabul. In the mountains trees provided ecological continuity and sustenance, and thus contributed to the economic and cultural well-being of the community. Tajik culture relied on trees.[47] The Soviet war and the Afghan Civil War saw the destruction of generations of walnut, pistachio, and mulberry trees, which had helped the populace resist droughts and famines. Additionally the wars helped destroy nonagricultural income and produced a ready pool of labor: an armed, unemployed army, which could be absorbed by the needs of poppy cultivation. Though poppy cultivation requires more labor time, Afghanistan's subsistence farmers shifted their production to this cash crop out of necessity. It was safer, more profitable, and easier to store, transport, and market than producing food for local consumption.

Forms of Late Neo-imperial Rule

With the full-scale military occupation of Iraq, U.S. imperialism seemed to have come full circle.[48] After the country's military defeat in Vietnam, U.S. foreign policy shifted from direct military involvement to wars through proxies, known as resistance or freedom fighters in the 1970s and 1980s, such as those in Angola, Mozambique, Afghanistan, and Nicaragua. These were often groups associated with right-wing death squads, radical Islamism, and the drug trade. With the collapse of communism revisions to this policy saw more direct U.S. military involvement, with NATO and UN backing. The 1990s was the period of "humanitarian intervention" which justified NATO bombing and UN intervention in the Balkans. The UN's involvement in Kosovo provides a context for Afghanistan in two ways. Despite the humanitarian rhetoric, short-term gains and political stability would trump issues of human rights and justified arming and supporting known criminals and drug dealers associated with the Kosovo Liberation Army.[49] These strategies provided the blueprint for the war against terrorism and the nation-building project in Afghanistan. However, only with the shift after 9/11 to unilateralism did the U.S. return to full-scale direct military occupation.[50] By 2006 the future looked much dimmer, the light at the end of the tunnel of occupation farther away from the earlier goal of nation building and democracy. Those who continue to engage the rhetoric of humanitarian intervention indicated that even the start of a democratic state is at least a decade away.[51] A shift in strategy from a war on terror to a war for the hearts and minds of the people also required more resources or more concentrated resources.[52] While the occupation of Iraq has similarities with the war in Vietnam, both in its scale and its complications, the political scope of the Afghanistan occupation has shifted toward a realpolitik judgment that a permanent foothold in the country—without

committing too many human resources—would require a working stale-
mate with the Taliban. The blueprint for the withdrawal from the pur-
ported goal of building a democratic nation-state is already apparent in
Iraq, where, with a dose of Orientalist logic, the retreat is blamed on tribal
and religious animosity. In this view Afghanistan is also considered a fragmented and failed state, a deeply divided "tribalized" society, inhabited by
war-like people from time immemorial. The narrative naturalizes Afghanistan's history and politics as though the country has not been fundamentally part of world politics from the nineteenth century on, through the
cold war, the collapse of communism, post–cold war politics, and the war
on terror.[53] It is an argument that conveniently forgets the Americans'
support for militant Islamists and the important role Afghanistan's powerful and nuclear-armed neighbor Pakistan has played in aiding factions and
the Taliban. And it is an argument that downplays U.S. and NATO support
for the most reactionary local leaders in an attempt to create a coalition
against the Taliban.

Nevertheless the capacity of Afghanistan's central authorities has depended on a patron-client relationship with various factions and the continued autonomy of the outlying regions of the nation. Before 1978 Afghanistan was considered, according to Barnett Rubin, a "rentier state," where
government expenditures and tax revenues were low and a clan- and tribal-
based patron-client system offered a source of security; the division between urban and rural areas both encouraged and resulted from this situation. Karzai's Kabul is a "rentier state" with the election dreams of a tech-
nocratic government fading into a "dysfunctional kleptocracy" based on
international aid.[54] Even paying taxes depends on bribing the tax collector
to register the tax as paid. And, argues Christian Parenti, "sections of the
government have to bribe each other to get simple tasks done."[55] It is a poor
copy of the Afghanistan regime before 1978, but still, things do get done.

It is not surprising that these patronage systems became international-
ized with the war economy. The United States and its allies have done
nothing to change the system, and the Karzai government was simply
mapped on top of already existing patronage networks. It is also not surprising that the drug trade and the arms trade remained the source of
income and power for local warlords, just as international donor aid is the
source of Karzai's income and power.

For late colonialism in the British Empire, indirect rule was a dual system based on a division between the urban and rural areas: the development of a European-type administration in the urban areas and rule through what the colonial administration considered "customary" in the rural areas.[56] The same model could be applied to contemporary Afghanistan. After September 11 the U.S. strengthened the "customary" warlords and thereby their patronage systems in the areas outside Kabul, while at the same time international aid organizations and NGOs helped reestablish civil society in Kabul and a few other urban areas. The election in 2004 also expressed this division: the constitution's insistence on a meritocratic cabinet and the belief in an open and free election on one hand, and on the other the "custom" of patronage outside the cities, which determines voting. The point here is not the thorough applicability of this system of rule but rather elective affinity, reinforcing the idea that the connection between the U.S. proxy war and post-Taliban Afghanistan will continue to be the geopolitical economy of opium. While clearly globalized in a contemporary world, the opium economy also replays older colonial dynamics in Afghan nation building as well.

The history of opium production is intimately linked to Afghanistan's nearly thirty years of war, which resulted in the destruction of its agricultural infrastructure and ecology. Unless aid organizations, the United Nations, and the European Union address the ecological destruction of Afghanistan from the ground up, and unless they include the Afghan farmers in their discussions, attempts at nation and state building will likely continue to be articulated through the politics of opium.

Notes

1 C. J. Chivers, "The Reach of War: Ambush Catches Joint Forces by Surprise as They Patrol Taliban Heartland," *New York Times*, 10 April 2007, sec. A.

2 A painting, *The Remnants of an Army* by Elizabeth Butler, of the sole survivor from the retreat from Kabul in 1842 of a British contingent of approximately fifteen thousand soldiers, made popular the idea that Afghanistan spelled the death of imperial armies.

3 In response to the *London Times* reports of British military blunders in the Crimean Peninsula in the 1850s, the British government sent Queen Victoria's photographer, Roger Fenton, to photograph scenes of the war. Included in the

more than 350 pictures of an orderly army is "Valley of the Shadow of Death," which became one of the most famous photographs of the war. It is a picture of a bleak and barren landscape dotted with thousands of cannonballs that stand in for human casualties.

4 This figure is based on an analysis by Sheila Bird, the vice president of the Royal Statistical Society.

5 Indeed the departing NATO commander, Lt. Gen. David Richard, remarked in February 2007, "We need to realize that we could fail here." M. K. Bhadrakumar wrote an article for the *Asia Times* titled "Afghanistan: Why NATO Cannot Win," 30 September 2006.

6 According to the U.S. Government Accounting Office poppy cultivation increased to 165,000 hectares in 2006, yielding a record 6,100 metric tons of opium, more than 90 percent of the world's illicit opium (*Afghanistan Drug Control*, 2006).

7 Parenti, "Taliban Rising," 14.

8 Ibid. Indeed Parenti argues that the eradication of poppy could plunge Afghanistan "back into all-out civil war."

9 Ibid.

10 Interviewed by Charlie Rose on 3 December 2006, Jimmy Carter represented the humanitarian interventionist position by arguing that in contrast to the war in Iraq, Afghanistan was a "just war." Furthermore if all resources could have been deployed in Afghanistan, genuine democracy could have been established.

11 The lack of institutional capacity is a critique shared implicitly by the Government Accounting Office and in essays in the special issue of *International Peacekeeping* edited by Christopher Freeman (2007).

12 A front-page article by Carlotta Gall, "Marines' Actions Called Excessive in Afghanistan," *New York Times*, 15 April 2007, reported excessive force against a potential bomber that covered ten miles of highway and left twelve civilians dead as marines hit bystanders and vehicles with machine guns.

13 In the whole country there were two suicide bombings in 2002; in 2006 there was about one every five days.

14 For example, see the BBC report of April 2005, "Afghanistan Women Stoned to Death." A study by the United Nations Development Fund for Women (UNIFEM) reported that 65 percent of fifty thousand widows in Kabul see suicide as the only option to rid themselves of their misery and desolation. UNIFEM estimates that one out of three Afghan women are beaten, abused, or forced into sex (see Joya, "The U.S. Has Returned Fundamentalism to Afghanistan").

15 Joya, "The U.S. Has Returned Fundamentalism to Afghanistan." Of course Karzai's second cabinet (in 2010) was soundly revised by the Parliament to address the issues of corruption and past criminal activity.

16 Even the suicide bombings inside Kabul, which caused an initial scare, have now been accepted as a way of life. Kabul even makes it to the front page of the *New*

York Times Travel section: in "The Mysteries of Kabul" (21 January 2007) Joshua Hammer writes, "The war ravaged Afghan capital is beginning to attract a new generation of travelers, many wondering what this city's post-Taliban future will hold."

17 For critiques of humanitarian aid in Afghanistan, see Donini, Niland, and Wermester, *Nation Building Unraveled?*; Goodhand, "From Holy War to Opium War?" For a useful earlier exposé of the consequences of humanitarian intervention in war situations, see De Waal, *Famine Crimes*.

18 Donini, Niland, and Wermester, *Nation Building Unraveled?*, 24.

19 The more active aid groups are frequently targets of attack by local militias. After being in Afghanistan for twenty-four years, Doctors Without Borders left in July 2004, saying that the government had done little to investigate the killing of five of its workers.

20 Earlier that year Karzai was reported to have said, "A jihad should start across the country. We must rid this country of poppy and return Afghanistan to legitimate forms of agriculture" (BNET, "Karzai for Holy War on Opium Trade"). Karzai's statements at that time sit oddly with his problematic action of releasing five convicted drug traffickers just prior to the presidential elections in 2009. According to Mehro Hameed, a senior judge, "If there are honest people within the judicial system who do their jobs honestly and convict these big criminals, only to find a decree is issued, then everything is back to zero" (quoted in Ben Farmer, "Afghanistan: Senior Female Judge Accuses Hamid Karzai over Release of Drug Lords," *Telegraph* [London], 9 September 2009, online [accessed 15 September 2009]).

I have inserted scare quotes around the term *nation building* to indicate that as a concept it needs to be problematized. If a state is built by force, whereas a nation is built through a concurrence of cultures, identity plays an important role. Thus tribal and ethnic identities affect the nation's configuration. Historically the Pashtuns have played a key role as the government and leadership class of Afghanistan. Building a nation thus takes a long time, much longer than those who use the term in policy documents care to consider.

21 Goodhand, "From Holy War to Opium War?"

22 I use the term *rebels* rather than *Taliban* or *al Qaeda* because those identified as al Qaeda are often localized.

23 The scare quotes are awkward, but these are always problematic labels if thought of as static and "primordial." Reading the contemporary history backward, we may easily view identity as fixed. The truth is that identities are political and constructed from particular kinds of inclusions and exclusions. The media, for example, understood the Balkans war and the Rwandan genocide as expressing ethnic animosities that were hundreds, if not thousands, of years old. It is important to consider ethnic identities as subject to change and manipulation as well as being interspersed with issues of patronage and power.

24 In contrast to the per capita cost of humanitarian intervention in Bosnia ($679), Kosovo ($526), and East Timor ($233), the per capita aid in Afghanistan is $57. On the cheap is a reference to British "indirect rule" in colonial Nigeria, which was supposed to be financially self-sufficient and thus cheap. Contrast this to Niall Ferguson's "white man's burden" revisionist rewriting of the history of British imperialism and his advice to the U.S. empire.

25 For American involvement in Southeast Asia and Latin America, see McCoy, *The Politics of Heroin*.

26 From the point of view of stopping poppy cultivation, the Taliban were successful. Brutal methods, which destroyed the country's only viable industry, led to starvation in many parts of the country. Cultivation dropped from 4,000 to 80 tons, and the U.S. awarded the Taliban $43 million in foreign aid. The Northern Alliance subsequently took the opportunity to fill market demand for opium poppies and increased cultivation production.

Though this is not the place to engage the literature about states, perhaps it is enough to note that historically the construction of states is violent and messy—note the Taliban's attempt to build state institutions—and what defines "the state" relies on at least two points. First, as noted earlier, states require hegemony, the monopoly of force, and consent over a given territory. States are not solely about democracy and democratic processes. A monopoly of force obliges consent; legitimacy is produced through the state's ability to produce security and thus to disarm rivals. A narco state, that is, a state involved in the drug trade, is thus not necessarily a nonstate or the absence of a state. The existence of competing armed groups within a territory, even if they are involved in "legitimate" business (in terms of world trade), however, is a problem for the state's existence. Second, in order for a state to exist it requires recognition in the world system. The Afghanistan state, as Barnett Rubin points out in "Rebuilding Afghanistan," was a founding signatory of the United Nations, and though a "weakened state" before the Soviet invasion was still recognized internationally. There are many weak states in the world; in fact some failed states still have the trappings of international statehood. Thus Afghanistan can be proclaimed a state even if Kabul does not have full control of the nation's territory.

27 According to the U.S. State Department, the Taliban played the market, "dumping opium stocks at prices higher than otherwise could have been achieved" (quoted in McCoy, *The Politics of Heroin*, 518).

28 On political Islamism, see Griffin, *Reaping the Whirlwind*.

29 Rubin, "Rebuilding Afghanistan."

30 Scott, *Drugs, Oil and War*, 46.

31 The secret deals between the CIA and the ISI have been described in a number of works. Important links with the CIA include Gulf Group Shipping, involved in shipping goods for U.S. aid programs, and the BCCI bank, with an important branch in London (and connections to the Bank of England), which laundered

drug money. See McCoy, *The Politics of Heroin*; Scott, *Drugs, Oil and War*; Truell and Gurwin, *False Profits*.

32 Nadia Mustafa, "Afghanistan's Turf Wars," *Time*, 3 June 2002. Available at http://www.time.com/time/magazine/article/0,9171,1002591,00.html.

33 McCoy, *The Politics of Heroin*, 526.

34 Christina Lamb and Jerome Starkey, "Karzai in move to share power with warlord wanted by US," *Sunday Times* (London), 10 May 2009. Available online at http://www.timesonline.co.uk/tol/news/world/middle_east/article6256675.ece.

35 See Candace Rondeau, "Afghan Rebel Positioned for Key Role," *Washington Post*, 5 November 2008, online (accessed 22 September 2009). Hekmatyar's power base contrasts with Karzai's, whose administration is based on a fragile alliance between warlords and backed by foreign powers. On the issue of ethnicity, inclusion, and exclusion in Afghanistan's institution building, see Simonsen, "Ethnicizing Afghanistan?"

36 Mamdani, *Citizen and Subject*; see McCoy, *The Politics of Heroin*.

37 Jalali, "The Future of Afghanistan."

38 Chris Horwood, "Stoned Again: A Filmmaker Gets Caught between Desperate Farmers and a Deadly Source of Income," *Financial Times*, 17 December 2006.

39 U.S. Government Accounting Office, *Afghanistan Drug Control*.

40 Each "lead nation" took one of the pillars: army, United States; police, Germany; justice, Italy; combating drugs, Britain; disarmament and demilitarization, Japan. See U.S. Government Accounting Office, *Afghanistan Security*.

41 See Jalali, "The Future of Afghanistan," for a discussion of general corruption in Afghanistan and the failure of funds to reach their intended targets.

42 See McCoy, *The Politics of Heroin*.

43 Ashraf Ghani, "Where Democracy's Greatest Enemy Is a Flower," *New York Times*, 11 December 2004, editorial.

44 See Goodhand, "From Holy War to Opium War?," 274–75.

45 Though the state had never been particularly powerful even under King Zahir and King Daoud in the 1960s and 1970s, it did enforce laws against poppy cultivation.

46 Goodhand, "From Holy War to Opium War?," 271.

47 Nigel Allan, quoted in McCoy, *The Politics of Heroin*, 506.

48 The connection between "late colonial" rule and "late cold war" politics in this section's title is suggested by Mamdani's two books, *Citizen and Subject* and *Good Muslim, Bad Muslim*.

49 See Ali, *Masters of the Universe?*, 354. The *L.A. Times* claimed that the Kosovo Liberation Army was linked to organized crime, narcotics, and al Qaeda. Tariq Ali quotes Ivo Daalder, top advisor to the White House on the Balkans: "If what we are proposing here is starting a major guerilla campaign to regain Kosovo, that is the Afghan syndrome" (354).

50 This continued in the 1980s in its sphere of influence in Panama and Grenada.

51 According to experts cited in the *Canberra Times*, such a scenario depends on being "fully engaged, politically, economically and militarily for at least another 10 to 15 years" ("Another Big Push to Fix the Afghanistan Mess," *Canberra Times*, 14 April 2007, B3).

52 The strategy of restraint on one side and excessive force on the other is a divide-and-rule counterinsurgency tactic as old as the colonial wars. The medium-term goal is to build lasting relations by avoiding military confrontations and train an Afghan police force to patrol secure zones where the population is shown how good life can be when they work with the government. These are show villages, part of a propaganda campaign. Each time the military leaves, however, the Taliban returns. See "Dutch Soldiers Emphasize Restraint in Afghanistan," *New York Times*, 6 April 2007, A1.

53 On the history of Afghanistan in a globalized world, see Rodney Steward's essay in this book.

54 Parenti, "Afghan Wonderland," 12.

55 Parenti, "Chaos and Fear Stalk Afghanistan on 9/11 Anniversary."

56 Mamdani, *Citizen and Subject*.

Afghanistan in a Globalized World

A Longer View

Rodney J. Steward

In September 1996 Taliban soldiers seized control of Kabul, sending President Burhanuddin Rabbani and his interim government fleeing into exile. Immediately Taliban officials declared Afghanistan *dar al-Islam* (an Islamic state) and imposed a strict interpretation of Sharia law. With only two-thirds of Afghanistan under their control, the Taliban launched a relentless campaign to eradicate militant opposition forces still in control of northern provinces. For the next three years battles raged back and forth across the Afghan frontier, through narrow passes high in the Hindu Kush, and in the streets of small towns and villages. To most of the world the Taliban seemed to represent the most extreme and the most violent fundamentalist faction the Islamic world had yet produced. The Taliban themselves greatly contributed to this perception by their reckless disregard for human rights and their willingness to publicly display the victims of their ultraorthodox policies. Furthermore the Taliban leadership's decision to ally itself with the Saudi terrorist Osama bin Laden and his al Qaeda network sent a misleading message to the world about their overall agenda and their vision for international Islamic reform. On the surface the radically fundamentalist principles espoused by Taliban leaders seem like a new phenomenon within the sphere of Islamic fundamentalism. They are, however, the result of decades of internal turmoil generated by the steady advance of globalization. Much recent critical attention focuses on Afghanistan under the Taliban,[1] and this book explores contemporary manifestations of Afghanistan's experience of globalization. I argue that the Taliban phenomenon has not occurred in a vacuum, but rather took shape over a long history of global politics.

The movement's roots stretch back to the early twentieth century and encompass major events in the Islamic world and throughout Central Asia, far beyond the borders of Afghanistan. Indeed Afghanistan's turbulent twentieth-century history foreshadows the emergence of a conservative backlash against reform policies aimed directly at its metaphysical and cultural underpinnings. If we are to understand the Taliban and the global conditions that made their rise to power possible, we must understand globalization's powerful drive to homogenize and the equally powerful drive to resist. In this book Gibson, Szeman, and Bergner explore contemporary dynamics of the homogenizing tendencies of globalization and the variety of forms of its resistance and subversion in Afghanistan after the fall of the Taliban to American-led military forces. I provide a historical understanding of the cohesive role Islam plays in facilitating social continuity within Afghanistan. In the twentieth century these internal factors intermingled with external factors such as the spread of communism and the cold war as well as Western cultural and political values to create an unstable religiopolitical environment. The persistence of that instability has fueled mounting social and political pressure, and in turn generated various crises of identity. Apparent in the unfolding of Afghanistan's troubled twentieth-century history are the dynamics which ultimately culminated in the emergence of the Taliban as seemingly disconnected from the global currents that contributed to its existence.

Islam in Afghanistan

Although Arab invaders carried Islam to the region known as Afghanistan in the middle of the seventh century, where, after decades of conflict, it gained a foothold in Kandahar in A.D. 699, Islam did not become the region's dominant religion until the fourteenth century.[2] Around 1745 an Afghan leader named Ahmed Shah Durrani forced both Safavids and Mughals out of Afghanistan and launched a campaign to seize territory north of the Hindu Kush. In 1767 Ahmed Shah concluded a treaty with the emir of Bukhara recognizing the Amu Darya River as the boundary between their territories. As a gift the emir presented Ahmed Shah with a cloak said to have belonged to the Prophet. Centuries later this cloak would come to play a significant role in the Taliban's rise to power.[3]

Islam penetrated to the heart of Afghan society, becoming the common link that transcended ethnic, linguistic, and cultural barriers. Scholars have noted that conversion to Islam posed no apparent threat to Afghans' tribal traditions in part because of striking similarities between pre-Islamic Central Asian cultures and Arabic culture. According to the historians Ludmila Polonskaya and Alexei Malashenko:

Both areas were characterized by active interaction and mutual alienation between the cultures of nomadic and settled ethnic groups. Long before Islam came into being, people leading a settled way of life developed psychological stereotypes that made them regard their nomadic neighbors as potential enemies. This influenced the spread of Islam and was mirrored in that religion.[4]

Islam reinforced traditional and tribal customs common to Afghan ethnic groups without threatening to erode cultural identity. Moreover Islam provided a lingua franca and a common religious culture that served to break down barriers separating the ethnic groups. To be sure, struggles between many ethnic groups persisted and at times exploded into major conflicts, but generally adherence to Islam brought with it a modicum of unity.

The complementary relationship between Islamic principles and Afghan tribal customs fostered a highly conservative outlook among many ethnic groups, especially among the Sunni majority. Nowhere is this more apparent than among the Pashtun majority, whose traditional law, the Pashtunwali,[5] is at odds with the Sharia on many points. For example, Pashtunwali "demands blood vengeance, even on fellow Muslims." It contradicts "Women," Sura 4 in the Quran, which says, "It is not for a believer to kill another believer unless it be by mistake," and enjoins that blood money be paid to the victim's family. It also diverges from the Sharia on other important matters. For example, "Proof of adultery in Sharia law is dependent on the evidence of four witnesses. In Pashtunwali, hearsay evidence is sufficient because the honour of the family is at issue, not the morality of the situation." In addition Pashtunwali prohibits women from inheriting property, which clearly contradicts the Quran's demand that the woman shall inherit half the share of the man.[6] This unusual blend of tribal custom and Sharia was plainly evident in Taliban policy and drew condemnation from Muslim legal scholars around the world.

Islam became the linchpin of Afghan society by uniting the various ethnic groups, albeit loosely, in a common faith. It emphasized the primacy of the paternal order and further reinforced the system of consensus in the decision-making process. Islam's focus on the equality of believers muted widely held beliefs of ethnic superiority. Afghans, however, placed their own indelible mark on the traditions of Islam. They adapted its rules to accommodate many of their deeply rooted traditions, thereby enabling them to submit to Allah on their own terms.

The Struggle for Afghanistan

Nineteenth-century Afghanistan represents somewhat of a paradox. During this century Afghan kings ruled Afghanistan more or less in its entirety, but as competition mounted between Britain and Russia for influence in Central Asia, Afghan rulers found it increasingly difficult to withstand the pull coming from either direction. Like the rope used in a tug-of-war between two giants, Afghan society strained under the pressure and gradually began to show signs of fraying. As Afghan kings struggled to exercise power and authority within their borders, Britain and Russia took steps to eliminate Afghanistan's sovereignty over its own foreign policy.

British and Russian interest in controlling Afghanistan underscores the region's strategic importance. In the eighteenth century czarist Russia conquered and subjugated most of Central Asia, spreading its influence ever closer to Afghanistan. In the nineteenth century Russia subsumed Tajikistan, Uzbekistan, and Turkmenistan, with the exception of a handful of ancient khanates in each of those regions. Britain, concerned for the safety of its Indian possessions, grew alarmed by Russia's steady advance toward Afghanistan. Both Russia and Britain sought to gain influence with Afghan rulers in an effort to throw up roadblocks in each other's path. Britain gained early ground when in 1809 Shah Shuja signed a treaty of mutual

defense with a British delegation against Russia and France. In 1837, however, when the British governor-general Lord Auckland sent a delegation to
Kabul to urge Dost Muhammad to renew the treaty, Dost Muhammad
refused. Not long after, a Persian army, led by Russian officers, invaded and
laid siege to Herat. The following year Lord Auckland sent an invasion
force to Afghanistan to reinstate Shah Shuja as king. The First Anglo-
Afghan War (1839–42), as the expedition came to be known, ended in
disaster for the British when Afghans rose up en masse in armed rebellion
against the invaders, forcing their withdrawal. On the road back to Peshawar Afghan fighters massacred a column of retreating British and Indian
soldiers led by Maj. Gen. William Elphinstone. In the spring of 1842 Auckland sent another invasion force to Afghanistan to exact revenge for the
previous year's slaughter. The British rescued prisoners taken the year
before, then destroyed large sections of Kabul, including the city's main
bazaar, and then headed for the Khyber Pass and the North West Frontier.[7]

Britain's and Russia's tug-of-war over Afghanistan reached a high point
during the Crimean War. In the second half of the nineteenth century the
British gained the upper hand over the Russians diplomatically, but Russia's direct administration of the Central Asian states beginning in 1868
fueled further tension. In 1879 Britain forced Emir Sher Ali to abdicate after
he shunned British delegates and opened a diplomatic dialogue with Russia. Yaqub Khan, Sher Ali's son, agreed to British terms and signed the
Treaty of Gandamak, which placed oversight of Afghanistan's foreign policy in the hands of the British. In 1880, following the assassination of
the first British foreign policy delegate in Kabul, the British commander
in Afghanistan, Lord Roberts, seized control of Kabul and forced Yaqub
Khan to abdicate. Later that year Abdul Rahman Khan, a relative of Sher
Ali, returned to Afghanistan after twelve years in exile in Samarkand and
St. Petersburg. After crossing the Amu Darya River in 1880 he gathered a
large following in the north, which proclaimed him emir of Afghanistan.
Britain recognized his claim and promptly withdrew its forces from Kabul. The British had high hopes that Abdul Rahman, like Dost Muhammad, would garner enough power to make Afghanistan an effective barrier
against Russia without posing a threat to India. The conclusion of the
Second Anglo-Afghan War (1878–80) left Britain with a clear understanding of the complexity of Afghan society as well as the futility of trying to

administer Afghanistan directly. Britain would devote itself to firming up a strong alliance with Emir Abdul Rahman, all the while believing it could manipulate the internal affairs of Afghanistan by exploiting Abdul Rahman's pro-British stance. They were wrong.[8]

When he became emir, Abdul Rahman Khan utilized all the political skills he had learned while exiled in Russia to consolidate his power and to politely but firmly keep the Russians at arm's length. He was an able, ruthless, and determined ruler whose ambition to modernize Afghanistan would sow the seeds of future conflict out of which the Taliban would eventually emerge. Deeply suspicious of all outsiders, and especially of non-Muslims, he sought to close off Afghanistan from the influence of outside forces. The historian Vartan Gregorian has observed:

During the reign of Abdul Rahman Kahn ... modest technological borrowings and institutional reforms were successfully used to centralize and stabilize the position of the Afghan monarchy. A policy of limited indigenous modernization and national self-sufficiency was anchored to a policy of self-imposed isolation and economic underdevelopment on the assumption that these policies best safeguarded the independence of a country caught up in the rivalries of two great imperialist powers.[9]

First, however, Abdul Rahman had to extend his authority beyond Kabul and snuff out considerable internal opposition to his rule. By 1896 he had brought all the territory between the Russian, Persian, and British spheres under his dominion. His feats of conquest were possible only with a heavy reliance on regular cash subsidies and supplies of arms from the British. Foreign aid enabled him to restructure his military from the ground up by substituting conscription, standardized training, and regular pay for the old feudal system wherein tribal leaders provided support for a particular campaign. Gradually he began laying the groundwork for a centralized government based in Kabul, where he and his advisors oversaw campaigns of expansion and further organized the government. Abdul Rahman crushed Pashtun opposition in the south and forcibly relocated hundreds of thousands of defeated Pashtuns to the region north of the Hindu Kush.

Abdul Rahman's reform and reorganization policies extended to tribal leadership and the *ulama* (legal scholars), supplanting ancient traditions of consensus and power sharing and replacing them with absolute monarchy.

Additionally he was the first Afghan monarch to invoke the concept of the divine right of kings, by formulating a religiopolitical justification for the monarchy. Abdul Rahman's reforms were limited by his distrust of Western powers and the attendant secularizing cultural forces as well as his use of religion to justify his power.[10] Efficaciously combining an earnest appeal for unity among Afghan tribes with the rhetoric of nationalism, he placed the threat of external aggression in a religious context in which the emir was the ultimate religious authority.[11] He embarked on a policy designed to curb the power of the mullahs (religious leaders) and bring them under royal authority. He contended that the preservation of orthodoxy demanded that the mullahs submit to his leadership. He also attacked them by arguing that they had taught "strange doctrines which were never in the teachings of Muhammad, yet which have been the fall of all Islamic nations in every country."[12] He stripped them of their right to declare jihad and denied them the right to prescribe the duties of the emir. He also struck at their economic independence by assuming control of the *waqf* (endowments), making the clergy dependent upon his treasury. He also initiated a policy whereby mullahs were required to take bureaucratic exams proving their ability to serve as functionaries of the state. His attack on the religious establishment would have long-lasting effects on future efforts to restructure Afghanistan.

The paradoxical nature of Abdul Rahman's secularizing changes and adherence to religious laws seems less contradictory when we focus on the political motivations for his policies (his concerted effort to take religious authority away from the mullahs and consolidate power under royal authority). Critics like Timothy Fitzgerald have reinvoked the integrated history of sacred and secular realms such as those operating in Afghanistan's case. Fitzgerald points to the medieval Christian Church, under which society (politics, religion, culture) were united as one body in Christ. He writes, "The holistic cosmology does not lend itself well to the modern idea of a religion-secular dichotomy, but it does lend itself well to the modern idea of degrees of sacredness and profanity which are relative to context."[13] In the cases of Abdul Rahman and his son Habibullah Khan the context and degrees of sacredness played a central role in the ways that religious and secular appeals circulated.

Abdul Rahman's nationalist reforms met with only moderate success.

His plan for safeguarding Afghanistan from imperialist schemes hinged on his ability to achieve a fine balance whereby modest legal, political, industrial, and economic reforms would not offset a general policy of self-imposed isolation. He pushed Afghanistan to modernize for the sake of self-sufficiency but worked diligently to prevent external influences from making inroads into the nation. He sought to order his country along the lines of a modern totalitarian state, wherein all institutions were subordinate to the state. As the divinely appointed defender of Islam in Afghanistan, the emir protected religious orthodoxy, and under his leadership the religious establishment was to exhort the faithful to submit to Allah and to the emir, his earthly delegate.

Abdul Rahman never fully realized his vision for Afghanistan. Although many of the reforms he initiated met little or no resistance, those policies curbing the autonomy of religious and tribal leaders and attempting to steer the various ethnic groups away from tradition were strongly opposed. He died in 1901, leaving the throne to his son Habibullah Khan. In his coronation speech Habibullah laid out his intention to pursue a policy of national unity, resistance to foreign aggression, and reform.[14] Keeping control over the various factions subdued by his father, however, would prove to be a difficult task.

Habibullah greatly expanded the scope of restructuring Afghanistan. Acting upon his father's religiopolitical justification for the monarchy, he formalized court ritual, giving it the appearance of divine sanction. According to Vartan Gregorian, during Habibullah's coronation

the *kahn-i-mullah*, winding a head cloth of white muslin around the new Amir's head, presented him with a copy of the Quran, some relics of the Prophet Muhammad, and a flag from the tomb of an Afghan saint; the intention was to emphasize the Amir's religious duties as well as the divine source of his power. A new and elaborate hand kissing ceremony designed to stress the sacredness of the office was also adopted. Both ceremonies indicate the degree to which the concept of monarchy had evolved.[15]

Habibullah sought to foster an aura of majesty in his court to further enhance the power of the monarchy. Like his predecessor, he first reorganized the army along the lines of professional European armies. He also sought to educate an officer corps by constructing the Royal Military

College. Improvements in education and technology became the hall-marks of his reform policy. He frequently exhorted his people to acquire knowledge, first of Islam and then of the Western sciences.[16] In 1904 he opened Habibiya College, the first secondary school for boys. The school's modest library was the first public library in Afghanistan's history. Habibullah looked to the Ottoman Empire as an example of how Muslims should embrace Western modernity without abandoning their traditions.[17]

Habibullah understood *modernity* as congruent with the modern nation-state. Oliver Roy describes how projects for improvement from Habibullah to his successor, Amanullah, corresponded with an overall agenda of modern nation building:

The constitution of 1923 defined Afghanistan as a nation in which every resident had a right of citizenship whatever his religion. . . . The rupture with Islamic forms of legitimation was also marked by the quest for a pre-Islamic "Indo-Aryan" past (hence the importance of archeology), and the invention of a folklore comprising a number of incongruous elements (the "national" sport was supposedly a Turkish game known as *bozkashi*; the "national" dance, called *atan*, was provincial, and came from Paktya). History was rewritten as if the political unit "Afghanistan" had existed from the earliest times. The school was, of course, the principal vehicle of this nationalist ideology.[18]

Habibullah was a great advocate of the pan-Islamic movement, which recognized the Ottoman caliph as the rightful leader of the Islamic world, but his nationalist tendencies and his pro-British orientation would ultimately prove to be the source of the monarchy's undoing. Stiff opposition to his Westernized education model soon arose from traditionalists among the marginalized religious establishment. The mullahs' resentment toward the monarchy, brewing since the days of Abdul Rahman, surfaced in vocal opposition to the emir's education reforms. Far more diplomatic than his father, Habibullah negotiated with the mullahs and agreed to make substantial concessions to them in regard to curriculum; this enabled the mullahs to get a foot in the door, making future resistance to their demands exceedingly difficult. Unwittingly Habibullah had restored the mullahs' power.[19]

The First World War provided an excellent occasion for Habibullah to renegotiate Afghanistan's relationship with Great Britain. During the war

Habibullah resisted demands from anti-British hawks within his administration to formally ally with the Central Powers. Instead he seized the
opportunity to exploit his country's neutrality by playing the two sides
against each other. In 1915 he welcomed the arrival of a Turko-German
mission sent to strike a formal agreement whereby Afghanistan would join
the Central Powers, receiving arms and a substantial amount of gold in
return for launching an invasion of British India with the support of Indian
rebels already prepared to act. Habibullah delayed signing the agreement
while he attempted to use this information as a bargaining chip with the
British to regain control of Afghanistan's foreign affairs. Britain caught
wind of the scheme, however, and arrested the ringleaders in India before
reaching a deal. The mission returned to Turkey with their meaningless
agreement in hand, and Habibullah, though frustrated that his plan had
failed, believed he had at least placated the war faction within his own
government. Memories of destructive British incursions into tribal lands,
however, still lingered in the minds of tribal leaders, and most of them
harbored deep anti-British sentiments. These men felt betrayed by what
they perceived as Habibullah's pro-British stance during the war. Although
Britain eventually agreed to relinquish oversight of Afghanistan's foreign
affairs, Habibullah had angered the anti-British faction by his refusal to
heed the caliph's call to jihad and join the Ottomans in their struggle
against the British, and also by the obvious extent to which the West influenced his policies. In 1919, while on a hunting trip in the mountains east of
Kabul, unknown persons assassinated him while he slept in his tent.

Habibullah made great strides in nationalizing and reforming Afghanistan. He overhauled public education, made improvements in healthcare,
introduced telecommunications, and built the infrastructure for a nascent
industrial complex. Unlike his father, who used forceful tactics to consolidate absolute power in the hands of the monarchy, Habibullah lost ground
to both the religious establishment and tribal leaders, in part because he
did not rely on force. During his reign the monarchy's power began to
unravel. Religious and tribal leaders grew disillusioned with the emir's role
as defender and sole interpreter of Islam. Many Afghans believed that the
Western values Habibullah promoted threatened to undermine the principles and culture of Islam. In Kabul, Amanullah Khan, Habibullah's son,
acted quickly to seize power. He seemed to be unaware that at the time

of his father's death Afghanistan seethed with discontent, and revolution lurked just beneath a veneer of stability. He established ties with Europe and the United States, sifting the international community for aid to fund his ambitious plans to more thoroughly Westernize Afghanistan.[20]

When the Treaty of Rawalpindi terminated British aid to Afghanistan, Amanullah faced a major financial crisis. According to the historian Barnett R. Rubin, Amanullah "received some military and technical aid from many countries, including the Soviet Union, Turkey, Germany, France, Italy, and Britain, but none of these sources proved regular or generous enough to constitute a reliable basis for state power." To finance the cost of technical assistance Amanullah had to develop domestic resources and shape them into a revenue-generating asset. The imperative was clear: he had to "reverse Abdul Rahman Khan's isolationism . . . and open the country to trade and to promote state-led capital accumulation."[21] The politics of Afghan tribalism and resistance to Western values, however, would make Amanullah's efforts to shape his country into a modern nation-state an explosive issue.

Amanullah's strategy for transforming Afghanistan's peasant-based agricultural economy into a market-oriented capitalist society was ambitious and all-encompassing. His reforms began with changes in taxation, land tenure, and transportation. According to Rubin, "Amanullah regularized the system of taxation, abolishing tax farming, and requiring that all taxes be paid in cash. He abolished many arbitrary taxes . . . and relied heavily on direct taxes on agriculture." Predictably his tax increases brought him into conflict with the landowning khans and tribal leaders. He also restructured customs duties and "actually tried to collect them, which in turn brought him into conflict with border tribes who lived by smuggling." His land tenure policies aimed to maximize the profitability of both land and labor. He abolished slavery, sold off vast tracts of government-owned land, legalized private landholding among small farmers, and thus "created a new class of peasant proprietors."[22] To encourage and facilitate trade he built a new network of roads and made improvements to old ones. To ensure that passage remained uninhibited he established garrisons along them, especially in border areas to prevent border tribes from illegally exacting duties, which further exacerbated tension between those tribes and the government. Amanullah also sought to make improvements in the army, mostly by increasing soldiers' pay. Lack of funds and general cutbacks, however, negated the soldiers' gains, causing morale to plummet. For reasons that defy explanation, Amanullah did not see the value in securing the army's loyalty. His failure to win the support of his top generals would ultimately prove disastrous.

The most contested of Amanullah's reforms were those aimed at education and those that struck at the power of the religious establishment. He wholly embraced Western education and opened Afghan schools to European influence. Between 1922 and 1927 French, German, and British schools opened in Kabul, where students learned the corresponding language and imbibed Western values. He established primary schools in every district of Afghanistan and made children's school attendance compulsory. He also developed a policy whereby the government sponsored elite students' education abroad and, according to Rubin, "shocked many Afghans by sending girls to study in Turkey and Switzerland."[23] He forbade the wearing of traditional dress in Kabul and exhorted Afghans to adopt Western attire. He scorned the practice of purdah and proudly circulated photographs of the royal family in Western dress.[24]

Amanullah's reforms went far beyond molding Afghanistan into a Westernized nation-state. Tribal leaders and the religious establishment perceived his Westernization scheme as an assault on the laws and customs of Islam and on the very character of Afghan society. The reforms also alienated certain ethnic groups economically by shifting the nexus of economic development. The Tajiks, for example, began to experience societal breakdown under the strain of Amanullah's new economic policies. Beginning in 1927 small rebellions broke out among Pashtuns, Tajiks, and Hazaras, and the army was sent to deal with them. In 1928 Amanullah embarked on a seven-month tour of Europe, which only fueled rumors that he was turning against Islam. Shortly after his return frustrated Tajiks and Pashtuns rose up in rebellion. The army had fallen into disarray, and several top generals deserted to join the rebels. A disgruntled Tajik named Bacha e Saqqao led the rebels to victory over Amanullah's dilapidated army. In 1929, after a brief but fierce civil war, Amanullah conceded defeat and fled to Italy, where he remained in exile until his death in 1960.[25]

The collapse of Amanullah's government at the hands of discontented rebels revealed to future Afghan leaders the perils of imposing sudden and pro-Western changes on the Afghan people.[26] Since the days of Abdul Rahman Khan, Durrani leaders had sought to impose upon Afghans the governing mechanism of a centralized modern nation-state by consolidating both sacred and secular authority in the hands of an absolute monarch and by personally dictating the terms of Afghanistan's transition to a modern state.[27] Their abrupt and autocratic approach to reforming Afghanistan's social, economic, and political profile threatened to undo the religious and tribal power structure upon which Afghan society rested. Herein lies Afghanistan's contemporary dilemma: how to form a central government, modernize, and safeguard independence without threatening the traditional distribution of power or compromising Afghans' Islamic identity by the imposition of Western values. This dilemma is the wellspring of much political, social, and religious discontent in modern Afghanistan, for it lays bare the geopolitical reality the country faces. Moreover it demonstrates Afghans' inability to reconcile the conventions of their faith and culture with ever-shifting paradigms in a globalized world order.

In 1929 Nadir Khan was crowned shah (king) of Afghanistan. His ascension represented a dynastic shift and the rise to power of the Musahibans, a branch of the deposed Durrani family.[28] In his bid to seize power Nadir Shah relied heavily on British aid, and as king he sought to reestablish friendly relations with Great Britain. He was a staunch conservative and sought to restore the traditional power structure, which the Durrani kings had worked feverishly to destroy. His vision for Afghanistan's future differed sharply from that of his predecessor. Politically Nadir Shah gravitated toward the British sphere, which encouraged his conservative agenda, in part because it helped to placate Pashtuns in the North West Frontier Province (now named Khyber-Pakhtoonkhwa) of Pakistan. His pro-British stance alienated Stalinist Russia, which had given support to Amanullah and his modernist policies. Once again Afghanistan found itself maneuvering between Britain and Russia.[29]

Unlike his Durrani predecessors Nadir Shah stressed the primacy of traditional modes of discourse as the basis of relations between tribal and religious leaders and his government. He did not exercise absolute authority, but rather formulated and administered policy with the help of his four brothers. Moreover his authority derived not from divine right, but from the consensus of an ad hoc *loya jirga* (council of leaders), convened to oversee the transfer of power. Early on he faced the perilous task of restoring power to the central government, which required skillful diplomacy. He and his brothers carefully presided over a political network of patronage that emphasized close relationships with the khans and other regional potentates. In an effort to gain the backing of certain powerful khans who had supported his bid for power, he offered exemption from taxation and conscription. These concessions hampered his efforts to rebuild and replenish the army, which was vital for retaining power. To accomplish this task he placed heavier taxation and conscription demands on other tribes and relied upon financial aid from Britain and technical assistance from German advisors.[30]

After two years in power Nadir Shah had extended his authority over most of the country, but the costs of restoring royal power and winning tribal support were high. He had resorted to brutal and repressive measures, driving a wedge between his government and some of the tribes and the small group of educated elites who owed their status to Amanullah's education reforms and remained loyal to him.[31] Furthermore his political reforms alienated the religious establishment. When he came to power in 1929 Nadir Shah declared that *hanafi sharia* law would be the legal code of his administration, thus assuring the religious establishment of his intention to respect their traditional authority. Controversy arose in 1931, however, over the new constitution, which detailed provisions for the coexistence of secular and Sharia law.[32] To the dismay of religious leaders, secular law gained a de facto popular mandate supported by the government. Gradually the Sharia slipped into a subordinate role and functioned only as a secondary legal code. Like Amanullah before him, Nadir Shah inadvertently marginalized powerful factions within his realm without anticipating their capacity to seek revenge. The persistence of political fragmentation portended an ominous future for the new king's government.

Nadir Shah also sought to reform Afghanistan, but he chose to proceed cautiously and at a much slower pace than Amanullah. His government pursued what Gregorian has termed a policy of "selective modernization."[33] He restricted the number of foreign technicians allowed to enter Afghanistan and channeled their efforts exclusively toward state-building projects. He established a central bank and authorized private corporations to develop Afghanistan's resources for export trade. In education, however, he reopened only a handful of Amanullah's controversial schools, most of which had closed during the rebellion. He also made changes to the curriculum, placing stronger emphasis on Islamic studies, and he banned schooling for girls. Ultimately Nadir Shah's patronage system, coercive tactics, and political reforms failed to placate the multitude of disgruntled factions stewing throughout his kingdom. Much like the last days of Habibullah Khan's government, Afghanistan under Nadir Shah seethed with discontent. In 1933 he was assassinated and his nineteen-year-old son, Mohammad Zahir Shah, succeeded him as king.

During the avuncular period (1933–53, when Zahir Shah's uncles served as regents and administered the state), after avenging their brother's murder, Zahir Shah's uncles devoted their attention to establishing peace and harmony among the members of the loya jirga. They revised the constitution, making Sharia the law of the land, and thus mollified disgruntled religious leaders. They agreed to concessions that strengthened the loya jirga's political voice but cleverly used the patronage system to keep the assembly under their control. Under their guidance Afghanistan kept a cool distance from the Soviet Union but never fully severed ties. In the 1930s the king's uncles continued to seek economic assistance abroad, mainly from the Axis powers. Although strong relations were cultivated with Germany, Italy, and Japan in the 1930s, Zahir Shah's uncles managed to preserve Afghanistan's neutrality during the Second World War. Economically, however, the outbreak of war all but halted economic development in Afghanistan, and the government sought desperately to reverse the economic stagnation besetting the country. Early in the 1940s, after protracted negotiations with the Allies, the regents agreed to expel all nonessential Axis diplomats in exchange for the Allies agreeing to purchase all the food and various other materials Afghanistan could produce.[34] The bargain stimulated agricultural production and averted an economic disaster, but by 1946 war debts forced Britain to make drastic cuts in foreign aid to Afghanistan, leaving Zahir Shah's government to fend for itself.[35]

In the postwar period the Soviet Union emerged as an aggressive superpower with an expansionist agenda and a renewed interest in establishing its hegemony over Central Asia. Under the czars Russia had posed a political and military threat to Afghanistan, but the threat from communist Russia was far more insidious. Officially atheist, Russia waged an ideological war among Central Asian Muslims, threatening to uproot Islam throughout the region. Fearful of the red giant on the other side of the Amu Darya River, Zahir Shah's government earnestly sought to cultivate closer ties with the United States.[36] American statesmen had long considered Afghanistan irrelevant, a political backwater of no strategic importance for gaining the upper hand in the cold war standoff taking shape in Europe. Hoping to improve Afghanistan's status among the community of nations and possibly attracting greater attention from the United States, the uncles sent a representative to the United Nations and an ambassador to Washington. The United States did offer aid and assistance to Afghanistan, especially with state-building projects like the Helmand Valley Project, but U.S. aid was never substantial enough to bolster Afghanistan's flagging economy.[37] Between 1946 and 1953 frustrated Afghan leaders tried in vain to foster a supportive relationship with the United States similar to the relationship they had once had with Great Britain.

Zahir Shah's uncles created a political environment plagued with corruption but wholly committed to preserving the status quo. Under their direction Afghanistan experienced a resurgence of interest in conservative Islamic culture, especially among the peasant majority. Moreover during this period Afghanis came to view the position of the government as an indicator of the state of Islam in Afghanistan.

On 27 September 1953 Zahir Shah's first cousin, Mohammad Daoud Khan, toppled the government and emerged as the new prime minister. Daoud drew his political power from the loyalty of the army, which he commanded. His government initiated sweeping modernization programs and pursued political reforms similar to those of Amanullah. With the backing of the army, Daoud suppressed internal opposition ruthlessly and devoted much of his time to promoting Pashtun nationalism, mostly across the border in Khyber-Pakhtoonkhwa, which according to the historian Hafizullah Emadi, "manifested itself in Afghanistan's policy toward Pakistan over the issue of the Durand Line."[38] Daoud pressed Pakistan aggressively for the development of an independent Pashtunistan carved from the tribal areas of the North West Frontier Province. The issue hardened into a full-blown controversy, culminating in Pakistan's closure of the border with Afghanistan in 1961.

Daoud's military forces paled in comparison with Pakistan's well-trained army and modern air force, and therefore he began seeking military assistance from the international community. In 1954 he sent his brother to Washington to request military aid, but the Americans refused to supply any aid until the Pashtunistan controversy with Pakistan was resolved. Not long after, however, Washington agreed to supply Pakistan with a substantial number of arms. Alarmed by what he perceived as an economic and military threat, Daoud convened the loya jirga for an emergency meeting to discuss the situation. The loya jirga voted unanimously to appeal to the Soviet Union for military assistance. By 1955 the Soviets had provided Daoud with over $600 million in military and economic aid.[39] Within two short years of coming to power Daoud had removed Afghanistan from the Western sphere of influence and placed the country squarely within the Soviets' camp.

During Daoud's tenure as prime minister small numbers of disaffected intellectuals, religious clerics, and members of the middle class expressed opposition to Afghanistan's exclusive and corrupt form of government and began forming liberal political movements. Because of their small numbers the government did not perceive them as a threat and allowed them to continue expressing their political views. Gradually these groups formed political parties and sought election to the Afghan Parliament. They also began producing journals and newspapers to further disseminate their political views. Most vociferous among these liberals was a group of young Islamists who called for sweeping governmental reform and advocated a reassertion of Islamic values.[40] In the parliamentary elections of 1952 the liberal parties failed to win a single seat, which led them to suspect the government of tampering with the results. Party journals immediately accused the government of election fraud, and members staged a massive protest in Kabul. Students from Kabul University joined the liberals, and together they demanded new elections. Incensed by the protest, Daoud ordered the army to disperse the demonstrators and arrest the leaders. The army arrested many protestors; some went to prison, but a substantial number of liberal leaders fled to Pakistan, including several leading Islamist agitators.[41]

Throughout the 1950s Daoud's government confidently pursued reform and modernization projects, particularly in urban areas. The Soviet Union supplied the bulk of material and expertise for such projects as road building, construction of military runways, and, grandest of all, the Salang Tunnel. The United States also supplied aid and assistance, but the Soviet Union dwarfed its contributions. Projects aimed at broadening educational opportunities rapidly expanded Kabul University's curriculum, and students from all parts of the country flooded the capital to take advantage. However, the vast majority of university students came from the ranks of the aristocracy and the well-to-do, which gave these new opportunities in education an elitist edge. The university's newest departments, all of which were secular, received the lion's share of funding from the government. Gradually the university's religious departments were relegated to seminary status. The elites studied the new secular curriculum, which included calculus, science, engineering, chemistry, and philosophy, while poor and undereducated students from the countryside enrolled in religious studies. In Kabul the religiopolitical implications were clear: Daoud's modernization efforts pandered to the wealthy and powerful while undermining and minimizing the traditions and authority of Islam.

Daoud stirred controversy again in 1959, when he and several of his top advisors appeared before a large crowd during a public ceremony with their wives and daughters unveiled. A massive protest from the religious establishment followed, but Daoud's Soviet-equipped army quickly moved in and dispersed the crowd with excessive force.[42] This incident triggered a flurry of protests and widespread opposition to the government, which ultimately led to Daoud's banishment from politics.[43]

Between 1961 and 1963 opposition to Daoud's government took the form of two organizations: the People's Democratic Party of Afghanistan (PDPA) and a collection of Islamist groups that coalesced around the Jamaat i Islami Party. Both endured a furious campaign of persecution from the government, which sought to eradicate all opposition. Daoud's henchmen murdered or imprisoned thousands of dissidents and forced many thousands more to flee to Pakistan and Iran. In spite of the government's purge, opposition surfaced among rural peasants whose living conditions had deteriorated to critical levels due to the closure of the border with Pakistan and to government neglect. The peasantry rallied behind a small but vocal group of mullahs who took offense at the government's clearly secular posture. The urban middle class voiced their opposition to Daoud's use of force and expressed their concern about the government's close ties with the Soviet Union, which many feared posed a grave threat to Afghanistan's independence. The public's discontent reached a critical point in 1963, and Zahir Shah intervened to demand Daoud's resignation. Daoud complied without a fight and handed power to his cousin peacefully.[44] Zahir Shah announced the formation of a new government and proclaimed general amnesty for all exiled political dissidents. Thousands returned to Afghanistan, and the people waited patiently for the new government to take shape.

Over the next decade Zahir Shah managed the government through a long series of prime ministers appointed to carry out his plans. The hallmarks of his new government were gradual modernization and liberal constitutional reform. Under Daoud the government had taken a liberal view on many issues, especially gender roles. Hundreds of women found government jobs, and some rose to positions of power within the Parliament. Traditionalists pointed to women's new status as evidence that the government had reneged on its responsibility to uphold the values of Islam and the customs of the Afghan people. Zahir Shah supported the new liberal policies, and he sought to make them the basis for the new constitution. In 1964 he established a Constitutional Advisory Committee, which included two women, to hammer out the details. According to Peter Marsden, "Among the more important provisions of the 1964 Constitution was the legal equality of both men and women. The Constitution also gave precedence to the secular legal code over the Sharia law."[45] The effects of legal gender equality and relegation of the Sharia to the status of near insignificance would be far-reaching.

Daoud's removal prompted Pakistan to reopen the border, unleashing a flood of relief supplies and trade goods. As relations with Pakistan warmed, Moscow stepped up efforts to win influence with the Afghan king. Although Zahir Shah made overtures to the West, he neither compromised his relationship with Moscow nor acquiesced to Soviet influence. His foreign policy strategy was to maintain a middle ground by which he could exploit his county's traditional neutrality, as many of his predecessors had done.[46] Moscow grew frustrated with its inability to develop a positive relationship with the Afghan king and therefore sought to secretly foster political opposition by exploiting the constitution's provision for political freedom. The Soviets gained influence with a leftist faction in the PDPA that advocated communism for Afghanistan. By the late 1960s the PDPA was polarizing into right-wing (nationalists) and leftist (socialists) camps. The Right, composed of middle-class merchants, some aristocrats, and several landowning khans, formed the bulk of the king's supporters and benefited greatly from his patronage. The leftists were mostly students, clerics, and educated elites who were dissatisfied with the king's experiment with democracy and called for a total redistribution of wealth by way of a communist revolution. Additionally several Islamist groups had gained followers, especially in the nontribal northern provinces among Tajiks, Uzbeks, and Turkmen who had fled to Afghanistan from Soviet Central Asia to escape the communists' persecution of Muslims. In spite of his efforts to bring about democratic reform, Zahir Shah was unable to quell the political volatility running rampant throughout his kingdom, and in July 1973 Daoud emerged from the shadows to take control once again. Zahir Shah was on a state visit to Italy when word reached him that Daoud had deposed him and seized control of the government.

The Soviet invasion that began in 1979 sent four million Afghan refugees fleeing to Pakistan and Iran and created a humanitarian crisis on a scale the world had never before seen. In both countries refugees huddled in sprawling camps not far from the border. Conditions were appalling, and shortages of food, clothing, water, and shelter soon made them disease-infested shantytowns where infant mortality soared and the average life expectancy plummeted. In Pakistan the seven mujahideen groups officially recognized by the Pakistani government organized their own camps; their names and leaders were Jamaat i Islami (Burhanuddin Rabbani), Hisb e Islami or Hekmatyar (Gulbuddin Hekmatyar), Hisb e Islami or Khalis (Younis Khalis), Ittihad i Islami (Abdul Rasoul Sayyaf), the Afghan National Liberation Front (Sibghatullah Mujadidi), Harakat i Inqilab i Islami (Nabi Muhammadi), and Mahaz i Milli i Islami (Pir Gailani). Each of these groups emerged out of Afghanistan's political chaos and persecution. Four were Islamist (fundamentalist), "in that they sought to create a political movement with an ideological basis that drew on a reinterpretation of the essential elements of Islam." The Islamist groups were Jamaat i Islami, Hisb e Islami, and Harakat i Inqilab i Islami. The other three groups were considered traditionalists, "in that they emerged from traditional tribal or other groupings within Afghanistan."[47] Each of these parties received military aid from the Pakistani government and organized their own militias, responsible for conducting military operations within Afghanistan. In 1985 these seven parties coalesced into the Seven Party Alliance and agreed to work in concert to drive out the Soviets and establish an Islamic state in Afghanistan.

In and around the mujahideen camps in Pakistan thousands of madrasas (Islamic schools) sprang up to offer Afghan boys a basic Islamic education. Because the peasantry's drift toward religious education had begun more than a decade earlier parents viewed madrasa education as a blessing and an opportunity for their sons to learn the fundamentals of their faith as well as to receive a basic education, which would see them through to victory over the atheist invaders of Afghanistan. Most of these schools were funded and operated by ulama of the Pakistan-based Jamiat ul ulama i Islam, a radical fundamentalist organization with close ties to Wahabi factions in Saudi Arabia.[48] As a result of Pakistan's Islamization program in the 1970s, sponsored by the dictator Muhammad Zia ul-Haq, the number of madrasas and Islamic institutions in Pakistan rose dramatically. Islamization fostered radicalism among the ranks of Pakistan's multitude of fundamentalist groups. As the number of madrasas increased, the quality of scholarship declined sharply. The madrasas that Afghan refugees attended had devolved into small stations for indoctrinating children in the religio-political ideology of radical Islamic fundamentalism. They also served to provide future mujahideen with a basic military education and thereby nurtured the Kalashnikov culture that characterized mujahideen camps in Pakistan. Most students, or *talibs*, trained in camp madrasas remained illiterate after completing their education but often assumed the title *mullah*. In camps and madrasas such as these an entire generation of Afghan boys received the basic knowledge and training that would inform their worldview.

In April 1988 the Soviets signed the Geneva Accords, which formalized the terms and conditions under which the Soviet army would withdraw from Afghanistan. A year later, in February 1989, the last Soviet regiment crossed the Amu Darya River, leaving Afghanistan in the hands of President Muhammad Najibullah, a Moscow-backed puppet of the PDPA. Almost immediately hundreds of thousands of refugees began returning, but many more stayed in the camps, fearful of what lay ahead. The mujahideen leaders returned to Afghanistan eager to begin asserting their political agendas, but soon the unity that had held them together during the years of Soviet occupation broke down.[49] Rural areas quickly became dangerous places where determined mujahideen factions battled each other in ever-increasing confrontations. The leaders turned on each other too, as one sought to seize control of a highway that lay within another's territory or to gain control of smuggling in a certain region. Within a year of Soviet withdrawal the mujahideen leaders who had once enjoyed a degree of respectability in the eyes of the world had degenerated into leaders of armed gangs, warlords among a war-torn people. Fragmentation among the mujahideen factions crippled the groups' ability to pursue their goal of establishing an Islamic state.

President Najibullah held on to power from 1989 to 1992 by taking advantage of this division, allying with one faction to fend off another. In 1992, however, a lull in the fighting allowed the mujahideen enough time to form a unified front against Najibullah's government. After a bloody campaign in which mujahideen factions shelled the capital for days on end, Najibullah relinquished his power and sought refuge in a UN compound in Kabul. The mujahideen factions agreed that Jamaat i Islami's leader, Burhanuddin Rabbani, should assume control of an interim government until a loya jirga assembled to vote for a new leader. Within weeks, however, another leader, Gulbuddin Hekmatyar, who felt slighted by Rabbani's appointment, launched an attack on Kabul, shattering the fragile peace and plunging Afghanistan into the bloody abyss of civil war.[50]

Between 1994 and 1996 the crisis in Afghanistan grew out of control. In rural areas unspeakable atrocities were committed against innocent peasants. The Taliban emerged from this chaotic situation in 1994, one of many factions seeking to gain control of the area around Kandahar, and within months they controlled one third of the country. The suddenness of their rise to power and their leaders' virtual anonymity has generated a good deal of myth about who they were, where they came from, and what they stood for. The Taliban (Pashto plural for "students") was composed of those madrasa students educated in the refugee camps of Pakistan. Many of them had fought alongside the mujahideen leaders during the Soviet occupation, acquiring significant military skills. As madrasa students they fell under the influence of fundamentalists in Jamiat ul ulama i Islam, who throughout the war in Afghanistan had sought to indoctrinate students with a heterodox ideology founded upon a strict application of Sharia and a strong emphasis on an outward display of Islamic morality and piety that coincided with the conventions of Pashtunwali law.[51] Although poorly educated and without substantial backing, the Taliban were dedicated to establishing a purified Islamic state in Afghanistan and to ridding their country of the corrupt mujahideen leaders, who, in their view, had abandoned the goal of establishing an Islamic state purged of outside influence. Their rise to power, however, must not be seen as the logical outcome of events whose roots stretch back across the century. If we view the Soviet invasion as the most aggressive effort to move Afghanistan out of its traditional position of relative isolation into the mainstream of world events, then the Taliban and their single-minded determination to safeguard Islam and traditional Afghan culture is their equally aggressive counterpart.

In 1993 the government of Benazir Bhutto sought an alliance with the Taliban, hoping to reopen trade routes with the Central Asian republics. In 1994 Pakistan's Inter Services Intelligence Directorate began funneling supplies and advisors across the border to the Taliban in advance of a trade convoy moving north from Pakistan to Herat. Taliban fighters easily defended the convoy from highwaymen and assured its safe passage. Later that year the Taliban toppled the warlord governor of Kandahar province, restoring order and disarming the populace.[52] Their leader, the mysterious mullah Muhammad Omar, himself a Pashtun from Kandahar, began laying the foundations for what would become the Taliban creed.[53]

Unlike their mentors in Jamiat ul ulama i Islam, the Taliban never had an ideology per se, but rather embraced a creed that served as their blueprint for building an orthodox Islamic state. First they would proclaim a jihad against the corrupt mujahideen leaders and rid Afghanistan of their influence. Their goal then was to implement a strict interpretation of Sharia and Pashtunwali law. They would safeguard the virtue of Afghan society and fully integrate all ethnic groups by proclaiming a government-led jihad against all Western influence. Finally, in all things they would seek to reestablish traditional gender roles and modes of conduct so that the honor of Afghan Muslims would be unblemished. Legislative authority would rest in the hands of *shuras* (council of mullahs and ulama), and the emir ul-muminin (leader of the faithful) would exercise executive authority.

When placed in the context of Afghanistan's twentieth-century attempts at political, social, and economic reform, the conservative nature of the Taliban and the creed they held up as a model for building an orthodox Islamic state possess a predictability heretofore overlooked. For decades nationalists and traditionalists have engaged in ever-widening battles over Afghanistan. Over the past one hundred years Afghanistan has experienced the "pressure cooker" effect of being sandwiched between two major imperial powers, and its own survival has depended upon the ability of its people to maintain the purity of their religious and cultural identity.

Notes

1 The most central, of course, is Ahmed Rashid's *Taliban: Militant Islam, Oil, and Fundamentalism in Central Asia*. Other works include Marsden, *The Taliban*; Goodson, *Afghanistan's Endless War*; Maley, *Fundamentalism Reborn?*; Gohari, *The Taliban*; Matinuddin, *The Taliban Phenomenon*; Crews and Tarzi, *The Taliban and the Crisis of Afghanistan*.

2 Polonskaya and Malashenko, *Islam in Central Asia*, 7–12.

3 Marsden, *The Taliban*, 14. The cloak presented to Ahmed Shah is known as "the cloak of the Prophet." Ahmed Shah built a mosque in Kandahar to house the cloak, where it remains to this day. In 1996 the Taliban leader Mullah Muhammad Omar stood on a rooftop before a large crowd of followers in Kandahar and wrapped himself in the cloak. This symbolic gesture triggered a thunderous roar of approval from the crowd below. Omar was then named emir ul-muminin (leader of the faithful), and he proclaimed a jihad against the mujahideen government in Kabul.

4 Polonskaya and Malashenko, *Islam in Central Asia*, 1. See also Barfield, *The Central Asian Arabs of Afghanistan*.

5 *Pashtunwali* is the Pashtun word for a specific code of values. According to the anthropologist Akbar S. Ahmed, Pashtunwali holds more sway in areas where people live at greater distances from other laws. Pashtunwali has been generally understood to include concepts such as *nang* (honor), *qalang* (rent for land use), *melastia* (hospitality), *nanawati* (sanctuary), and *badal* (revenge). Pashtunwali forges particular kinds of social and political relationships. For example, renting from a landlord, according to Ahmed, codifies the "symbiotic roles of patron and client" (*Millennium and Charisma among the Pathans*, 75–76).

6 Marsden, *The Taliban*, 85–86.

7 Ibid., 16–19. After signing the mutual defense treaty with Britain, Shah Shuja was overthrown and forced into exile in India. By 1837 Britain's concern about Russia's intrigues in the region was near climax. The British dispatched a host of spies and

delegates to Afghanistan to gather intelligence and to gain influence with Emir Dost Muhammad. Britain's best-known delegate was Capt. Alexander Burnes, who was impressed with Dost Muhammad and recommended to his superiors that Britain seek an alliance with him. Dost Muhammad was unwilling to compromise his neutrality—a point he demonstrated by receiving the Russian delegate to Tehran. He also insisted that Britain force the Sikhs out of Peshawar and the North West Frontier. Infuriated, Burnes left Kabul and returned to India. The British then decided to support Shah Shuja's bid to reclaim his throne. Shah Shuja struck an alliance with the British and the Sikhs and successfully overthrew Dost Muhammad in 1839. See Magnus and Naby, *Afghanistan*, 32–34.

8   Klass, *Afghanistan*; Marsden, *The Taliban*. See also Grover, *Afghanistan*.

9   Gregorian, *The Emergence of Modern Afghanistan*, 8.

10 See Magnus and Naby, *Afghanistan*.

11 Ibid., 130; Poullada, *Reform and Rebellion in Afghanistan*, 5–8.

12 Magnus and Naby, *Afghanistan*, 135.

13 Fitzgerald, *Discourse on Civility and Barbarity*, 76.

14 Gregorian, 181.

15 Ibid, 182.

16 In general scientific history the Muslim world experienced a "golden age" of scientific work between A.D. 900 and 1200 which operated within greater Islamic structures of thought. Aaron Segal illustrates how Muslim centers in the Middle East such as Cairo, Baghdad, and Cordoba vied for dominance with Chinese science and that Islam was the force that propelled scientific discovery. Between the thirteenth and eighteenth centuries the Islamic world experienced a general decline in scientific advancement while European knowledge began its ascent. See Segal's "Why Does the Muslim World Lag in Science?" for a discussion of this history as well as factors that have helped or hindered Islamic science in more recent times. See also al-Hassan and Hill, *Islamic Technology*.

17 Fitzgerald, *Discourse on Civility and Barbarity*, 184–85. The Ottoman Empire, 1302–1922, covered parts of North Africa, the Middle East, and the Mediterranean.

18 Roy, *Islam and Resistance in Afghanistan*, 18.

19 See Dupree, *Afghanistan*; Poullada, *Reform and Rebellion in Afghanistan*; Gregorian, *The Emergence of Modern Afghanistan*; Maley, Fundamentalism Reborn?

20 Marsden, *The Taliban*, 20–21.

21 Rubin, *The Fragmentation of Afghanistan*, 54.

22 Ibid., 55.

23 Ibid., 56.

24 Purdah is the practice of secluding women from the gaze of men who are not directly related to them. The practice has an international history, not limited to the Muslim world. See Jennifer Heath's excellent collection, *The Veil*. In Afghanistan the seclusion of women is very directly connected to Pashtunwali as well as

class affiliation. Here, as in other parts of the world, women from the upper classes were more generally secluded than women working outside the home. In various contexts the adoption of the veil has not necessarily been equated with submission to patriarchal institutions. Women who have actively taken on the veil have done so in order to afford greater mobility in the public world or as a political statement that affirms Islamic or anti-Western positions. See Mernissi, *Beyond the Veil.*

25 Marsden, *The Taliban*, 21; Poullada, *Reform and Rebellion in Afghanistan*, 196–212.

26 Newell and Newell, *The Struggle for Afghanistan*, 38.

27 Abdul Rahman Khan, Habibullah Khan, and Amanullah Khan were all part of the Pashtun Durrani dynasty, which dates back to the eighteenth century. Its founder, Ahmad Shah Durrani, forced the Safavid and Mughal emperors out of Afghanistan.

28 Newell and Newell, *The Struggle for Afghanistan*, 38–39.

29 For the definition of the "Great Game," see Altaf Ullah Khan's essay in this book.

30 Ibid.

31 Newell and Newell, *The Struggle for Afghanistan*, 38–39. See also Marsden, *The Taliban*, 21–22; Magnus and Naby, *Afghanistan*, 34; Rubin, *The Fragmentation of Afghanistan*, 54; Gregorian, *The Emergence of Modern Afghanistan*, 295.

32 Marsden, *The Taliban*, 21.

33 Gregorian, *The Emergence of Modern Afghanistan*, 292.

34 The Allies included the UK, France, the Soviet Union, the United States, Australia, Brazil, Canada, New Zealand, India, Poland, Czechoslovakia, the Union of South Africa, Denmark, Norway, Belgium, Egypt, and Greece. The Axis powers' main participants were Germany, Japan, Italy, Hungary, Romania, and Bulgaria. The Second World War spanned 1939 to 1945.

35 Dupree, *Afghanistan*, 480–82.

36 Ibid., 482–85.

37 Ibid., 483. See also Marsden, *The Taliban*, 23.

38 Emadi, *State, Revolution, and Superpowers in Afghanistan*, 32.

39 Ibid., 33–34.

40 See this book's introduction for a discussion of Islamism.

41 Emadi, *State, Revolution, and Superpowers in Afghanistan*, 34–36.

42 Marsden, *The Taliban*, 22.

43 Ibid., 23; Emadi, *State, Revolution, and Superpowers in Afghanistan*, 36–37; Collins, *The Soviet Invasion of Afghanistan*, 17–26. In this passage Collins gives a concise overview of Soviet-Afghan relations from 1945 to 1963 which offers insight into Daoud's growing dependence upon Soviet aid and support.

44 Key events in Daoud's first term as prime minister included a tense standoff with Pakistan over the Pashtunistan issue and the closure of the border in 1961, which brought great economic hardship on the peasantry. Daoud's ties with Moscow opened the door for the Soviets to spread their influence throughout Afghani-

stan, especially among the radical wing of the PDPA, which split during the Constitutional period (1963–73). Daoud also made a bitter enemy of the religious establishment, which he perceived as the greatest threat to his government. He was particularly brutal with Islamist opponents; some historians suggest that he even sought to reach an agreement with certain factions within the PDPA to unite in an effort to squash the Jamaat i Islami.

45 Marsden, *The Taliban*, 23.

46 See Emadi, *State, Revolution, and Superpowers in Afghanistan*, 65–79.

47 Marsden, *The Taliban*, 29–33.

48 The Jamiat ul ulama i Islam (JUI), like several other fundamentalist factions in Pakistan, traces its roots to the Deoband tradition. It emerged in Pakistan in 1947 and immediately went about establishing madrasas, especially in the Pashtun territories of the North West Frontier Province and Baluchistan, to win over converts. The JUI advocates the founding of a strict Islamic state wherein Sharia law is the only legal code. Their acceptance of Pashtunwali as a cornerstone in their fundamentalist ideology has drawn the condemnation of Islamic scholars from around the world.

49 The Geneva Accords anticipated the mujahideen's playing a governmental role in post-Soviet Afghanistan, but Najibullah was very reluctant to share power with them. During Soviet occupation he served as commandant of the Kabul prison, infamous for its torture rooms and execution galleries, and a price was placed on his head. Toppling Najibullah was the mujahideen leaders' first priority.

50 See Rashid, *Taliban*.

51 Ibid.

52 Marsden, *The Taliban*, 43–51; A. Davis, "How the Taliban Became a Military Force."

53 Maley, *Fundamentalism Reborn?*, 43–55. See also Marsden, *The Taliban*, 57–66.

The "Afghan Beat"

Pukhtoon Journalism and the Afghan War

Altaf Ullah Khan

Prologue: Journalism at the End of 2007

This essay spans a period of almost six years in a part of our globe whose
notorious position in the world scene is not going to end in the near future.
The focus of my original analysis in 2002 was a group of Pukhtoon journalists operating out of Peshawar in Pakistan.[1] These journalists, who reported the war in Afghanistan, had an affinity with the people and events
they covered. Since then the coverage of Afghanistan, the status of that
state, and Pukhtoon journalism have continued to change. For instance,
stability, nation building, and development have largely replaced the rhetoric of hunting for global outlaws: Osama bin Laden and al Qaeda. Pukhtoon journalists are being reoriented from reporting on war to reporting on
development projects and conflict management and resolution. Since my
original survey, technological developments in gathering and disseminat-
ing news and information and the development of newer forms of analysis
from global perspectives have altered journalism in the region. There have
also been efforts to bring together Pukhtoon journalists from both Afghanistan and Pakistan to develop new journalistic formats, fusing the professional boundaries between ethnically Pukhtoon professionals in the two
countries.[2] With international agencies stepping in to provide professional
and financial support for this training, the process of change in Pukhtoon

journalism might become a role model for development in other spheres of nation building distinct from nation building as articulated by NATO or the West.

Western coverage of the assassination of Benazir Bhutto reflects the current framework of meaning-making in global media. The Western media analyzed the assassination (at least on CNN and BBC World, which are accessible in Peshawar) far more intensely than did Pakistani private TV networks, which were restrained by the regime at the time. For Western news networks the primary concern was to link the assassination with the tribal areas of Pakistan and Khyber-Pukhtoonkhwa (previously known as North West Frontier Province), the Taliban operating in this area, and al Qaeda and the Taliban. During the period of my study Western media corporations depended upon local Pukhtoon journalists for analysis, or at least presentations, of the conflict. Since 2007 it is much more common for Western media to simply use footage from private television channels in Pakistan and provide their own analysis. Hence while the cooperation between Pukhtoon and Western journalists in the early years of this current war in Afghanistan may have reflected the internationalization of journalism in the region, presently the region is experiencing greater media globalization. In the aftermath of the assassination of Benazir Bhutto, Pukhtoon journalists such as Rahim Ullah Yusufzai, whose work is discussed below, have not been called upon to analyze the role of the Taliban or the engagement of militant groups in the tribal areas. Thus the globalized system has made it possible for Western journalists to do their own analyses, focusing upon issues from their own standpoint while utilizing local media resources.

Media in Pakistan has been in a state of flux since 2002. The introduction of private television and FM radio in the country has changed the system of journalism as well as the working routines of journalists. This has naturally affected the roles of Pukhtoon journalists in Peshawar, the professionals who in the early years of the current war reported on the conflict while recognizing their connection to the parties involved. The war, however, is no longer simply in Peshawar's backyard. Competing radio stations, each propagating its own brand of hatred, have acquired greater numbers of listeners, and the local journalist is no longer the sole interpreter of events. It is becoming increasingly difficult to synthesize the local reality with the global picture of events. This antagonistic relation between the local and the global frameworks and perspectives has made the profession not only more difficult, but also more dangerous. The Pukhtoon journalist is no longer a spectator with heart-felt sympathies for a people with whom he shares ethnic affiliation. His own house is also on fire. Waziristan, the southern districts of the Khyber-Pukhtoonkhwa, and all the tribal areas are embroiled in this conflict, and the national boundaries between Afghanistan and Pakistan are even less stable than before. Furthermore the global village is challenging traditional social structures in this remote area. Tribal areas on both sides of the Pakistan-Afghan border have become the focus of the global media. In fact news from this area has become a component of Western audiences' daily media experience. For example, weather forecasts for Afghanistan (especially Kabul) have become important in the West, since troops from many Western countries are stationed in Afghanistan and have dealings within the tribal areas in Pakistan.

The boundary dividing Pakistan and Afghanistan has become ever more blurred, which can also be seen as a result of globalization. As Jalalzai and Jefferess point out in the introduction to this book, "Globalization accounts in part for the permeability of national and regional boundaries in the current Euro-American presence in Afghanistan, a site of contemporary warfare and resistance that likewise cross and redefine national boundaries." The ethnically Pukhtoon border has remained a riddle, still awe-inspiring and ambiguous. Nobody is sure where al Qaeda might be hiding. While a prudent observer senses confusion among the media at all levels, the media regime of the NATO forces and the Pakistani government (represented by Inter Services Public Relations), have more control over news and information than they did at the turn of the millennium. Ironically the Taliban has also become more adept at utilizing the media for their own ends. They harass and kidnap journalists and force them to cover their version of the story; the distinction between fact and fiction does not matter on either side of the divide.

Globalization has not only changed the technological dimensions of journalism in the Pukhtoon-dominated areas of Pakistan and Afghanistan, but has also added to the global journalist's body of knowledge. Western experts' ability to analyze independently is due to their changing perception of the world. The world in its entirety has become critical, and if one decides to deal with any part of it, one must—to some degree—know it. Hand in hand with this newer perspective goes the technological communication revolution. The prevalence of mobile phones in the remotest parts of the globe has made it possible for information to travel faster and made it easier to sift truth from partial truths. It has become possible for marginalized groups, the usual scapegoats for autocratic governments in Pakistan, to put the record straight by giving their side of a story. For example, when the government alleged that a militant group had perpetrated Bhutto's assassination, a representative of their leader, Bait Ullah Mehsud, phoned media channels on 29 December 2007 to reject responsibility. These voices of otherwise marginal groups at moments of global importance have challenged national constraints and laid the foundations for other kinds of global connections.

Although Rodney Steward (see his essay in this book) is not incorrect in saying that the persistence of instability has fueled social and political pressure and "generated various crises of identity" which might be seen as contributing to the Taliban's fundamentalism, there are developments in Afghanistan that challenge traditionalism. While there is no comparison between Afghanistan or the tribal areas of Pakistan and Western democracies, and while there are significant problems with using Western terms to identify the "rights" and "wrongs" in this part of the world, current struggles to get one's voice heard through the media may be seen as having democratic potential. The continued growth of local media in the region, including the work of Pukhtoon journalists, challenges fundamentalism. It is through these small victories that democracy can be achieved.

Efforts to train and equip tribal journalists as well as their fellow Afghan professionals are already under way in the areas of development journalism and conflict management and resolution. This marks the beginning of a new era in journalism in this region, a new phase of analysis and narration from the standpoint of humanist development. The training and re-orientation of the tribal journalists along with the Afghan journalists will develop a new intelligentsia, a new group of organic intellectuals (to borrow from Antonio Gramsci) who will actively fulfill their social responsibility.[3] This group of professionals can be found in every sphere of modern life. Their rise and fall causes the rise and fall of their parent institutions and the society that supports them.[4] In light of these developments, this essay best serves as a historical document, attesting to the pace of change in the region.

The Afghan War: A Pukhtoon's Perspective

Presenting the views of a sensitive group of professionals, such as Pukhtoon journalists, about one of the most controversial wars in modern history is a difficult task. Even more difficult is putting their views in a global perceptive. The most readily available way to investigate the views of Pukhtoon journalists on the U.S.-led invasion of Afghanistan, and their role as journalists and intermediaries between foreign journalists and local people affected by the war, is by the empirical method of individual interviews using an open-ended questionnaire. The fieldwork which served as the basis for this essay takes us through the end of 2001 and therefore captures the moment following the September 11 attacks and the beginning of the Afghan war; it does not include the journalistic response to postwar Afghanistan and the reconstruction period.

My discussion focuses on three concerns as they developed in response to the questionnaire: (1) the views of journalists on American involvement in the Afghan war at the end of 2001, (2) the impact of this war on journalism in Peshawar, and (3) how the notion of globalization affects the role and position of Pukhtoon journalism. The aim of this discussion is to present the perspective of Pukhtoon journalists who are interpreting global events in local contexts.

After September 11 Pukhtoon journalists saw the conflict in Afghanistan as a culmination of the historical events of the previous twenty years. For them the Afghan war was a continuous process of death and destruction, beginning with the Soviet invasion of Afghanistan in the late 1970s. The Soviets created a jingoistic atmosphere in Afghanistan from which Afghan nationalism arose in order to resist foreign occupation. The West, led by the United States, also used Afghanistan and its people in their cold war against Soviet socialism. After the defeat and disintegration of the Soviet Union, the states supplying the Afghans with arms and ammunitions were not interested in offering developmental assistance. Afghanistan was forgotten by the West and suffered under the influence of its neighbors, particularly Pakistan. The Afghans were forced to host everyone with a half loaf to offer.[5]

Although Afghanistan was linked to the September 11 catastrophe, Pukhtoon journalists did not see any evidence that Afghans were responsible for the attack. They did interpret the U.S. and its allies' military involvement in Afghanistan as an act of aggression against innocent Afghans, and they did witness the ensuing death and destruction as well as the loss of sovereignty in their homeland. This viewpoint developed out of a complicated set of connections between Peshawar and Afghanistan issuing from ethnic affinity, geographical proximity, religious unity, and eyewitness sympathy. Pukhtoon journalists' interaction with Western media companies and journalists transformed their dissent and sense of estrangement into hatred against the Western media and media managers. At the same time, Pukhtoon journalists worked with the Western media to earn good money and to make a living covering the war, neither of which would have been possible without Western support. As a result they could not criticize the West; to do so would not only cost them their jobs, but possibly their lives. The threat of being labeled an active al Qaeda member still loomed large. There was a time in very recent history when Pukhtoon journalists dreamed of having the freedom to write and report like their colleagues in the West; independent, professional reporting was the goal of many young reporters. Their ideals were shaped by the work of Western journalists; in particular the Watergate scandal illustrated Western journalists' freedom to report and write. But now most Pukhtoon journalists no longer believe in the integrity of the Western media. Globalization is no longer perceived as the emergence of a global fraternity, but as the West's hunt for energy resources, cheap labor, and markets, as well as global hegemony that controls and manages dissent around the globe.

Historical Background of Afghan Journalism in Peshawar

The Soviet invasion of Afghanistan and the subsequent war were turning points in the history of Afghanistan and Pakistan. It changed the demographics of both countries: Afghanistan became a deserted place, while Pakistani cities swarmed with Afghan refugees. The impact of the April Revolution (1978) on Pakistani society is multifaceted. The political map of Pakistan changed, and the Afghan factor became a major determinant in the active politics of Pakistan. The Pukhtoon politicians in Pakistan's North West Frontier Province and Baluchistan used anti-Afghan rhetoric as recurrent themes in their political demagogy. With little commitment to serve the people, they took Afghan bashing as the easy way out that excused their own incompetence.

Because there is a close connection between journalism and politics in the developing world, one of journalists' major roles is covering the statements of the political elite. This practice has also developed a specific nomenclature: "statement journalism." It was in consonance with this tradition that Afghanistan made the front pages of Pakistani newspapers. Another important factor making Afghanistan one of the most cherished beats in Pakistani journalism was the international involvement in the war against the Soviets, then Enemy Number One of the West. The Western media and Pukhtoon journalists filled the deserted newspaper offices in Peshawar in the late 1970s. Local journalists earned money as well as exposure at a level they had never before imagined. One must keep in mind that the majority of the journalist community in Peshawar was left-leaning at that time; they were active communists or were at least sympathetic to the ideology. Their criticism of private property was the natural outcome of their life experiences; many came from poor families from rural areas, especially in Khyber-Pukhtoonkhwa, where village chieftains with an extra tract of land dominated the area. These journalists had espoused communist ideology to reject the dominant social and political structures and were not necessarily well versed in Marxism. But the charm of a better career and a heavier purse was good enough to make the majority of journalists comply with the new reality.

Thus the coverage of the Afghan problem by the journalists in Peshawar remained a mercurial activity. It was very much in consonance with the local mood as well as the spirit of anticapitalism at the University of Peshawar and other educational institutions in the Pukhtoon areas of Pakistan. Although the general response in Pakistan to the war was more or less in tune with Western media coverage of Afghanistan, this was not true for these journalists. They generally remained anticapitalist in a broader sense, if not clearly Marxist in their worldview.

Apart from these controversial issues, the wars in Afghanistan positively affected the development of journalism in Peshawar. Journalism thrives on crises; sensational events bring in money to established media organizations, and the best chance of a boom is where blood spills. This gory reality is very much the truth in the case of Peshawar journalism. Peshawar was not a media center in Pakistan before the Soviet-Afghan war. Even in the early 1980s there was no journalist of recognizable stature heading a newspaper in Peshawar. When a major English daily, *The Frontier Post*, was launched in 1985 from Peshawar, the late Aziz Siddiqui was invited to be its editor. Siddiqui was not a Pukhtoon, nor did he hail from any Pukhtoon area in Pakistan. But within a short period of ten to fifteen years Peshawar had developed exceptional journalists like Rahim Ullah Yusufzai, who is not only an expert on Afghanistan in Pakistan, but also works with many international media organizations around the world. Besides Yusufzai there are many other young journalists working with leading national and international media organizations. The Afghan war has not only given stature and prestige to Peshawar journalists, but there are journalists in other parts of Pakistan who owe their fame to what journalists call "the Afghan beat." One example is Hamid Mir, who began as reporter/editor of a leading Urdu daily and now hosts a popular show at the leading private Urdu TV Geo. Hamid Mir earned fame and fortune by interviewing Osama bin Laden. Thus the Afghan war, and especially the Afghan beat, has been instrumental in creating quite a few famous figures in Pakistani journalism.

Besides providing individual fortunes, the Afghan war has led to the expansion of the newspaper industry in Peshawar. The past few years have witnessed not only the mushrooming of newspapers from Peshawar, but also ever greater attention to Peshawar in the major national dailies. As corroborated by the interviews in my study, Peshawar, the Afghan issue, and Pukhtoons gained more and more space in the national press. One journalist in Peshawar attested, "There are days when the front pages of major daily newspapers are held back till the latest news from Peshawar reaches the head offices of the papers."[6] More and more exclusive Peshawar pages are being added to the major dailies to cover Pukhtoon issues extensively: "The daily *Dawn* has to adjust its policy of treating individual news according to the peculiar working environment in Khyber-Pukhtoonkhwa after it started publication from Islamabad," said one senior journalist.

All this makes Peshawar perhaps the most important media center in Pakistan. No newspaper in Pakistan can operate at the national or international level without having sufficient resources and manpower to cover Peshawar, which became the center of Afghan politics during the Soviet war in Afghanistan. Apart from the Afghan activity, the ethnic affinity between the Pukhtoons on both sides of the Pakistan-Afghan border made the coverage of Pukhtoons in the Khyber-Pukhtoonkhwa and Baluchistan a very important media function in Pakistan.

The issue is whether the focus on Pukhtoon-dominated areas in Pakistan boosts journalistic activity and professional competence more generally. The Pukhtoon journalists are of the opinion that the focus on the Afghan war has by no means minimized the importance of the coverage of other local and regional issues of the region. Underscoring the previous underrepresentation of Pukhtoon issues, one journalist asserted, "The Afghan war has given Peshawar much needed recognition on the national and international scale. As far as the national scene is concerned, we have used this opportunity to highlight the problems of the Pukhtoons in general. On the international level it was not possible for us to do much for our people, because the priorities of the Western media are very different."

According to these testimonies and the changes in local and international reporting practices, the Afghan war helped boost the profession. It gave the journalists more exposure, won more space for Peshawar and Pukhtoons in national dailies, and encouraged journalism in the region. Seen in this context, the Afghan war has opened a new chapter in the development of journalism in Peshawar, the first one of its kind.

Views on War and the Role of the Media

The U.S.-led attack on Afghanistan can be seen as a continuation of the war that has lasted more than two decades, beginning with the April Revolution in 1978. The present Afghan psyche is thus marked by decades of war. Even older people are so much under the stress of the current crises that they are not able to give a clear picture of life in Afghanistan before 1978. Since the journalists in Peshawar have been the continuous witnesses to this war, their ideas might also be in consonance with those of the Afghans themselves. It would therefore be prudent to begin with the difference between this war and the violence that preceded it. When asking questions about the Afghan war we must keep in mind the priorities of the Pukhtoon journalists. Because of their Pukhtoon ethnicity the Afghan war resonated in ways particular to them, unlike the experience of other journalists, Western or Pakistani.

For most Pukhtoon journalists the Afghan people were the center of the conflict in Afghanistan. This humanitarian perspective is distinct from that of the international humanitarian organizations helping the victims of war in Afghanistan in that it is expressly self-interested. The people of Afghanistan are the Pukhtoon journalists' own folk. As Pakistani Muslims, they share a religion with the Afghans but identify professionally with Pakistani and Western journalists. Pakistani journalists saw the conflict as a regional problem, or viewed the Afghan war in light of the nation's sufferings as an Islamic country. The degree of detachment intensified to a considerable extent in the case of Western journalists; their job had become more or less covering the enemy, the people responsible for the catastrophe of 9/11.

Pukhtoon journalists saw American involvement in Afghanistan as a continuation of foreign control of Afghan politics. "When will the Afghan people see a better day is the question," said one journalist. "Bombing Afghanistan is not the answer to the situation that has arisen since 9/11. It can be the beginning of a *New Dark Age*, if the rehabilitation process is not followed with the same vehemence as the bombing. This, to date, doesn't seem to be happening," A senior journalist in Peshawar asserted, "The poor Afghans lived under the tyranny of the Kings, were captives of the communist regimes that brought the Russians into the land, and were handed over to the whims of the Taliban after the Soviets left the ravaged country. And what next? We have the rest of the world against a people whose only sin is that they live in a place from where one can control the energy resources badly needed to run the capitalist mill."

Consciousness about energy politics and the use of terms like *the New Great Game* can be traced back to the 1990s.[7] During that period the Area Study Centre for Central Asia, Russia, China, and Afghanistan made vigorous contact with the local press, and a series of articles on the topic were published in Peshawar newspapers. The journalists also got involved in the workshops and seminars organized by the Centre. Against this backdrop journalists in Peshawar doubted the veracity of the Western claim that the Afghan war was a war against terrorism. This perspective is strengthened by the perception that the situation in Afghanistan has not wholly improved despite persistent assurances by NATO and American authorities.

For this group of professionals, interpreting global events in a local context, Osama bin Laden and Mullah Omar were not very popular, although journalists have historically not said much against them because of the dangers involved in speaking critically. One reporter who responded to the questionnaire remarked, "Why doesn't Osama try to free his own folk from the tyranny of the few? Aren't there any problems in Arabia needing the fighting spirit of many determined strivers?" "Who is this Mullah Omar?" said another. "How can a person just come out of nowhere and become so strong in a society where people know the grandparents of each other, especially in relation to the leaders?" Many Pukhtoon journalists believed that their own experience with the Taliban and their leaders did not correlate with the kind of destructive potential evidenced by catastrophes like 9/11.

One did not find adequate answers to the question of who was ultimately responsible. The journalists did have opinions, but ones they never clearly asserted. "This is a terrible New Great Game. The players have new intentions and the machinations are new. But there is one thing that the New Great Game has in common with the old one: namely, the exploitation of the whole region. But this time all this will be done in a very ruthless way as far as Afghanistan is concerned."

Discussions with Pukhtoon journalists about Afghanistan's role in the September 11 attacks on the U.S. and the aims of the U.S.-led invasion of Afghanistan generally indicated a deep distrust of the present global community. These journalists saw the world as an arena marked by power struggles, where the stronger seeks to destroy the weaker. Their general perspective on the struggle was that nations seem to have only their own financial interests in mind, and everyone wants to dominate. Closely associated with this desire is the energy requirement of both the up-and-coming and the entrenched powers, as well as the goal of destroying the new enemy, so-called Islamic fundamentalism, and containing the old, already humiliated enemies, the former Soviet Union and present-day China.

As far as the question of war between religions or civilizations (i.e., Huntington's "clash of civilizations") is concerned, there are not very many journalists who agreed with this thesis. Most Pukhtoon journalists did not see the war as a clash between Islam and Christianity, or between Islam and the West. They reacted critically to the words floating in the Western media, interpreting the events in the exclusive context of militant Islam:

"Words like 'Crusades,' 'Islamic Militants,' 'Militant Islam,' etc. are really humiliating simplifications of the problem." Further they are dangerous in the Afghan context. "What we see are innocent people reeling under the tyranny of jingoistic groups for more than twenty years, groups that were products of global politics," said one journalist.

But the greatest skepticism persisted about the future of Afghanistan, and specifically the survival of Afghanistan as the homeland of the Pukhtoons, as well as the revival of Pukhtoon culture. Many Pukhtoon journalists had little hope:

The people of Afghanistan have gone through a tyrannical period and have lost all they had. Their culture has been destroyed through continuous experimentation of differing kinds. The Communists tried to impose their will upon the simple freedom-loving people of Afghanistan. The Islamists from Arabia and those from within have done their best to gain personal benefits and legitimize their own misdeeds in the name of Islam. But what do we have now? The experiments are over. The land is defeated, and there is no more courage left to think into the future.

The human catastrophe evident during the war fed this pessimism. Journalists from around the globe saw the catastrophe as observers rather than as participants. They could not have the same empathy toward the suffering of Afghans that the Pukhtoon journalists did. The Pukhtoon journalists feared that what happened in Afghanistan could also happen to them in the near future: "They always refer to the Afghans as 'Afghan people.' This obscures the real problem. These are no impersonal beings, nobodies from Mars. These are men and women, old and children. We see it in this way: for us they are not 'people.' They are us." But not all of them are pessimistic about the future of Afghanistan: "The Afghans have strong and deep cultural roots. They have survived such destruction and atrocities before. Their resilience and perseverance in the face of hardships is axiomatic. The Afghan culture will reemerge with all its strength once these hard times are over."

The Pukhtoon journalists are part of the Pakistani media system. They work with the national dailies and earn their living and their reputation from these organizations. There are but a few features that differentiate them from other journalists as far as Afghanistan is concerned. They have two qualities that make the task easier for them than for other Pakistani journalists: ethnolinguistic affinity and geographical proximity. As a result

Pukhtoon journalists have easier access to resources than other Pakistani or foreign journalists. They can easily develop and keep in contact with their sources due to their shared culture. Furthermore Peshawar is the largest Pukhtoon city, the center of Pukhtoon culture, and most of the families of the Afghan politicians and other elite families live in Peshawar. Most of the international humanitarian organizations operate from Peshawar, and the families of many these staff members also live in Peshawar. This makes it easier for the Peshawarite Pukhtoon journalist to collect information through personal contact, which is also the reason why national and international media assign local Pukhtoon journalists the task of covering Afghanistan.

The relationship of the Pukhtoon journalist to Western media is manifold. On one level, the Pukhtoon journalist is the confidant of the foreign journalist. Working side by side they both witness and facilitate their methods of covering the Afghan (or Pakistan) issue. Yet the financial dimension plays an important role as well. The Pukhtoon journalists I interviewed liked the money they earned because it helped them live a better life. Indeed the pay was the main reason they want to work with the Western media. The Afghan war, however, brought another unpleasant reality to light: the exploitation of local journalists. One complained, "They buy our services for a few dollars and then sell the stories in tens of thousands. This is not fair. We are the ones who make the stories. They don't even know the language, the culture, nothing. They cannot even know a bit about anything, if we are not there to help them." But the journalists knew well that this equation was inevitable. Tied to the financial disparity was the question of personal behavior. "They treat you very harshly," one young journalist told me. "They even interfere with personal matters. They try to dictate even our personal behavior. They pay for the services and they think they have bought the person." But perhaps the worst aspect of these relationships involved foreign journalists renting the services of junior journalists to hunt for news. One of my former students told me that they paid the people in the streets to make anti-American or pro-Taliban comments before the camera: "There were many who only did it for the kick of being filmed. There were yet others who didn't comply voluntarily. They were then paid." The young man I interviewed was paid two hundred dollars on this shooting day.

One can easily imagine what the response of the Pukhtoon journalist might be when he sees this slanted version of reality. "They have really presented things out of context," said one. "This was not the way things happened. But more dangerous was the interpretation and context formation of events that has made an altogether different story of the reality as we know it." In addition to the obvious problem inherent in the misrepresentation of the events of the Afghan conflict, the close relationship Pukhtoon journalists have had with foreign journalists destroyed their faith in the ideal that in the marketplace of ideas truth will prevail. "None of them tried to part themselves from the bandwagon. All have tried to serve the interests of the mighty and sacrificed truth at the altar of homogeneity," declared one journalist. "They have followed only one standard, and unfortunately not only that of earning money. It was simply hatred against us. For them we were the wretched of the earth. Distortion of our image for the aggrandizement of the West was not morally objectionable for them." In this statement one clearly sees the withering away of the borderline between the ordinary Afghan and the Pukhtoon journalist. This tension between their role of representing the conflict and their relationship to the ordinary Afghan is in fact the *focal point* of the conflict between the Pukhtoon journalist and the foreign journalist as far as the coverage of Afghanistan is concerned. This affinity is not simply one of empathy, but is in fact a question of identity.

These journalists saw Pakistani media as divided into pro- and anti-Taliban camps, where the pro-Taliban camp was in fact an anti-American one. "It was the sense of loss of sovereignty that pushed a few among us into the camp that in some way sympathized with the Taliban," said one senior journalist. "It is in fact a complicated issue. The way of the Taliban is not the way of Islam, but the way of the West is also not that of liberal democracy. And when there is a conflict between two evils, you normally opt for the known one." The other reason for anti-American sentiments among the journalists is the Pakistani government's highhanded way of dealing with the press during the present conflict: "Our hands were tied. We could not show both sides of the picture. The only way to survive was to line up with the West in Taliban bashing." But for most this was impossible. Their readers did not believe in the black-and-white portrayal of issues. As one journalist told me, "There ought to be a balance. And to achieve this balance was (and still is) the hardest task to accomplish."

Conclusion

The development of Peshawar as a media center in the 1980s and its present importance to national and international media is an example of how global issues transform the very structure of media and journalism in remote and forgotten parts of our modern world. The very process of professionalization is going on in the wake of this global-interactive milieu. Journalists are developing their journalistic ideals through their interaction with the Western media and journalists on the international level. On the national level covering Afghanistan is becoming increasingly important, giving local journalists as well as the media possibilities they would never have otherwise imagined.

This is an environment that naturally molds professional ideology into an international frame, since going beyond borders into Afghanistan is an international activity. In the same vein, getting the news published in global media and interacting with counterparts from around the globe is itself globalization in action. There are positive and negative aspects of this work across frontiers. Positively speaking, it broadens professional horizons, both intellectually and in terms of procedures. A negative aspect is the tendency to develop opinions based on extreme generalizations. The actions of individual Western journalists are generalized, as are the attitudes of Western media toward Pakistani journalists and media. This also applies more broadly to the general Western attitude toward Pakistan and the Islamic world. Individual grievances are generalized into clashes of values and even civilizations.

The same was true for opinions about the war in Iraq and the war against terror in general. These events were conflated in confusing ways. Internal acts of terror were also blamed on U.S. policy toward Muslims; these events stem from a vicious circle of injustice and oppression that makes life difficult for the common person in Pakistan. In Pakistan America was perceived to be the root of all trouble, an oversimplification of conspiracy theories which exist in systems with controlled information regimes. In present-day Pakistan such theories add fuel to the existing fire of anti-American sentiment, making intercultural harmony impossible. Bridging this gap requires intercultural dialogue based on the principles of equality and mutual respect as well as honest soul-searching on both sides of the divide.

Notes

1 For a discussion of the variations of the term *Pukhtoon*, see the introduction to this book.

2 For instance, the University of Peshawar, besides engaging in the training of professionals on the Pakistani side of the border, has also formed associations with sister universities in Jalalabad and Kabul in Afghanistan.

3 Gramsci, *Selections from the Prison Notebooks*, 5.

4 Said, *Representations of the Intellectual*, 67–69.

5 The aim here is not to test the veracity of this perspective, but simply to present it.

6 The direct quotations from journalists remain anonymous in order to protect their professional positions and their safety. Their statements are taken from an email questionnaire or from individual telephone interviews.

7 *The Great Game* refers to the nineteenth-century struggle in the region between Great Britain and Russia. Threats of Russian and British incursion into and influence over Central Asia heightened tensions between the empires, particularly over Afghanistan and, by extension, India. See Rubin's *The Fragmentation of Afghanistan*.

Veiled Motives

Women's Liberation and the War in Afghanistan

Gwen Bergner

On 16 November 2001 the Bush administration announced that U.S.-led forces had liberated Kabul, Afghanistan. Both the administration and the American media represented this military action as a human rights mission for the benefit of Afghan women. The next day Laura Bush used the president's weekly radio spot to "kick off a world-wide effort to focus on the brutality against women and children by the al-Qaida terrorist network and . . . the Taliban." Widely covered by the media, Laura Bush's address characterized the Taliban's abuses of women and children, noting specifically that "children aren't allowed to fly kites; their mothers face beatings for laughing out loud. . . . Only the terrorists and the Taliban threaten to pull out women's fingernails for wearing nail polish." Noting that women had been confined to the home, Bush credited our military with freeing women to "listen to music and teach their daughters without fear of punishment."[1] Alongside coverage of Bush's radio address, American media paraded images of unveiled Afghan women as evidence of victory and Afghanistan's liberation. CNN's 16 November web story "Kabul Liberated" featured eight photographs, seven of which focused on Afghan women.[2] Significantly most of these focused on whether women were veiled or unveiled. Over the next weeks and months major newspapers and magazines,

1 "Afghan Girl," photograph by Steve McCurry, *National Geographic*, June 1985 cover.

from *USA Today* to *Time*, ran stories on Afghan women with huge color photos of exotic Afghan girls, their kohl-rimmed eyes framed by heavy bangs and the drapery of their head scarves, reminiscent of the famous *National Geographic* cover from 1985. Surprisingly the Bush administration and the media thus represented Afghan women as a primary cause for U.S. military action to effect regime change in Afghanistan (though years later that rationale has dropped from sight). The burqa, a full-body covering, became a symbol of the abuse of women under the Taliban; unveiled women demonstrated the success of America's ostensibly humanitarian mission to rescue women.

The representation of Afghan women in post-9/11 American media and politics serves as a textbook case of the gendering of nationalism in a global

Special report **Hope returns to Afghanistan**

2 "Special Report:
Hope Returns
to Afghanistan,"
photograph by
Ami Vitale,
USA Today,
28 August 2002.

frame. As a number of feminist postcolonial theorists have noted, male
national power is often consolidated by means of constructions of gender
difference. Women represent the nation symbolically in order to motivate
male nation building. This paradigm forecloses women's participation in
national agency: women bear the nation, while men build it.[3] The so-called
war on terror transposes this dynamic onto a transnational frame. In America's crusade for worldwide liberal democracy (and capitalism), Afghan
women represented the non-Western, non-Christian victim (of al Qaeda
and the Taliban) to be rescued by muscular American democracy.

In a reprise of colonial logic, brown women must be saved from brown
men by white men.[4] But the U.S. freed Afghan women not to participate
in the machinery of a new democratic nation, but—as Laura Bush, CNN,
the *New York Times,* and the *Christian Science Monitor* claim—to wear

makeup, act as good mothers, and make themselves visible to the male gaze.[5] Through these images the United States co-opted and colonized the iconography of Afghan familial and domestic space in order to extend America's political, military, and ideological purview. Thus the technologies of gender difference worked to define national difference and rationalize uneven power relations between groups of men. The internal gendering of nationalism inherently drives international power politics.

The intense attention to the oppression of women by the Taliban after 9/11 stands in marked contrast to earlier media accounts. Despite efforts by feminist organizations in the United States such as the Feminist Majority to raise awareness about the plight of Afghan women, the American press had consistently belittled their claims, quoting government and academic authorities who testified that their reports of abuse were emotional, exaggerated, and oversimplified.[6] Thus a comparison of media representations before and after September 11, 2001, reveals how images of Afghan women were mobilized for the purposes of U.S. foreign policy and nationalism. Images of this veiled or unveiled exotic feminine body—"liberated" like their children to laugh, sing, and wear makeup—demonstrate how, as Lauren Berlant writes, "democracies can . . . produce a special form of tyranny that makes citizens like children, infantilized, passive, and over-dependent on the 'immense and tutelary' power of the state."[7] In the case of Afghanistan there is a gendering not just of the national, but of the transnational imaginary: the infantilized Afghan woman mobilizes the American "citizen's faith in the nation" as a rescuing, not conquering, hero.

The Bush administration's rhetoric about liberating Afghan women and media manipulation of the veil to frame the war seemed embarrassingly cliché in its tiresome, if terrifying repetition of hoary imperial discourse. And yet, as Imre Szeman reminds us in the conclusion to this book, "our astonishment at the endless political perversions and hypocrisies are somewhat misguided: the idea that the U.S. could even now engage in a militaristic adventure in Afghanistan betrays a strange fantasy" that such events are aberrations in the progressive narrative of modernity. The saturated image of the veil as the sign of Islam's radical difference—and in the case of post-9/11 Afghanistan, its association with terrorism—is similarly unsurprising. Working like Homi Bhabha's endlessly repeated, ambivalent stereotype, such an image of fixed difference "connotes rigidity and an un-

changing order as well as disorder, degeneracy, and daemonic repetition."
The stereotype as discursive strategy "is a form of knowledge and identification that vacillates between what is always 'in place,' already known,
and something that must be anxiously repeated. . . . It is the force of
ambivalence . . . that gives the colonial stereotype its currency: ensures its
repeatability in changing historical and discursive conjunctures."[8] Through
the metonymic stereotype of the burqa, discourse in the United States
represented the Taliban as premodern and ahistorical, thereby erasing the
contingent particularity of this political nexus.[9] As several recent commentators argue, this ahistorical representation ignores American involvement
in Afghan politics that helped precipitate the rise of the Taliban, omits
Afghan women's active resistance to oppression, and glosses over subsequent rollbacks of women's rights in the U.S. as well as in Afghanistan. The
flatly embarrassing stereotype thus provides a point of discursive entry to
rehistoricize the transnational politics of Afghan women's rights.

In the three years prior to September 11, 2001, American newspapers
published only a handful of stories about the Taliban's treatment of Afghan
women. This is not to say that they knew little about it. In fact foreign
papers covered the issue widely, and the op-ed pages of some American
newspapers regularly ran letters to the editor from citizens and columns by
commentators such as Ellen Goodman and Howard Kleinberg asking the
government to address Afghan women's rights and to cut the U.S. government's financial support to the Taliban.[10] Moreover the nonprofit group
the Feminist Majority had been waging a major campaign to raise awareness about the Taliban's oppression of Afghan women. Although the Feminist Majority's email petition circulated widely, they failed to win much
media attention until they recruited Mavis Leno, the wife of Jay Leno, to
bring some Hollywood glamour to the issue.

When Mavis Leno organized a "star-studded" Hollywood event, a small
number of papers finally covered the issue, albeit in the Arts and Leisure
sections, and even these articles minimized the Taliban's abuses, belittled
the Feminist Majority's claims, and trivialized American women's concerns. For example, a *Boston Globe* story on the Feminist Majority's awareness campaign that ran on 24 March 1999—in anticipation of the Hollywood gala slated for the next week—reported, "While American women
are reacting on a gut-level revulsion to the Taliban regime, many familiar

with Afghanistan caution against oversimplifying a chaotic fabric of politics and culture."[11] The article quotes Swanee Hunt, a former U.S. ambassador and the director of Harvard's Women and Public Policy Program, and Abdul Hakeem Mujahid, an Afghan representative to the UN, to mitigate claims by the Feminist Majority and Physicians for Human Rights. Hunt defends the Taliban for having brought law and order in the wake of chaos left by the end of Soviet occupation in 1989. Mujahid is quoted as saying that the Feminist Majority is "anti-Islamic" and filled with "disinformation." He claims the burqa is the choice of many women in Kabul and argues that women are not prevented from seeing male doctors; they just prefer to see female doctors. In reality the Taliban prevented most female doctors from practicing and forbade women to see male doctors.

Although the *Globe* article quotes authorities both in support of and against the claims of the Feminist Majority, other reports are not so balanced. On 30 March 1999, the day after the Hollywood gala, the *Washington Post* ran a piece in the Style section titled "A Cause Unveiled: Hollywood Women Have Made the Plight of Afghan Women Their Own—Sight Unseen." Starting with the title's play on the politics of the veil, this article renders the "cause" of Afghan women simply a Hollywood fashion fad. "In six months the Taliban's 'war on women' has become the latest cause célèbre in Hollywood," it breezes. "Tibet is out. Afghanistan is in." Citing only Leno, the Feminist Majority president Eleanor Smeal, and one other woman connected to the Feminist Majority as sources on the Taliban's abuses, the article quotes no fewer than six "specialists on Afghanistan" to dispute claims that Afghan women lack access to healthcare and education. These specialists include the director of Save the Children for Afghanistan; the head of the Women's Commission for Refugee Women and Children; an anonymous UN official; a Reagan administration expert on Afghanistan; a pro-Taliban, Afghan-born woman living in the U.S.; and Mujahid, the Taliban's U.S. representative. These experts lament what they claim are the Feminist Majority's misinformed embellishments. Judy Benjamin, head of the Women's Commission for Refugee Women and Children, says, for example, " 'This is a terrible snow job. . . . It's amusing almost, but sad. With the Jay Leno connection they have struck it rich and gained Hollywood, but trust me, they're terribly misinformed.' "[12] Not only is the Feminist Majority misinformed, according to this phalanx of experts, but their campaign will harm Afghan women if it results in loss of aid to Afghanistan.[13] Ultimately the *Post* article favors the detractors of Leno and the Feminist Majority, reporting that the group's "sweeping statements" declaring that Afghan women and girls are prisoners in their own homes "are largely inaccurate, according to those familiar with the country." This ostensibly wrongheaded claim of Afghan women's imprisonment would be taken up by Laura Bush less than eight months later.

After 9/11 the Bush administration and the American media suddenly turned their attention to the Taliban's treatment of women.[14] Significantly Laura Bush's radio address was titled "The Taliban's War on Women and Children," suggesting that the U.S. invasion of Afghanistan was an act of defense rather than a first strike. That the First Lady, who had remained practically silent on political issues until this point, gave the radio address marking the liberation of Kabul was meant to signal, perhaps, that American women are not "veiled" or silenced and that they should sympathize with Afghan women on the basis of their shared roles as mothers. Eschewing a discourse of rights in favor of a discourse of femininity, she speaks of the Taliban's "degradation of women" and "brutality against women and children," lamenting, "Our hearts break for the women and children in Afghanistan." Afghan women's freedom was justified only in terms of maternal duty: education for girls will be restored so that "women can teach their daughters."[15] This emotional appeal used the inclusive first-person pronoun to domesticate Afghan women while radically differentiating the listeners from the Taliban: "We respect our mothers, our sisters, our daughters." But who constitutes this civic "we"? It would seem that Bush appealed to the chivalry of an implied audience for whom women exist relationally—not individually—as mothers, sisters, and daughters. Implicitly she called for the protection of women and children by the U.S.[16] Afghan women would be freed to play conventionally Western feminine roles—to laugh, wear nail polish, listen to music, and be better mothers.

If the pre-9/11 media debate over the status of women in Afghanistan—staged between a Western feminist organization on one hand and international aid groups, diplomats, and select Afghan expatriates on the other—excluded the voices of Afghan women and women's rights organizations, the post-9/11 administration rhetoric and media coverage similarly eclipsed Afghan women's agency and desire. Laura Bush's appeal to

save women and children worked by representing Afghan women's interests as identical to our own: that of liberal humanist subjects or of ordinary
soccer moms.

In these conventionally gendered terms the Afghan woman could be
rescued only if Afghan women were not actively fighting for rights, but
groups such as the Revolutionary Association of the Women of Afghanistan (RAWA), founded in 1977, was advocating women's rights long before
the U.S. invasion.[17] Furthermore the rhetoric of rescue and reform deployed by the Bush administration and the media after 9/11 occludes the
history of U.S. foreign policy that helped create the very conditions from
which U.S. military might and morality will ostensibly save Afghan women.
Carol Stabile and Deepa Kumar trace this history, recounting that, beginning in 1979, the United States worked to precipitate the Soviet invasion in
1980 as part of the cold war strategy to weaken the USSR and funded the
mujahideen in this proxy war. When the Soviets withdrew the U.S. ceased
aid and involvement, thereby allowing the mujahideen to fill the resulting
power vacuum (they formed the Northern Alliance in 1992) and to begin
the assault on women's rights. After the Taliban came to power in 1996 the
U.S. supported the regime, despite its intensified crackdown on women's
rights, so as to garner cooperation for building an oil pipeline that would
benefit an American company.[18]

In Laura Bush's address Afghan women's liberation symbolized America's just cause, but the freedoms promised are more symbolic than sub-
stantive. Likewise the media visually engaged Afghan women to epitomize
America's military and cultural victory. In the days after the invasion the
unveiling of Afghan women by the removal of the burqa became the clear-
est symbol of Kabul's "liberation" and the Taliban's defeat. In CNN's online
report "Kabul Liberated," we find a series of photos of veiled and unveiled
women. In one photo a gang of teenage boys press against a CNN van. The
caption reads, "Men and young boys gather around a CNN van—in it a
woman is unveiled. Some say they haven't seen a woman in six years."

As a picture of women's liberation this photo and the caption's passive
voice beg the question of who does the unveiling. Is the woman unveiling
herself, or is someone doing it to her? Is she a Western woman who never
was veiled? In fact the photo represents not so much women's agency as
the viewers' voyeurism—both the Afghan boys' and ours—in desiring a

3 "Men viewing unveiled
   woman." "Kabul Liberated,"
   CNN.com, 16 November 2001.

glimpse of this woman unveiled. In typical Orientalist fashion, the American public is titillated by the idea of revealing an exotic "harem" of women, heretofore available only to the men—fathers, brothers, and husbands—who control them. Another CNN photo shows a woman with bare head and face as an example of women who "proudly removed their burqas" now that the Taliban were defeated. The caption on a third photo, of female hospital workers, states, "Women who work inside this hospital unveil their burqas, wear makeup and work alongside male doctors." There is no mention of women doctors. Yet a fourth photo shows a woman who persists in wearing the veil because, as the caption explains, "no one has yet announced they can take it off." The editorial voice interprets the woman's persistence in wearing the veil after the Taliban's ouster from Kabul as a form of naïve passivity, negating the possibility of cultural difference.

In this series of photos, unveiling the Afghan woman for the American gaze represents stripping power from the Taliban. This "clash of civilizations" is, in part, a war between men over women's bodies.

The case of the war in Afghanistan is not the first time the veil has functioned as contested ground between East and West or between colonized and colonizer. In an essay published in 1959 Frantz Fanon explores what he calls the "historic dynamism of the veil" in Algeria's fight for independence from French colonial rule. The French assumed that veiled Islamic women were oppressed and therefore incapable of playing an active

4-6   From "Kabul Liberated,"
CNN.com, 16 November 2001.

role in the revolution. This enabled Algerian women to smuggle bombs and arms under their garments, using the veil to act as political agents in a nationalist project.[19] The veil is not simply a sign of women's subjugation; its meaning varies with historic and political context. But though Algerian women used the veil to oppose the French, their anticolonial role did not guarantee their access to similar agency within a decolonized Algeria. Nevertheless the meaning of the veil is contingent upon a number of cultural, historical, and political factors, as the Vietnamese feminist and postcolonial theorist Trinh T. Minh-ha wrote in 1991:

If the act of unveiling has liberating potential, so does the act of veiling. It all depends on the context in which such an act is carried out or, more precisely, on how and where women see dominance. Difference should be defined neither by the dominant sex nor by the dominant culture. So when women decide to lift the veil, one can say that they do so in defiance of their men's oppressive right to their bodies. But when they decide to keep or put on the veil they once took off, they might do so to reappropriate their space or claim a new difference [as women].[20]

Significantly Trinh makes clear that the veil offers these potential valences of defiance and reappropriation only if women control it.

Trinh claims the veil, in part, to emphasize differences among women, to disrupt the homogenizing category *woman*, and to assert the mutability of identity. In this she echoes the efforts of many postcolonial and Third World feminists to resist, in Chandra Mohanty's words, "hegemonic 'Western' feminisms" and instead to develop "autonomous feminist concerns and strategies that are geographically, historically, and culturally grounded." Mohanty warns against the "assumption of women as an already constituted, coherent group with identical interests and desires, regardless of class, ethnic or racial location, or contradictions [which] implies a notion of gender or sexual difference or even patriarchy that can be applied universally and cross-culturally." If we substitute "Afghan women" for Mohanty's "Third World women," we can no doubt argue that Laura Bush's anti-Taliban rhetoric "colonize[s] the material and historical heterogeneities of the lives of [Afghan] women . . . , thereby producing/ representing a composite, singular ['Afghan Woman']—an image that appears arbitrarily constructed but nevertheless carries with it the authorizing signature of Western humanist discourse."[21] A feminine humanist subject, already constituted under the veil, awaits liberation. In the American imagination she is recognizable as a mother who wants healthcare and literacy and, more immediately, to sing, wear nail polish, and laugh with her children.

In contrast to Bush administration rhetoric, the Feminist Majority more consistently made their case for Afghan women in terms of human rights rather than feminine or maternal roles, decrying the Taliban for refusing women work, education, and healthcare—and also for violently enforcing the veil. They did not use Afghan women simply to marshal American nationalism for a war whose political and material scope went far afield of women's liberation. Therefore I would not equate the means or ends of the Feminist Majority with those of Laura Bush and the administration she represented. Just as the meaning of the veil can vary according to a woman's deployment of it, so perhaps can the humanist rhetoric of Western feminism vary according to strategic use. Nonetheless it's hard to dispute claims that popular feminism in the United States contributes to a consumerist femininity veiled as liberal humanism.

The contradictions of popular feminism, along with celebrity charity, consolidate spectacularly in the performance of *The Vagina Monologues*, staged at Madison Square Garden and hosted by the playwright Eve Ensler, at which Oprah Winfrey unveiled a burqa-clad Afghan woman. This performance dramatized the Orientalist canard that the passive Afghan (Muslim) woman needs liberation by Western feminists. The scripted performativity of the spectacle underscores its work as ideological fantasy: the unveiled Afghan woman was actually a representative of RAWA named Zoya and an active feminist leader. She has since written an account of the event, reporting that the organizers asked her to wear the burqa so that Oprah could unveil her. As if the symbolism of unveiling were not concrete enough, in her account of the event Zoya describes being rendered physically dependent on her American sponsors when, as she climbed the stairs to the stage, she was blinded by a combination of the burqa and tears caused by the powerful arena lights; by the time she got to the stage she really did need to be rescued.[22]

The Feminist Majority and the international movement to combat violence against women, V-Day, sought to raise awareness of the Afghan women's cause through celebrity spectacle that underscored the cultural contradictions of capitalist charity feminism. We might refer to the largely unacknowledged contradiction within American feminism between liberation and consumption as Victoria's Secret. At a time when American women's efforts to achieve economic and political equality are largely stalled and the gap between industrial and underdeveloped nations grows, the lingerie empire offers a salient if silly reminder of some of the contradictions between the rhetoric of women's rights and the consumer-consumed binary of contemporary American femininity. On 18 November 2001, two days after Kabul's liberation, ABC broadcast the much-ballyhooed Victoria's Secret fashion show. In the *New York Times* Alex Kuczynski noted the uncanny juxtaposition of that day's network newscast images of "Afghan women removing their burkas, revealing their faces as the Taliban regime retreated," and that evening's program, in which "models had peeled away their clothing and were showing off thong panties." According to Kuczynski, the show featured lingerie-clad supermodels, "portrayed with a cheerless mock innocence as angels, or as Christmas packages to be unwrapped, . . . hitting their paces hard so breasts bobbled atop demibrassieres in time to the music, which included lyrics like 'took her to the bedroom / she was stripped down' to a driving beat." Kuczynski laments "the folly of what can only be described as soft pornography on a television network" at a "moment when Americans are desperate to see a fine example of their culture, something that can send the global message that the nasty critics of U.S. vulgarity and commercialism must be wrong."[23] In other words, the spectacle of Tyra Banks sporting white angel wings paired with a harem-style bra and diaphanous pants and sarong (think *I Dream of Jeannie*) begs the question, Is this what women's liberation looks like?[24] The hour-long pornomercial packaged as legitimate cultural phenomenon attracted the predictable feminist debate between those who claimed that empowered women buy Victoria's Secret lingerie to make themselves feel beautiful and those who argued that women are in thrall to the fashion and beauty industries, which foster hypersexualized ideals of femininity to keep women consuming their products. That entrenched debate can only circle the imbricated logics of America's capitalist democracy and individualistic freedom.

Since the invasion of Afghanistan academic feminists have rightly noted that the sensationalist use of images of veiled and unveiled Afghan women, even by Western feminists, renders Afghan women passive, silent, and victimized; occludes the history of Afghan women's organized and non-organized resistance; and elides differences among Afghan women of ethnicity, class, and geography.[25] As Gillian Whitlock writes, "The image of the veiled woman in particular is a powerful trope which both invokes the passive Third World subject, and enables and sustains the discursive self-presentation of Western women as secular, liberated, individual agents."[26] These criticisms necessarily evoke the question of how Western women can advocate Afghan women's rights without committing the sins of appropriation, exploitation, and neocolonization. Is there a place from which we can speak? In Whitlock's words, "How does one begin to learn a more nuanced language which makes the veil a vehicle for a reflective and ethical practice of cross-cultural engagement?"[27] Transnational feminists will similarly need to revise their local strategies in this globalized political apparatus, as Chishti and Farhoumand-Sims effectively demonstrate in this book, by revising strategies based on Western values while also devising effective action.

Though academic discourse is quick to critique the consumerist ethnocentrism of popular Western feminism, the RAWA and V-Day association demonstrates the complexity of transnational feminism's pragmatic strategies given political and economic conditions. After all, as Whitlock notes in her analysis of Oprah's unveiling and Zoya's account of it, RAWA also commodifies the images of Afghan women abused by the Taliban in order "to fund local strategies of feminist resistance to Islamic fundamentalism."[28] In fact RAWA's website includes a page on the Madison Square Garden event, written by "U.S. Supporters," that foregrounds the significant activist work Zoya achieved by participating in various V-Day activities. She networked with international feminist groups before the performance, addressed the sold-out crowd directly after she was unveiled, and spoke at the U.S. House of Representatives the following week. Zoya might have sung for her supper, so to speak, by agreeing to the unveiling, but she also made her voice heard by working with American feminists. To further complicate the transnational relationship between RAWA and American feminists, Zoya's unveiling occurred during Oprah's performance of a monologue on Afghan women that Ensler had written after visiting Pakistan and Afghanistan under RAWA's auspices.[29] Though Western feminists have disproportionate access to money and media, the Afghan women's group made effective use of these resources for their own purposes.

Nevertheless the need for more nuanced, local, and contingent strategies of advocacy are made apparent by Afghan women's responses to Western "liberation" in the wake of the U.S.-led invasion, including those of resistance. What happens to representation when Afghan women fail to embrace their liberation according to our expectations? One example is CNN's photo caption explaining that the veiled woman in Kabul has not removed her burqa because no one has told her she could. *National Geographic*'s "Afghan Girl" presents a more direct challenge to our entwined narratives of Western humanism, human rights, and women's liberation. She first appeared on the magazine's cover in 1985 as an anonymous teenager living in a refugee camp in Pakistan. The striking photo became so widely known, especially after the U.S. invasion of Afghanistan, that the photographer, Steve McCurry, returned to Pakistan seventeen years later to look for her. After several unsuccessful efforts a *National Geographic* team located her in Afghanistan early in 2002. McCurry photographed her again, but only after obtaining permission from her male relatives.[30]

As the story on *National Geographic*'s website explains, Sharbat Gula "lives a traditional Muslim life behind the veil." After receiving permission from her male relatives, she chose to come "out from the secrecy of the veil to tell her story." According to the article, "Sharbat said she fared relatively well under Taliban rule, which, she feels, provided a measure of stability after the chaos and terror of the Soviet war." The photographer and the journalist report that after this interview and a second photograph showing her unveiled, she wishes to withdraw permanently from the media's eye and to continue her life in purdah. Though she revealed her face for the camera once again, when granted a voice she refused to be liberated from "the customs and traditions of her culture and region" by *National Geographic*'s offer of aid. Perhaps as compensation, *National Geographic* started an Afghan Girls Fund "to assist in the development and delivery of educational opportunities for young Afghan women and girls."[31]

In critiquing representations of Afghan women I do not mean to minimize the Taliban's oppression of women or deny that they disciplined women to their interpretation of Islam by mandating the veil. Rather I want to point to the significance of the veil in the Western imagination,

specifically in relation to current discourses of terrorism. If terrorism signifies covert, small-scale, even domestic warfare against "us" as a nation,
then the veiled Muslim woman is paradoxically and metonymically coded
as both a victim of Islamic orthodoxy and a sign of clandestine terrorist
tactics that are now largely synonymous with the Islamic world in much
American discourse. As Fanon wrote, "In the Arab world . . . the veil worn
by women is at once noticed by the tourist. . . . It generally suffices to
characterize Arab society. . . . For the tourist and the foreigner, the veil
demarcates both Algerian society and its feminine component."[32] In other
words the veiled woman represents the limit of American cultural and
economic imperialism. For example, a front-page photo from the *New York
Times* (4 April 2004) shows a phalanx of veiled Iraqi women, identified as
belonging to a Shiite militia, marching in Baghdad to protest the U.S.
occupation of Iraq.[33] In contrast to photos of "liberated," unveiled Afghan
women, the uniform anonymity of these veiled Iraqi women represents the
resistance to U.S. "liberation" that the Bush administration had not anticipated. Just as the veiled woman resists our gaze, so her culture resists our
colonization.

Unveiling the Muslim woman signals our victory, but not necessarily
Afghan women's freedom. That the Bush administration's claim to have
liberated the women of Afghanistan was premature and perhaps disin-
genuous is borne out by the fact that Afghan women (especially in many
provinces outside Kabul) remained subject to much the same abuses they
experienced under the Taliban, in part because the Bush administration
refused to finance or maintain security beyond Kabul. Consequently Afghan women outside the capital were commonly forced to wear the veil,
denied access to healthcare (Afghanistan long had the highest and now has
the second-highest maternal mortality rate in the world), and subjected to
rape, strip searches, and other means of sexual discipline meant to limit
their autonomous travel. Still, in other ways women's lives did change
significantly after the fall of the Taliban. Women voted in the presidential
election in October 2004, a phenomenon widely covered by the American
press. Nonetheless Human Rights Watch reports, "A pervasive atmosphere

7 "Sharbat Gula, the 'Afghan Girl,' holds the image of herself," photograph by Steve
   McCurry. From Cathy Newman's "A Life Revealed," *National Geographic*, April 2002.

8 "The Al-Mehdi Army Protests the Occupation in Iraq," photograph by Scott Nelson, *New York Times*, 4 April 2004.

of fear exists for women involved in politics and women's rights in Afghanistan, despite significant improvements in women's lives since the fall of the Taliban in late 2001."[34] Female voter registration in some provinces was as low as 10 percent; some female election workers were killed or injured by terrorists, and the sole female presidential candidate was barred from speaking at certain public events at which other candidates spoke.[35] Female voter turnout was even lower in the presidential elections of 2009. The new Afghan constitution does make some provisions for women's participation, for example reserving 25 percent of parliamentary seats for women. But there has been retribution against women's political participation and access to education.

Afghan women's full participation in civil and political life depends to a large extent on whether the U.S. makes a long-term commitment to women's rights in Afghanistan. The ongoing violence there and the resurgence of the Taliban since late 2006 and early 2007 in some areas reminds us that liberty and democracy cannot be granted at the drop of a hat—or a veil. The rebuilding of Afghanistan is a complex process that will extend years

beyond the moment of military "victory" and involve a new conglomera-
tion of global agents because international nongovernmental organizations administrate much of the nation-building apparatus in post-Taliban
Afghanistan. But though the work of these organizations is no doubt crucial to the future of Afghanistan's women, the U.S. government still plays a
powerful role in this transnational terrain. The risk is that it will now see
Afghan women's rights as inconsistent with American interests. Just as the
Bush administration used Afghan women to further national interests in
invading Afghanistan, so now the U.S. government might abandon that
commitment in favor of pressing political goals such as achieving stability
in Afghanistan. It is not unreasonable to worry that the U.S. can retreat
from a full commitment to women's rights under the guise of respecting
Afghan sovereignty, but legitimate goals of political stability and cultural
autonomy must not trump women's rights.

Notes

I would like to thank the National Geographic Society and the photographer Ami
Vitale, respectively, for granting permission to publish without cost the photographs labeled here as figures 1 and 2. I am also grateful to Adrienne Germain,
president of the International Women's Health Coalition, for information relating to Afghan women's healthcare under and after the Taliban.

1 White House, "Radio Address by Laura Bush to the Nation."
2 CNN, "Kabul Liberated."
3 McClintock, " 'No Longer in a Future Heaven,' " 90. See also Yuval-Davis and
   Anthias, *Women-Nation-State*, 7.
4 Numerous commentators, including many of those I cite in this essay, have linked
   the colonial formula of white men rescuing brown women to rhetoric about the
   war in Afghanistan and, more generally, to contemporary Western representations of the veil.
5 The *New York Times* article by Barry Bearak, titled "Kabul Retraces Steps to Life
   before Taliban," 2 December 2001, on the restoration of normal life in Kabul after
   the Taliban's retreat, is accompanied by a photograph by Robert Nickelsberg of
   the "once-secret beauty shop of Mahbooba, who crowded hairspray, lipsticks and
   photos of Indian movie stars into her Kabul apartment." A *Christian Science
   Monitor* online article about Laura Bush's pledge of "U.S. support to ensure
   [Afghan] women participate fully in public life" is accompanied by a photo of
   "2003 Beauty School Training graduates" (31 March 2005).
6 See below for a detailed discussion regarding the tensions in media coverage of

the plight of Afghan women. The Feminist Majority Foundation is a women's advocacy group founded in 1987. Its website states that they are "a cutting edge organization dedicated to women's equality, reproductive health, and non-violence. In all spheres, FMF utilizes research and action to empower women economically, socially, and politically."

7 Berlant, *The Queen of America Goes to Washington City*, 27. The embedded quotation is from Tocqueville's *Democracy in America*.

8 Bhabha, *The Location of Culture*, 66.

9 Anne-Emmanuelle Berger, writing before 9/11, notes that the West dehistoricizes the contemporary veil in a way that allows us to see it as premodern and cultural rather than as a political response to the Westernizing processes of decolonization. She argues that because the veil is politically contingent rather than culturally static, it is possible for Western commentators to make a political critique of veiling without automatically engaging in cultural imperialism ("The Newly Veiled Woman"). For another discussion of the postcolonial politics of veiling, see Nesiah, "The Ground beneath Her Feet." For two discussions of the recent resurgence of the veil among Muslim girls and young women in France, see Ardizzoni, "Unveiling the Veil," and Kramer, "Taking the Veil."

10 For examples of editorials, letters to the editor, and opinion pieces, see Sima Wali, "The Voice of Afghan Women," *Boston Globe*, 16 September 2000, sec. A; "Where's the Outrage?," *Buffalo News*, editorial, 23 August 2000, sec. B; "Statues and Statues," *Buffalo News*, editorial, 6 March 2001, sec. B; Ansar Rahel, Laina Farhat-Holzman, Philip Dacey, and Will Webster, "Treatment of Afghan Women Needs Attention," *Christian Science Monitor*, 9 May 2000, 10; Howard Kleinberg, "Where's the Outrage about Plight of Afghan Women?," *Milwaukee Journal Sentinel*, 11 March 2001, sec. J.

The few news articles covering the Taliban's abuse of women's rights include Barbara Crossette, "Afghan Women No Longer Permitted to Work with Relief Groups," *New York Times*, 12 June 2000, sec. A; Janelle Brown, "The Taliban's Bravest Opponents: Women," *Chicago Sun-Times*, 3 September 2001, 14, which reports on a documentary by the BBC reporter Saira Shah called *Beneath the Veil*.

11 Stephanie Schorow, "Veil of Tears: Bostonians Join a Nationwide Campaign to Address the Plight of Afghan Women," *Boston Globe*, 24 March 1999, Arts and Life section, 59.

12 Sharon Waxman, "A Cause Unveiled: Hollywood Women Have Made the Plight of Afghan Women Their Own—Sight Unseen," *Washington Post*, 30 March 1999, sec. C.

13 These perplexing claims by international aid organizations that women are not systematically abused under the Taliban points to the complex role of such NGOs in transnational politics, an issue discussed in relation to postinvasion Afghanistan by Maliha Chishti and Cheshmak Farhoumand-Sims in their essay in this book.

14 On the same day as Laura Bush's radio address, the U.S. State Department released a report on the status of women in Afghanistan by the Bureau of Democracy, Human Rights and Labor, "Report on the Taliban's War against Women."

15 Bush mentions rights for women only once, near the end of the address: "The fight against terrorism is also a fight for the rights and dignity of women."

16 This justification of violence in defense of virtuous womanhood recalls not only colonial logic but also white supremacist rhetoric that justified campaigns of terror against African Americans as a mission to save white womanhood from black "brutes." This is not to say that the two situations are analogous or that the Taliban are victimized and Afghan women are not. Rather the Bush administration's rhetoric of war worked similarly to infantilize women and veil the self-interested motives for the invasion.

17 Revolutionary Association of the Women of Afghanistan, "About RAWA." As Chishti and Farhoumand-Sims note in this book, the extensive network of Afghan women's resistance is only now, in the post-Taliban era, receiving scholarly attention.

18 Stabile and Kumar, "Unveiling Imperialism." For an account of Afghanistan's own struggles and vicissitudes in relation to women's rights, see Ahmed-Ghosh, "A History of Women in Afghanistan."

19 Fanon, *A Dying Colonialism*.

20 Trinh, "Not You/Like You," 416.

21 Mohanty, "Under Western Eyes," 255, 258, 256–57.

22 I am indebted to Gillian Whitlock's discussion of Zoya's account of the unveiling in "The Skin of the *Burqa*." I thank Sanjukta Ghosh for first calling my attention to this event.

23 Alex Kuczynski, "Victoria's Secret on TV: Another First for Women," *New York Times*, 18 November 2001, sec. 9. Because the Victoria's Secret fashion show has become an annual holiday TV special since this initial broadcast, and viewers are increasingly inured to media images of underwear-clad women, it is now difficult to grasp the whiff of scandal surrounding the broadcast in 2001.

24 The debate about whether freedom for Afghan women would take a Western tack intensified when Afghans saw international television broadcasts of Vida Samadzai, an Afghan-born California college student, wearing a red bikini in the Miss Earth beauty pageant in Manila in October 2003. The Afghan Supreme Court denounced her for violating the tenets of Islam and the culture of Afghanistan. See Marie Cocco, "Bikini Unveils Hypocrisy on Afghan Feminism," *New York Newsday*, 4 November 2003, sec. A.

25 In this book Chishti and Farhoumand-Sims discuss how transnational feminism's failure to consider the perspectives of a broader base of Afghan women negatively affects postinvasion efforts to establish women's rights, especially in rural Afghanistan.

26 Whitlock, "The Skin of the *Burqa*," 57. Stabile and Kumar note that this narrative

of modernity suggests that Western humanist values have achieved a state of fully realized women's rights; it glosses over the neoconservative erosions of American women's reproductive rights in the past couple of decades, for example, and the lack of commitment in the U.S. to international women's rights, exemplified by the fact that the U.S. is one of only two countries not to ratify the Women's Convention (the other is Afghanistan; "Unveiling Imperialism," 774–78).

27 Whitlock, "The Skin of the *Burqa*," 55.

28 Ibid., 58, 70.

29 Revolutionary Association of the Women of Afghanistan, "U.S. Supporters Welcome RAWA at V-Day in New York City and Washington, DC."

30 Steve McCurry, "Sharbat Gula, the 'Afghan Girl,' Holds the Image of Herself," *National Geographic News*, online.

31 Braun, "How They Found *National Geographic*'s 'Afghan Girl.' "

32 Fanon, *A Dying Colonialism*, 35–36.

33 Scott Nelson, "The Al-Mehdi Army Protests the Occupation in Iraq," *New York Times*, 4 April 2004, sec. A, published with the caption "A Show of Strength in Baghdad: Iraqi women who belong to a Shiite militia, the Mahdi Army, marched yesterday in a Baghdad neighborhood to protest the U.S. occupation of Iraq. The march also drew thousands of other protesters."

34 Human Rights Watch, "Afghanistan."

35 Human Rights Watch, "Women and Elections in Afghanistan."

Transnational Feminism and the Women's Rights Agenda in Afghanistan

Maliha Chishti & Cheshmak Farhoumand-Sims

Globalization has invariably contributed to reconfiguring the international political landscape by enabling international nonstate actors to exert greater influence and decision-making capacities within the domestic affairs of states. New methods and systems of governance have emerged to transcend borders, linking states and nonstate actors in complex and interdependent relationships, from the supranational to the local level.[1] In Afghanistan new patterns of authority and power are taking form, manifested by the unprecedented growth and entrenchment of international actors (donor governments, multinationals, the UN, the World Bank, and international NGOs) operating in the country to pick up where the state has ostensibly left off. These international networks are constructed as the long-awaited "corrective" to decades of conflict in Afghanistan and the former belligerent state practices of the Taliban government. Neoliberal marketization alongside immediate political democratization are the dominant blueprints for postconflict recovery in Afghanistan, entailing an externally directed reordering and restructuring of the Afghan state. Integrally part of this new international apparatus is the transnational feminist movement advocating for gender reform as a sociopolitical corrective to the history of exclusion and oppression endured by Afghan women. Although

women's organizations based in Europe and North America have per-
sistently increased international attention to the plight of Afghan women
since the 1990s, advancing the rights of Afghan women is by no account the
original and exclusive domain of transnational feminist networks. In contrast, the vast and impressive Afghan women's movement is only recently
receiving more scholarly attention. Although the Afghan women's movement in the post-Taliban era is still in its infancy, the Afghanistan context
reveals a diverse and extensive network of Afghan women's resistance,
organizing, public participation, and political activism.[2]

Since the fall of the Taliban many have sought to structurally improve
the situation of women and girls across many parts of Afghanistan. Although not exhaustive and most certainly fraught with tension, many inroads have nevertheless been made; there are new institutional instruments to facilitate and support women's rights, such as the Ministry of
Women's Affairs, the Gender Advisory Group, and the Office of the State
Minister for Women;[3] increased attendance of girls in schools; improvements in formal-sector female employment; and a burgeoning of nonprofit
women-centered organizations. Most significant perhaps are legal and governance reforms pertaining to women's rights as well as constitutional
provisions to promote and protect their active political participation.[4] For
example, in the parliamentary elections of 2005, sixty-eight women won
parliamentary seats; 25 percent of the seats were reserved for them under
the new constitution. Afghan women represent roughly 27 percent of the
National Assembly and hold 16 percent of the seats in the Upper House.[5]
These rather impressive developments require the caveat acutely observed
by Valentine Azarbaijani-Moghaddam, reminding us of the history of both
intermittent gains and losses of Afghan women's rights since the late nineteenth century under many different regimes. She warns that current celebrated successes should not occlude sustained strategies to ensure far-
reaching transformations in gender relations that will inevitably require
more time, commitment, and resources.[6] Indeed the ongoing challenge
remains translating the well-intentioned framework for gender equality
into meaningful practice that is actualized each day by the lived experience
of both urban and rural Afghan women. However, by all estimations the
constraints and limitations for Afghan women remain tremendous (as seen
after the elections in 2009), and Afghan women activists and parliamen-

tarians have publicly questioned the intentions and strategies of the Afghan government and foreign powers operating in the country, particularly their failed agenda to improve the lives and livelihoods of women.

The challenge for national and transnational feminist networks is to connect to the very material, complex, and multifaceted lives of women in Afghanistan, while at the same time ensuring that national and foreign interests hold true to their commitments on advancing women's rights. This essay examines the intersections between the transnational feminist apparatus and the Afghan women's movement in terms of political, sociocultural, religious, and ideological contexts that inform gender politics in Afghanistan. We define *transnational feminism* as the spectrum of actors, instruments, policies, and programs that bring gender issues into the forefront of politics and society in Afghanistan that have either been formulated or supported by those located in the West, often within a Western liberal feminist discourse. We distinguish transnational feminism from the Afghan women's movement. Many Afghan women and Afghan women's organizations are, however, part of the transnational feminist apparatus, which consists of the gender policies and programs alongside individual consultants, advisors, international women's rights NGOs, international agencies such as the United Nations Development Fund for Women (UNI-FEM), and international instruments such as the Convention on the Elimination of All Forms of Discrimination against Women (CEDAW), UN Security Council Resolution 1325 (SCR 1325), and the Beijing Platform for Action that have arrived more or less in Afghanistan after the fall of the Taliban government.

Examining the relations that exist between the transnational feminist apparatus and Afghan women's organizing is critical not only to assess the front lines of collaborative and supportive work practiced among women, but to help identify and overcome gaps in understanding and to promote women's rights in the country. This analysis is imperative given current discussions within the feminist community over what is increasingly considered a systemic failure of gender mainstreaming in international policy initiatives to secure women's full participation in conflict and postconflict states. Although aid interventions in Afghanistan may have shifted traditional gender roles to some degree, they do not necessarily indicate renegotiated gender relations. More research is needed to examine how aid interventions have modified the specific roles of and relations between men and women.

Based on our own research and work with Afghan women's organizations, we argue that the presence of the transnational feminist apparatus is most certainly not separate or distinct from the larger international aid apparatus, nor is it disentangled from the active military campaign waged in the country as part of the global war on terror. Those working in the field of gender equality must reflect on the implications of the increased militarization of the international aid apparatus, in addition to the latter's unprecedented decision-making power within the politico-economic structures of the Afghan state and civil society. As Chandra Talpade Mohanty emphasizes, "Western feminist scholarship cannot avoid the challenge of situating itself and examining its role in such a global economic and political framework. To do any less would be to ignore the complex interconnections between First and Third World . . . and the profound effect of this on the lives of women in all countries."[7] In this sense, we argue that the gender agenda in Afghanistan likewise does not escape the underpinnings typically associated with the interactions between the outsider "givers" and the insider "receivers" of aid. Focusing on gender reform and the aid regime, we argue that the types of relationships forged most often operate from unequal and neo-imperial power relations typically characterizing outsider-insider dynamics. In Afghanistan, however, we believe these relationships are premised on a tension between promoting the universal applicability of gender reform and the impulse to resist all forms of Western imperialism that seek to transform Afghan cultural, political, traditional, and religious paradigms. The politics of gender in Afghanistan once again thrusts Afghan women into the larger ideological, political, sociocultural, and religious battlefields unfolding in the post–September 11 environment, pitting the highly simplified binary of an "us" against "them," against the backdrop of a highly visible international presence in the country.

Certainly these tensions need not exist in all interactions between the Afghan women's movement and the transnational feminist apparatus, nor are they the only barrier to improving gender relations in the country. We do insist, however, that the tensions between insider and outsider, Afghan and non-Afghan, and indigenous and neo-imperial directly or indirectly contribute to gender politics in Afghanistan. We trace these tensions first from the transnational feminist campaign to rescue and reform Afghan women leading up to the fall of the Taliban, to international aid in rebuilding Afghan society and efforts to promote gender equality within an Afghan context. Greater understanding of the broader relationships forged in the pre- and post-Taliban periods is a necessary starting point to address the potential impact, efficacy, and nature of the women's rights agenda. A new communicative and political practice must be forged among women across their diversities that works in principled solidarity and critically moves away from the traps of neo-imperialism.

The Politics of Representation:
Reforming and Rescuing Afghan Women

The transnational women's movement has made significant inroads in prioritizing women's rights internationally. Over the past three decades the movement has realized several impressive accomplishments, which include codifying women's socioeconomic and political and civil rights in international conventions (CEDAW), gender reform in policies and programs at national and international levels (such as donor aid policies and the work of the United Nations and World Bank), and advocating for women's rights in international law (SCR 1325). Although the transnational women's movement has heightened gender sensitivity among many Western states and international institutions, very seldom do international women's organizing and advocacy directly impact interstate relations by exerting direct pressure on powerful states to formulate foreign policies and regulate their interactions with other states based on the violations of women's human rights. Certainly the rather persistent and high-profile advocacy campaign against the Taliban government waged by women's rights activists since the mid-1990s contributed to successfully persuading powerful governments, such as the United States, to officially *not* recognize the Taliban government and urged the UN to practice greater gender inclusion in peacemaking and humanitarian efforts in the country. The tragic events of 9/11 and the subsequent war on terror rapidly recentered the plight of Afghan women, culminating in the rather swift initial military defeat of the Taliban government by the United States in late 2001. Although the overthrow of the Taliban government was certainly not instigated by the concerns and campaigns of Western feminist networks, the task of liberating Afghan women was nevertheless conveniently grafted onto the war agenda as a positive outcome. This moral impetus to "rescue and reform" Afghan women from what was constructed as a "backward and arcane" culture justified war, inevitably sparking debate within feminist academic and activist circles over what appeared as the temporary engagement of women's rights discourse within the nexus of militarization, racism, and imperialism that characterized the content as well as the context of the new global security framework. The military defeat of the Taliban government by the United States brought to the forefront the racialized and gendered dimensions of the war on terror and the need to raise critical questions about how feminist rhetorical and political practices are taken up and implicated in broader geopolitical contexts. The Afghanistan context is important in the study of global women's rights advocacy in examining not only the very high profile and rather sensationalist politics of representations of Afghan women leading up to the war, but also how subsequent international pressure to structurally "reform and rescue" Afghan women even in post-Taliban Afghanistan is fraught with complexities, particularly in the context of globalization.

Since the 1990s the relentless and sensationalist images of burqa-clad Afghan women and accounts of their struggles have symbolized oppression and served as demonstrable proof of the oppressive political rule of the Taliban. The pervasive images of the veiled, secluded, and oppressed Afghan women were politically mediated by feminist groups (including the Revolutionary Association of the Women of Afghanistan and the Feminist Majority) to bring international attention to the plight of Afghan women. (For a detailed analysis, please see Gwen Bergner's essay in this book.) Operating with the best of intentions, these women's rights activists dedicated tremendous resources to consistently revealing the brutal violations of basic rights endured by Afghan women, which arguably would not otherwise have registered on the radar of international concern. However, the campaigns invoked an archetypal image of the downtrodden, oppressed, and veiled Afghan woman that very problematically muted the historical, sociocultural, religious, and political complexities that shape the lived realities of the majority of Afghan women. The feminist gaze thereby obstructed not only the multiple forms of resistance and resilience that informed the lives of many Afghan women, but displaced a more textured reading of their lives that would not have positioned gender as disassociated from the multiple locations they inhabit—across ethnicity, class, geography, and historical experience.

Furthermore, in assessing the politics of feminist representations of Afghan women we need to make salient the historical and political legacy of how racially minoritized women and Muslim women in particular have been represented in order to advance imperial relationships, particularly between the West and the Islamic world. Leila Ahmed's historical analyses of Muslim women across the Middle East, for example, show how women were used as political pawns to warrant colonial intervention in the name of civilizing and emancipating other cultures.[8] Colonial writings of Muslim women as oppressed and victimized reinscribed European dominance over the Orient by advancing colonial expansionist agendas that masqueraded as euphemistic expressions to civilize and tame barbaric societies. In this sense images of women were historically constructed as politicized sites of contestation, control, and conversion. As Jasmine Zine notes, the result of the 9/11 tragedy revived Orientalist images of Muslim societies, such that the liberation of Muslim women served to justify all forms of military action. She writes, "Once again, Muslim women's bodies are being positioned upon the geopolitical stage not as actors in their own right, but as foils for modernity, civilization, and freedom."[9] The feminist campaign to liberate Afghan women colludes with Orientalist tropes by constructing a singular, monolithic Afghan Woman, whose agency and heterogeneity is appropriated and controlled to advance a neo-imperialist agenda as part of the war against terror.

In the absence of a nuanced political analysis the U.S. and other outside agents positioned culture and religion as the key culprits fueling the oppressive nature of the Taliban regime. The representations of Afghan women were thereby conveniently packaged in a dichotomized simplicity of equality versus inequality, freedom versus oppression, and civilization versus barbarism.[10] The events of 9/11 and the immediate war-mongering brewing in the United States and in Europe widely appropriated these existing images to legitimize a war that would pit the civilized world against the uncivilized. Images of the oppressed and downtrodden Afghan women that were long part of the dossier of feminist advocacy against the Taliban regime merged into the jingoism and patriotism fueling the U.S. government's efforts to gain support for the war on grounds of promoting liberty, freedom, and an end to evil and terror. As Gwen Bergner examines in this book, the Bush administration, and Laura Bush in particular, promulgated an American rescue of Afghan women in such a way as to infantilize them, thereby masking the true motivations for the war. This merging of women's rights discourse into the agenda of militarization, racialization, and imperialism was self-evident and rightly resisted by a vast number of feminist academics and organizations around the world.[11] While many Western feminist groups debated the issues, the images of Afghan women nevertheless were reinscribed to pursue a more aggressive foreign policy that did not question the racist and imperialist motivations of the war or elucidate the historical and political complexities that informed the conflict. Instead the fall of the Taliban regime was situated in an "us" versus "them" binary, placing Afghan women at the center of the mission to reform Afghanistan under the supervision and watchful eye of the West.

This framing of Afghan women to legitimize the war requires more scholarly attention, particularly in terms of how this (mis)information influenced and determined the women's rights agenda in the country and the types of relationships fostered between the transnational feminist apparatus and Afghan women in the postwar period of reconstruction and rebuilding. Inevitably the sensationalized stories of Afghan women leading up to the war precipitated particular kinds of interventions. The stereotypical images created misleading, simplistic, and superficial understandings of gender relations and Afghan women. In many ways the archetypal image succeeded in dislocating Afghan women's agency and was hence reinscribed into many of the post-Taliban gender policies and programs. For instance, gender programs assume that culturally and religiously conservative women are less likely to advance women's rights compared to more educated, nonreligious women (or, for example, rural women compared to urban women, or women who wear the burqa compared to those who do not). As Azarbaijani-Moghaddam notes, international feminists were set on working with women who shared their values, who could converse and engage in written English communication, and who were less outwardly religious. In doing so the transnational feminist apparatus initially focused on a small group of Afghan women who mirrored their own politics, thereby compromising Afghan women's agency and access to the women's rights agenda. Azarbaijani-Moghaddam is convinced that gender issues have been oversimplified by advisors who lack a general understanding of the complexities of religion, culture, and history. She argues that weak analyses, oversights, and oversimplifications can make interventions very disruptive: "Badly conceived and facile analyses based on the assumption that Afghan women are vulnerable individuals living in a vacuum may eventually isolate rather than reintegrate women."[12] Elaheh Rostami-Povey's study of Afghan women provides a much needed corrective to the history of women's organizing. In her research she "writes back" by repositioning Afghan women's agency and ownership of their struggle and by highlighting the history of women's secret organizations and solidarity networks under the Taliban regime. Her study counters the dominant sensationalist images of Afghan women and hence implores the transnational feminist apparatus to build on existing capacities and work with all Afghan women—conservative and moderate, urban and rural, literate and illiterate.[13] Clearly an accurate reading and engagement of the complex lives of Afghan women across their diverse locations will ensure social and political gender reform that acknowledges their struggle and inculcates more nuanced approaches required to advance women's rights across Afghanistan.

The Women's Rights Agenda and International Aid Apparatus in Afghanistan after 9/11

Afghan women quickly became the trophies of liberation, their images paraded around the world as proof of a just and moral victory over the Taliban regime. While the media presented stories of women's clothing stores and beauty salons reopening in Kabul, the swift military defeat of the Taliban regime was accompanied by the unprecedented arrival of international agencies setting up shop, many for the first time, in a country now witnessing an unprecedented influx of foreign expatriates and substantial donor funds. During the Taliban period Afghanistan received on average U.S.$250 million annually in aid, with only a couple of hundred international expatriates working in the country. In contrast, since the fall of the Taliban aid money pledged in the billions at large donor conferences is transforming the country into an expatriate haven for seasoned postwar expert agencies, consultants, and organizations. It was anticipated that the "liberators" would prioritize the needs of ordinary Afghans, yet after six years of foreign intervention many Afghans are frustrated and disenfranchised due to the lack of sustained and visible impact, particularly in the rural areas. The hopefulness we observed in 2003 has transformed into the impression that outsiders are politically ambivalent toward the needs of local people. The Asia Foundation's national survey in 2006 revealed growing skepticism and animosity among Afghans toward the international presence and the Afghan government. The key issues raised in the survey include concerns over security, the lack of reconstruction, the weak economy, and high levels of unemployment.[14] Both the illicit economy and the informal economy continue to account for 80 to 90 percent of the total economy, and according to the World Bank, among others, the deteriorating economic condition threatens government legitimacy and stability and in many regions helps to increase the power of the warlords.[15]

Transnational feminist networks are not isolated from the messy terrain of real and perceived failures of aid interventions in the country. Frustrations about the national interests of foreign powers are looming, specifically against the outright political bargaining with warlords, which significantly undermines any efforts to advance women's rights. Despite aid flowing into the country women's formal rights are not translated into lived experience, particularly since forced marriages, domestic violence,[16] threats and intimidations, kidnappings, honor killings, and daily harassments are all major obstacles to the safety and security of women across the country. The lack of security has been identified as a significant problem for the majority of Afghans, but women and girls bear the brunt of it as it impairs their active participation in the reconstruction and development process, clearly corroborated by the events after the second presidential elections.

In 2006–7 the security situation deteriorated significantly, with an increased number of explosions, suicide bombings, and armed attacks. In Kandahar the assassination in September 2006 of Safiye Amajan, the head of the Department for Women's Affairs, illustrated the dangers facing women, especially those active in human rights organizing. It has been repeatedly stressed that in public spaces all women and girls are potential

targets of resurgent opposition forces, local warlords, and powerful criminal groups, who threaten, intimidate, and enact physical and sexual violence. In this fraught environment gender programming will have only a
superficial impact if the majority of women continue to be constrained and
the underlying political changes are not made. The foreign agenda in the
country, and the transnational feminist engagement with it, must take
greater responsibility for what Azarbaijani-Moghaddam describes as a situation in which women's rights are being "transacted" by foreign powers to
pursue their multiple and contradictory agendas in the country.[17] Efforts
to support Afghan women become trapped inside the complex web of
political and military objectives, priorities, and criminalizing partnerships.

Transnational feminist advocacy needs to reveal the dangerous implications of imperial play in Afghanistan and the role of internationals that, on
the one hand, engage the rhetoric of gender equality and promote safety
and security for all women, but on the other simultaneously undermine
state legitimacy and the rule of law through their continued direct and
indirect support of warlordism. In this sense the end of the first Taliban
regime ushered in a new and different era of challenges for women. The
situation, as Denize Kandiyoti acutely observes, is one in which "women
continue to be wards of their communities and households and have little
recourse to protection or justice outside these domains."[18]

Provincial Reconstruction Teams and
the Militarization of Aid

The militarization of aid found expression in Afghanistan in 2003, when
the United States established the first provincial reconstruction teams
(PRTs) in the three provinces of Gardez, Kunduz, and Bamiyan.[19] This was
followed shortly by Britain's establishing PRTs in Mazar-e-Sharif in the
north and Canada's establishing PRTs in Kandahar in the south. Over the
past several years more than fourteen countries have established PRTs
across Afghanistan, emblematic of the new security face of postconflict
development operations. Among the aid community in Afghanistan, the
purpose of the PRTs remains unclear even though their official and stated
objective is to "advance the central government's presence throughout
Afghanistan and to provide direct support to the reconstruction efforts."[20]

Observers argue that the PRTs were primarily created to engage soldiers in aid, development, and reconstruction in order to "win the hearts and minds" of the people and promote the success of the military campaign. Feminists too have had mixed responses to the growing politicization and securitization of aid in Afghanistan that very quickly blurred distinctions between strictly political, military, and humanitarian motivations. The multiple and arguably contradictory motivations of PRTs have created frustration and concern among aid workers and recipients. Aid and development NGOs, researchers and activists alike, argue that the militarization of aid is not conducive to sustainable peace or development and threatens the integrity of this important work for decades. They argue that the militarization of aid has greatly diminished humanitarian space, and aid agencies are finding it increasingly difficult to distance themselves from the war on terror's active combative campaigns in the country. Any efforts on the part of aid actors to interact and establish trust and good relations with communities on exclusively humanitarian terms is met with suspicion or ambivalence. The blurring of lines between military and humanitarian work has consequently compromised the safety and security of aid workers, as demonstrated by a noticeable and disturbing increase in violent attacks against foreign aid workers and their Afghan colleagues, who are accused of collaborating with the foreigners. As a result many NGOs with a long history of working in the harshest and most challenging of times in Afghanistan have suspended their operations.

Feminist scholars and practitioners must pay closer attention to the authoritative presence of internationals, particularly in terms of the implications of the war on terror's varied geopolitical and military interests that not only frame the postconflict agenda, but implicate (by extension) gender programs in Afghanistan. Across the country the current foreign (military as well as civilian) presence has evoked concern and a desire to "protect" Afghan women from the "foreign gaze," thereby not only hindering women's participation in aid projects, but further restricting their access to public space. The PRTs in particular reinforce working primarily with Afghan men as the key development partners, since women are largely prohibited from engaging with men who are not directly related to them by blood or marriage (such as soldiers). Although the militarization of aid is posited as creating more peace and security for communities, these goals are highly suspect given the premise that the use and threat of violence are the means to conflict resolution. Unless these fundamental contradictions are all taken into account and addressed, the militarization of aid will hinder rather than serve the cause of peace in Afghanistan and negatively impact the local populations, particularly the women.

International Aid and the Politics of Women's Organizing

The lack of accountability not only of the multiple political mandates in the country but also the billions of dollars entering the country is a key concern, especially in terms of how this money is being distributed and who benefits. The failure of the international community to maintain a consistent course of aid further exacerbates the weariness and suspicion among Afghans, already troubled by the lavish and revolving presence of the expatriate community. In our own work in Afghanistan in the spring of 2003, we observed that Afghan women from both rural and urban areas recognized the scattered international agenda and criticized aid agencies particularly for their distance from the lives of the majority of Afghans. Indeed the international aid apparatus has set its own subculture and infrastructure, operating in what Antonio Donini calls the "Kabul Bubble."[21] They work within a hierarchical, donor-driven structure of policies and practices, dispensing aid money unevenly across Afghanistan. The practices and politics of women's rights are most often defined by the international aid apparatus in terms of its relationship to transnational feminism networks. We have observed that in the context of Afghan women's organizations, transnational feminism, consistent with the international aid apparatus, promotes the institutionalization of women's organizing to encourage an urban-based humanitarian aid framework in the country. Women's organizing is specifically directed to create "functional and efficient" NGOs that are structured like their international counterparts. The transnational feminist apparatus needs to recognize that tensions arise when policies and practices re-create demarcations made by the international aid community between the secular and religious, the formal and informal, the urban and rural, and so on. This agenda often disempowers the illiterate, rural-based Afghan networks of women organizers and puts them in competition with the more urban-based, educated, and

professional Afghan women's organizations. More often than not, the informal networks of women are perceived as inexperienced, hindered by
their own cultural and religious conservatism, and are assumed to lack the
skills to properly manage their financial resources. These perceptions can
further exacerbate the disparities among women's groups and inevitably
challenge national and transnational feminist hopes for building a politics
of solidarity across the diversity of women's locations and experiences.
This can lead to a divisive fragmentation of the women's movement if, for
example, English literacy and donor history are the key determinants to
receiving support.

Transnational feminists operating within the postconflict aid apparatus
in the country need to be diligent against donor-driven agendas, which can
nurture a rigid and privileged hierarchy of Afghan women's organizing.
The protracted exclusion of these women not only dislocates their agency
as co-constructors of a women's rights agenda, but will have a detrimental
impact on Afghanistan's overall capacity to instigate long-term changes in
attitudes and perceptions. To work against the normative structures of the
international aid community, the transnational feminist apparatus must
implement flexible and creative approaches that depart from normative
donor practices that all too often facilitate the entry of women into institutionalized civil society at the expense of building alliances and pooling
resources (financial and human) in order to work toward mutually agreed
upon goals and objectives.

The Convention on the Elimination of All Forms of Discrimination against Women and the Afghan Women's Rights Agenda

In an effort to ensure that women's rights are firmly entrenched in the
critical early stages of nation building in Afghanistan, the transnational
feminist apparatus actively sought to advance two important international
United Nations documents that ostensibly would protect and promote
women's rights and participation in peace building and reconstruction: the
United Nations International Convention on the Elimination of All Forms
of Discrimination against Women (CEDAW) and the United Nations Security Council Resolution 1325 on Women, Peace, and Security (SCR
1325).[22] Although not perfect and certainly fraught with limitations and

controversy, these documents are nevertheless considered instrumental in advancing and guaranteeing women's rights, particularly in the formative period of social, political, and economic state building in Afghanistan. The advocacy efforts of transnational feminist networks and of Afghan women themselves enabled both CEDAW and SCR 1325 to bear some influence over the drafting of Afghanistan's new constitution and in ensuring that Afghan women's rights were prioritized under the Bonn Agreement.[23]

The first of these two documents, CEDAW, was adopted on 18 December 1979 by the UN General Assembly and came into force on 3 September 1981 after twenty countries ratified it. Despite debates about and criticisms of CEDAW and its applicability in a diverse international community, 185 states were party to the Convention. The Convention was the "culmination of more than thirty years of work by the Commission on the Status of Women," whose work was "instrumental in bringing to light all the areas in which women are denied equality with men."[24] Of all the UN declarations and conventions CEDAW in particular is the most critical and comprehensive document created to address the advancement of women and the fulfillment of their human rights. It not only defines equality, but also addresses a wide range of human rights issues relating to women. It also provides an agenda for action for those states who are party to the Convention, often referred to as the Women's Convention and International Bill of Rights for Women. The Convention's preamble and thirty articles address civil rights and the legal status of women; it is the first treaty in history to consider issues relating to human reproduction and the impact of culture on gender relations.[25] The Convention discusses such varied topics as freedom of religion; freedom of movement, opinion, and association; nationality; sexual and reproductive rights;[26] and rights to education, healthcare, and the political arena. It defines discrimination against women as "any distinction, exclusion or restriction made on the basis of sex which has the effect or purpose of impairing or nullifying the recognition, enjoyment or exercise by women, irrespective of their marital status, on a basis of equality of men and women, of human rights and fundamental freedoms in the political, economic, social, cultural, civil or any other field."[27]

By ratifying CEDAW states commit to incorporating the principle of the equality of men and women in their legal system, abolishing and revising all discriminatory laws, establishing tribunals and other public institutions to ensure the effective protection of women against discrimination, and eliminating all acts of discrimination against women by persons, organizations, and enterprises. Although the UN does not have enforcement mechanisms, the strength of the Convention is rooted in the requirement that state parties who have acceded to the Convention are legally bound to put its provisions into practice.

As with other treaty bodies the implementation of the Convention is monitored by a committee composed of "independent experts." The CEDAW committee is composed of twenty-three experts who are nominated by their governments and elected by the Economic and Social Council to serve four-year terms. Experts are chosen based on their "high moral standing and competence in the field covered by the Convention."[28] The committee meets three times a year with a designated number of state delegations who have submitted their reports. States are expected to submit reports to the treaty body once every four years. In their reports countries are expected to outline measures they have adopted to bring their country's laws and practices more in line with their obligations under the Convention. At the reporting sessions the delegations from each country provide a summary of their written report, including statistical information and updates, which allows the committee to then question the delegation on its progress in implementing CEDAW and to provide general recommendations concerning the elimination of discrimination against women. The committee reports to the Economic and Social Council and the General Assembly with a list of its activities and recommendations based on its examination of reports and information received from state parties and NGOs. States parties to CEDAW present their first report to the committee one year after ratification, and every two years thereafter.

Afghanistan's history of engagement with CEDAW began on 14 August 1980, when the country signed onto the Convention. By signing, Afghanistan made a salutary endorsement whereby it agreed not to undermine the spirit of the Convention while it carried out an internal review to determine whether or not to ratify.[29] Over the years of conflict and unrest, however, the Convention was forgotten; it regained attention only after the fall of the Taliban and the arrival of the international aid apparatus in the country. Grassroots women's organizations and UNIFEM immediately began to provide training workshops on CEDAW, and there was a growing interest in the Afghan women's movement to learn about the Convention and consider ways it could be used as an advocacy tool for women's rights in Afghanistan. In addition to this growing interest within civil society, the interim Afghan government wanted to demonstrate its commitment to gender equality in the face of intense international pressure to improve the situation of women. It was in this climate that the interim government unexpectedly undertook measures to formally ratify the Convention on 5 March 2003.[30] Afghanistan's ratification of CEDAW was an important milestone for women's rights, not only in that country but also across the Muslim world. Afghanistan made history by becoming the first Muslim state to ratify CEDAW without reservations.[31]

The timing of Afghanistan's ratification of CEDAW was extremely significant given that it preceded the drafting and adoption of the new Afghan constitution in January 2004. The transnational feminist movement along with national actors within the Afghan women's movement quickly mobilized to lend support and help embed CEDAW commitments within the new constitution. In the months leading up to the constitutional *loya jirga* much of their advocacy centered on demanding that international human rights principles pertaining to women, such as equality before the law and advances in political rights, be included in the constitution. Adoption of CEDAW did have opponents, however; there was a clear campaign to discredit the Convention as Western, un-Islamic, and incompatible with Afghan culture and religion. Despite great resistance by conservative elements before and during the constitutional loya jirga, however, international and local feminists achieved some successes that were celebrated by women in Afghanistan and their supporters around the world. The chairperson of CEDAW, Ferida Acar, noted:

The newly approved Constitution explicitly guarantees that men and women have equal rights and duties before the law. This is a significant victory for women and girls in Afghanistan who barely three years ago were completely excluded from all spheres of life and faced systematic violations of their human rights on a daily basis. Gender equality is a crucial factor not only in achieving sustainable peace but also in ensuring respect for human rights, democracy and the rule of law in all societies. Enshrining the principle of gender equality within the Constitution is a vital starting point for the transformation and reconstruction of Afghanistan. It legitimizes the important role played by women and girls in Afghanistan in reshaping their future and in rebuilding their country.[32]

Still, Afghan women were only guardedly optimistic. While they celebrated the explicit inclusion of gender equality and other positive developments in the constitution, according to Lauryn Oates and Isabelle Solon-
Helal, "they remain[ed] cautious due to other constitutional provisions
that proclaim[ed] Afghanistan an 'Islamic Republic' and declare[d] that
'the beliefs and provisions of the sacred religion of Islam' [had] precedence
over any law in Afghanistan."[33] This apparent conflict will pose an obsta-
cle to the advancement of women if extremist interpretations of Sharia
are used to determine women's rights and responsibilities in Afghanistan.
Their concerns are well placed; the vast majority of the reservations to
CEDAW are entered by Muslim governments who argue that Islamic Sharia
law supersedes international law and therefore prevents them from fully
complying with CEDAW.[34] By attaching a reservation to a particular article
a state party articulates its decision not to be held accountable to that
article.

Given the potential for women's rights to be undermined, the transnational feminist network's agenda in Afghanistan sought to strengthen
the women's movement there by creating awareness and generating widespread grassroots support for CEDAW and SCR 1325 in public and legal
discourses. It was assumed that once Afghan women's organizations became familiar with these international instruments they would be able to
contextualize their own struggles and activism from within these political
frames and diligently monitor government accountability and compliance.

While training Afghan women on CEDAW in Afghanistan in May 2003,
we were inspired by their intense interest in and serious consideration of
the applicability and relevance of the Convention to Afghanistan. In working with formal (urban-based) and nonformal (rural-based) Afghan wom-
en's organizations and networks from across the country, we found that in
many cases introducing the contents of these international documents
generated an overall positive response by many women, who felt these
documents were useful tools for advocating women's rights. In training
sessions on CEDAW we noticed that some of the participants were con-
fused about or opposed to it because of anti-CEDAW propaganda they had
heard on the radio or read in local newspapers. Upon a closer reading and
examination of the Convention, however, many of these women were able
to have some of their misconceptions and concerns addressed.[35] Nevertheless the suitability and applicability of the Convention in helping to trans-

form gender inequities in the country produced intense discussions. This is not surprising, as various other Muslim states have raised concerns or opposed CEDAW specifically around women's rights to free movement and nationality (article 9) and other rights related to marriage and family life (article 16). Traditionally the desire to limit a woman's role to that of wife and mother has prevented her from entering public life and being an active member of society through social and political participation. While working in Afghanistan we saw some of the same concerns raised by those apprehensive about CEDAW's impact on that country. While a great majority of women were eager to learn about these instruments and use them to their advantage, a very small group of equally passionate traditionalists (men and women) harbored suspicion of CEDAW as part of a "Western imperialist agenda." As in other Muslim states, the forces of opposition led by conservative clergy and their supporters invoked religious grounds for noncompliance. Ariane Brunet and Isabelle Solon-Helal of the organization Rights and Democracy, who have worked extensively in Afghanistan, suggest:

In Afghanistan, women's rights are viewed as part of a Western agenda; they are used as a propaganda tool by all sides and linked to cultural and religious values. Every possible roadblock to the realization of women's rights and to the participation of women in decision-making processes has been installed: the perpetuation of warlordism, the lack of security, and the lack of effective gender policy coordination.[36]

One of the difficult tasks we encountered was how to promote CEDAW across the country without disavowing Afghan culture and religion while simultaneously not supporting patriarchal attitudes and structures that undermine the rights of women. Although discussions of CEDAW are a platform for dialogue and critical engagement among women, as one Afghan women's rights activist recently noted, the task is not easy:

Despite years of CEDAW related activities in Afghanistan, most women's political activists were not really aware of what CEDAW is exactly about, but when we began our activities and campaigns for women's political rights, it became the discourse among political activists. But due to the sensitivity of the topic, we were always arguing based on all international human rights conventions signed by Afghanistan, and tried not to focus on CEDAW.[37]

A critical challenge is to address the suspicions Afghan men and women have about CEDAW, primarily as a Western imperialist imposition that will abruptly modernize and secularize Afghanistan's cultural and religious traditions. Clearly, using international provisions to change and challenge women's and girls' realities in Afghanistan must therefore be predicated on the ownership of these instruments by Afghans themselves. This entails a multifaceted approach whereby national and international actors must collaboratively work through the messy terrain of dialogue and action to engage CEDAW from within a negotiated cultural and religious framework. This is not to say that Afghan women must concede to misogynist and extremist perspectives, but if women—and men—believe that international tools do not respect their religious and cultural traditions, they will not support their application in domestic practice. What we found in Afghanistan was a split between those who thought these tools did not go far enough in protecting and promoting women's human rights, and those who were concerned about the impact of their application on the status quo. The former group challenged CEDAW for not implicitly discussing violence against women in the private sphere as a human rights violation; they believed the Convention should demand that states make domestic abuse a criminal offense. One woman commented, "All the rights in the world are meaningless if I have to suffer abuse at the hands of my husband and his family on a regular basis. Why does this Convention not protect me from this?" The other group believed that private sphere rights should not be codified in international law in order to preserve Afghan and Islamic cultural and religious practices pertaining to women's familial and social roles. These women seemed to be resisting women's rights in order to protect their own social status. As Rostami-Povey argues, "The responsibility for the injustice and violence lies not only with the immediate family but also with individual communities, religious organizations, health and education institutions, professionals and law enforcers."[38]

To dispel fears and concerns about CEDAW local women's NGOs in Afghanistan have been engaged in educational campaigns that serve two important purposes: familiarizing women with these international provisions and allowing them to develop independent opinions about their content and relevance, and encouraging locally based plans of action to implement these provisions and ensure that CEDAW and SCR 1325 directly relate to the needs of Afghan women and not be perceived as externally imposed. These efforts have resulted in increased dialogue, particularly about Afghanistan's responsibilities as a signatory to CEDAW, but the security situation and other barriers to women's participation in public life have made it only marginally possible for women to demand changes to the status quo. Lack of security is preventing women from enjoying freedom of movement and demanding their rights without being threatened. This was clearly demonstrated in loya jirgas where women delegates suffered verbal abuse and threats to their physical safety because of their outspoken demands for rights and their criticism of the status quo. Public discourse clearly impacted the Constitutional Drafting Commission whose mandate called for "broad participation of women in the constitution-making process" and the inclusion of nine women members serving on the Commission.[39] The mandate also made a commitment to work with the Women's Ministry and UNIFEM to hold public education programs about the constitutional rights of women throughout the country in order to reach out to women and to increase public awareness. Without a doubt, the development of a national women's movement is critical to promoting change. Brunet and Solon-Helal reflect on their extensive work in Afghanistan:

The elusive gains made with Afghanistan's ratification of CEDAW, the very new concept of a Ministry of Women's Affairs, the weak coordination among donor countries regarding women's rights, the varied and contradictory gender policies proposed in a variety of U.N./ATA [Afghanistan Transitional Authority] documents, and the lack of gender-focused staff appointments at the United Nations Assistance Mission to Afghanistan (UNAMA), indicate that women's human rights also need to be protected by civil society organizations and by the building of a women's movement that is educated and capable of being a valuable interlocutor to a State that should be governed by the rule of law. This cannot happen over a few years, let alone over a few months.[40]

In our work we found women expressing a desire to connect with women and women's groups outside Afghanistan to share experiences and lessons, particularly in addressing the issue of Islam and law. Case studies of women's activism in other Muslim countries and in the rest of the developing world provide these organizations with encouragement, support, and valuable ideas about how to meet the challenges they face as

Muslim women struggling to realize their rights within an Islamic framework. Our references to the work of women's movements in Iran, Pakistan, Egypt, and other Muslim states were met with great enthusiasm and pride by the Afghan women we worked with, who felt that they shared similar challenges and would benefit from meeting with other Muslim women on such issues. Despite this need for regional cooperation and networking among women's groups, the transnational women's movement has made little effort to facilitate this process. A small number of NGOs are spearheading this effort,[41] but without international financial support these efforts will prove arduous.

The engagement of Afghan women is absolutely critical to creating frameworks that implement CEDAW and other international instruments that speak to women's lived realities in Afghanistan. Universal human rights norms come to life only when they find relevance to those they serve. Attempting to apply only one model will not only fail, but will give impetus to opponents of these valuable tools. Efforts to promote CEDAW and SCR 1325 must not only educate women but also sharpen their analytical abilities so that they may interpret CEDAW within the framework of Islamic legal and cultural discourses.

Challenges to the Convention

Although misunderstandings of CEDAW abound, the following discussion of key articles illustrates that international human rights need not be incompatible with Islamic customary and legal discourse, and that dialogue and education would serve to bridge the gap and benefit women in Afghanistan. The most challenged CEDAW articles include article 4, on special measures; article 5, on sex-role stereotyping and prejudice; article 6, on prostitution; article 9, on nationality; article 15, on law; and article 16, on marriage and family life. In our training programs we were met with extensive questions about the meaning and intent of articles 6 and 16, which had received negative press in the media and had been challenged by critics, including various local and national Islamic scholars. Article 5 addresses the universality of women's human rights and encourages state parties to the Convention to modify social and cultural patterns of conduct to eliminate the idea of one sex as superior and stereotypical roles for men and women. This is a particularly challenging article in the Muslim world because of the debate around women's roles and responsibilities in Muslim society and the need to preserve cultural norms.[42] Some Muslim scholars who have debated this issue argue that the question is not one of the universality of human rights but rather the application of universal norms to protect and preserve "legitimate" cultural traditions that do not promote the suffering of groups based on ethnicity, sex, nationality, religion, or any other category. Clearly the solution to this dilemma lies within the Muslim world itself.

Another revealing discussion about CEDAW dealt with article 6, which requires states to take all appropriate measures, including legislation, to suppress the trafficking of women and the exploitation of prostitutes. Media discussions of this article gave the impression that it "promotes" promiscuity. When we began to discuss this article in detail, its relevance became increasingly clear to our female participants, who discussed the plight of widowed women who had to turn to prostitution to earn a living, and the increasing number of trafficked women who have worked in Afghanistan since the arrival of foreign troops. Article 9, on the right of women to hold nationality independent of their husband, is particularly problematic in Afghanistan and the Muslim world, where a woman's—and her children's—nationality and freedom of movement are tied to the husband or father. Article 16 allows women to decide whether to get married and to choose their spouse. It allows a woman the power to decide the number of children she would like to have and their spacing and gives her an equal say in their custody and guardianship. She would also have equal rights to ownership, acquisition, management, and administration of property. Despite opposition to the rights articulated in this article, Afghan women noted that Sharia law already provides Muslim women with many of these rights. Some women noted that only extreme interpretations of Sharia law and women's ignorance of their Islamic rights lead to disagreements about the roles and responsibilities of Muslim women in the family.

The Muslim world is not a homogeneous entity, and religious precepts are clearly influenced by historical, regional, and cultural factors, which in turn impact the interpretation and the practice of religion. As Abdullahi An-Na'im argues, "It is not difficult to establish the responsibility of many Islamic states to change aspects of religious law in accordance with their obligations under international law. The question is how to effect such change in practice."[43]

We would argue that a good way to start effecting change is for transnational feminists working in Afghanistan to build solidarity by creating more spaces for the exchange of ideas, critical reflection, and mutual learning. By engaging, not disavowing, traditional religious sources of the Quran and Sunnah, in addition to centering the nuances of culture, our discussions with Afghan women were able to move into those difficult spaces where a closer reading of each article helped to clarify and contextualize its varied meanings and purposes. Our collective assessment that these principles could be applied in a culturally and religiously appropriate manner served to overcome many of the initial concerns and skepticism.[44]

Conclusion

Women's organizing is not a new phenomenon in Afghanistan. Afghan women have a long tradition of activism and resistance in the face of insecurity and grave human rights abuses. Their activities have continued throughout twenty-three years of protracted conflict and have led to a burgeoning women's rights movement that is committed to the advancement of Afghan women and their full enjoyment of their most basic rights, including access to education, healthcare, and economic opportunity and important civil and political rights. According to the Beijing Declaration and Platform for Action, "Equality between women and men is a matter of human rights and a condition for social justice and is also a necessary and fundamental prerequisite for equality, development and peace."[45] In Afghanistan "the low social status of women, and the consequent power imbalances between women and men that it generates, are the underlying reasons for harmful and discriminatory practices and physical and sexual abuse against girls and women."[46] The international feminist movement has a strategic role to play in supporting and building solidarity networks with the existing women's movement in Afghanistan. However, it is critical to note that the global and local complexities and contradictions that underpin the rights agenda in Afghanistan can also backfire, with the very real possibility of a backlash against Afghan women seen as betraying Afghan culture and traditions by participating in foreign aid projects. At the very least the feminist international apparatus needs to be aware of perceptions on the part of *both* Afghan women and men that equate women-centered and gender-targeted programs as a direct challenge to traditional culture and religion. The expansive internationally directed rights agenda across Afghanistan is perhaps already fueling and further legitimizing rigid interpretations of sacred texts in order to "rescue" Afghan women from the tyranny of Western neocolonial quests to reconfigure Afghan womanhood. Both local and international actors must therefore be attentive to the messy terrain of advancing and improving the lives of Afghan women and girls in the current postconflict dynamics of outsider–insider politics. As Zine acutely observes, we must be aware of "the way bodies and identities are scripted in service of neo-imperialist goals and from within fundamentalist worldviews. Both ideological views limit [women's] agency, autonomy, and freedom and seriously circumscribe their lived conditions, choices, and experiences."[47] Moving beyond this ideological battlefield is perhaps an impossibility, but principled solidarity based on collaborative efforts and genuine dialogue can help facilitate mutually defined goals to further promote the overall well-being of Afghan women in postconflict Afghanistan.

Notes

The coauthors of this essay are listed alphabetically.

1 For an extensive discussion, see Mark Duffield's *Global Governance and the New Wars*.

2 See Elaheh Rostami Povey's study "Women in Afghanistan."

3 We recognize that these institutions are still in their infancy and have yet to meet their full potential. For example, see International Crisis Group, "Afghanistan: Women and Reconstruction."

4 For a concrete analysis of Afghan women's participation in the constitutional process, see Oates and Solon-Helal, *At the Cross-Roads of Conflict and Democracy*.

5 Afghan Research Education Unit, *A House Divided*, 15.

6 Azarbaijani-Moghaddam, "Afghan Women on the Margins of the Twenty-first Century."

7 Mohanty, *Feminism without Borders*, 20.

8 L. Ahmed, *Women and Gender in Islam*.

9 Zine, "Muslim Women and the Politics of Representation," 2.

10 Chishti, "The International Women's Movement and the Politics of Participation for Muslim Women," 86.

11 Interview with Lauryn Oates by Cheshmak Farhoumand-Sims, 25 October 2007.

12 Azarbaijani-Moghaddam, "Afghan Women on the Margins of the Twenty-First Century," 103.

13 Rostami-Povey, "Women in Afghanistan."

14 Asia Foundation, "Afghanistan in 2006."

15 World Bank, "Afghanistan." See also Senlis Council, "Afghanistan Five Years Later" and "Losing Hearts and Minds in Afghanistan."

16 Oates, *National Report on Domestic Violence against Women: Afghanistan.*

17 Azarbaijani-Moghaddam, "On Living with Negative Peace and a Half-Built State."

18 Kandiyoti, *The Politics of Gender and Reconstruction in Afghanistan*, 32.

19 For a more thorough discussion and analysis of PRTs, gender issues, and Afghanistan, see Farhoumand-Sims, "The Three Block War."

20 Peace Operations Working Group of the Canadian Peace Coordinating Committee, "NGO / Government Dialogue on Provincial Reconstruction Teams (PRTs) in Afghanistan and the Militarization of Humanitarian Assistance."

21 Donini, *Nation Building Unraveled*, 2004.

22 For a more complete discussion of CEDAW, see Cheshmak Farhoumand-Sims's dissertation, currently in progress, "Implementing CEDAW in Afghanistan."

23 For the United Nations Division for the Advancement of Women, see the UN website.

24 Ibid.

25 Ibid.

26 The Convention is very careful in addressing this issue and refers only to women's right "to decide freely and responsibly on the number and spacing of their children and to have access to information, education and means to enable them to exercise these rights" (CEDAW, article 16:1e).

27 CEDAW, article 1.

28 Their mandate is outlined in articles 17–30 of the Convention.

29 Medica Mondiale Basic German Women's Group, "Information about CEDAW and CEDAW in Afghanistan."

30 Farhoumand-Sims's interviews with Afghan women activists and workers in the Ministry of Women's Affairs and the Ministry of Foreign Affairs reveal that no one seemed to have known that the Ministry of Foreign Affairs was pursuing CEDAW ratification until it was announced in March 2003.

31 Turkey is the only Muslim country that has removed all reservations to the Convention.

32 Women's International League for Peace and Freedom, "CEDAW Chairperson Applauds New Afghan Constitution."

33 Oates and Solon-Helal, *At the Cross-Roads of Conflict and Democracy.*

34 Farhoumand-Sims, "Implementing CEDAW in Afghanistan."

35 One of the major weaknesses of CEDAW that the women highlighted was the absence of any discussion about domestic violence. We explained that this was due to resistance and opposition, largely by Muslim states, against any inclusion

in the Convention of women's private sphere rights. Articles dealing with other "private" rights, such as marriage, are highly contested by Muslim states and continue to elicit reservations. The feeling was that if such an article about violence against women were added to CEDAW fewer parties would sign it. It would be better to have countries sign on and work toward full compliance rather than alienate them.

36 Brunet and Solon-Helal, "Seizing the Opportunity," 20.

37 Email communication with an Afghan women's rights activist who wishes to remain anonymous, 16 November 2007.

38 Rostam-Povey, "Women in Afghanistan," 175.

39 Brunet and Solon-Helal, "Seizing the Opportunity," 12.

40 Ibid., 7.

41 See website for Women Living under Muslim Laws, http://www.wluml.org/.

42 For a fuller discussion of the challenge of women's human rights and cultural relativism, see the works by An-Na'im, Afshar (co-editor of *Development, Women and War: A Feminist Perspective*), and Azarbaijani-Moghaddam cited in this essay as well as Mayer, *Islam and Human Rights*.

43 An-Na'im, *Human Rights in Cross Cultural Perspectives*, 182.

44 Women Living under Muslim Laws is an excellent organization doing work in this area.

45 See Beijing Declaration and Platform for Action.

46 Rostam-Povey, "Women in Afghanistan," 175.

47 Zine, "Between Orientalism and Fundamentalism," 11.

Global Frames on Afghanistan

The Iranian Mediation of Afghanistan in International
Art House Cinema after September 11, 2001

Kamran Rastegar

In the tiny, roiling world of international
film culture, any movie even tangentially related to
Afghanistan now rivets the attention.

KENT JONES, "Center of the World,"
Film Comment, January/February 2002

A press photo for the popular art house film *Five in the Afternoon* (2003)
shows the film's Iranian director, Samira Makhmalbaf, leaning over the
shoulder of the Afghan actor Aghaleh Rezaei (see Figure 1). The photo
perhaps unintentionally symbolizes the relationship between Iranian film
production and Afghan subjects, an issue which has been especially significant in global art house cinema since the invasion of Afghanistan in 2001.
Five in the Afternoon is one of several feature-length fictional films about
Afghan subjects to enjoy varying degrees of commercial success and critical attention on the international film festival circuit and in the art house
film market since the invasion.[1] It is noteworthy that many of these films
have been directed or produced by Iranians or made with a high degree of
involvement by Iranian film professionals—films such as *Journey to Kandahar* (2001), *Osama* (2004), *Barefoot to Herat* (2002), *Silence between Two
Thoughts* (2003), and *Five in the Afternoon*. Afghan subjects also occupy a

1   Director Samira Makhmalbaf and actor Aghaleh Rezaei in a press photo for
Five in the Afternoon.

central role in many Iranian films, such as *Baran* (2001), *Djomeh* (2000),
and *Delbaran* (2002), which explore the experiences of Afghan refugees in
Iran. All received enthusiastic receptions at festivals in Europe and the
Americas.

   In addition to Iranian productions specifically concerning the plight of
Afghan refugees in Iran, a handful of films concerning Afghanistan have
been made without significant involvement from the Iranian film industry;
these include the American production of *The Kite Runner* (2007), based
on Khaled Hosseini's best-selling novel, and the French-produced *Soil and
Ashes* (2004), directed by the Afghan director Atiq Rahimi.[2] These films
have played an important role in producing a cinematic framework for
viewing the contemporary history of Afghanistan; nonetheless, in the years
immediately following the 2001 overthrow of the Taliban, global cinematic
discourse, and to some extent public discourse arising from these films, was
very largely based upon films produced by or with a significant involvement of Iranian film producers.

Given the role of Iranian filmmaking in the production of a global cinematic discourse on Afghanistan, it is natural to ask how we may assess the mode of relation between international filmmakers and their Afghan subjects. How do the economic and cultural frameworks that have given value to these films in the global cinema market affect their production, and how do filmmakers of different nationalities function in producing a cinematic discourse on this subject?[3] In the press photo for *Five in the Afternoon* Samira Makhmalbaf leans over the shoulder of her Afghan actor, her eyes fixed on a point on the horizon, her lips slightly open as if in midsentence. Rezaei's gaze is somewhat modestly cast downward; she is not speaking. The contrast in dress, self-presentation, and physical position separate filmmaker and subject from one another. The proximity of their bodies connotes an intimacy and comfort between them, although Makhmalbaf's position over Rezaei's shoulder lends her an air of superiority and supervision. What she is whispering may well be an instruction for the actor's next scene.

The photograph hints at the problematic relationship that naturally binds a filmmaker and her subject. The relative power and authority of the filmmaker is a question of much investigation in cinema, no less for Iranian auteur filmmakers than for those of European or American provenance. Yet in terms of their reception in the global film markets that operate in conjunction with the major international film festivals (sometimes termed the "A-list" festivals), such as the Cannes, Venice, Berlin, and New York festivals, it is clear that the relationship of Iranian filmmakers to the subject of Afghanistan is much less exposed to critical reflection than the relationship of European or American filmmakers to the same subject. Global art house cinema has played an important role in providing a visual or cinematic discourse for viewing Afghanistan in recent years.[4] This cinematic discourse has arguably been influential in setting political and cultural discourse in Europe and the U.S., as elite commentators, journalists, and activists are very often among the audiences of art house cinema, particularly cinema that addresses topical or controversial international issues.

Through an examination of *Journey to Kandahar, Osama,* and the earlier *The White Balloon,* both as cinematic texts and in terms of the contexts of their production, we may be able to discern the outlines of the development of cinematic discourse on Afghan subjects in globalized cinema.[5]

Doing so will bring into view the nuanced role of Iranians as legitimizing intermediaries between Afghan contexts and narratives and global art house cinema markets, presenting the outlines of a complex relationship that is defined by Iranian domestic politics and regional histories and by the peculiar position of Iran in relation to Europe and the U.S.

Iranian Cinema and Afghanistan in Iranian Domestic Politics

The deployment of Afghan themes in the global reception of Iranian cinema goes at least as far back as the release of *The White Balloon* (1995), one of the first postrevolutionary Iranian films to gain not only critical but also a measure of commercial success in international terms.[6] *The White Balloon*'s last shot is a freeze-frame on the image of an Afghan refugee boy who sells balloons in a middle-class Tehran neighborhood around the time of a national holiday.[7] The film is often cited as a harbinger of the widespread success Iranian cinema was to enjoy in the late 1990s on the international film festival circuit and, more important, in gaining distribution in the small but relatively lucrative cinéaste markets of Europe and the U.S.: "By 1999 [*The White Balloon*] had the highest commercial gross among Iranian films in distribution in the U.S."[8] Yet few critics emphasized the film's delicate positioning of the Afghan character among a wide range of other, often socially marginalized characters—provincial soldiers serving in the capital, European expatriates, ethnic minority merchants, among others—to ask questions about the mutability of national identity in Iran. Instead much of the press and public reception of the film focused on the child protagonist, the relative exoticism of Iranian traditions relating to Noruz (a New Year's celebration observed by Iranians, Kurds, and other nationalities), and the particular narrative structure of the film. In many readings *The White Balloon* was simply discussed as an ethnographic window into Iranian urban culture caught between tradition and modernity, leaving the Afghan balloon seller largely ignored by European and American commentators. In the words of one reviewer, "*The White Balloon* quietly introduces us to another culture and another way of looking at film."[9]

Since *The White Balloon* the plight of Afghan refugees in Iran has been the subject for a number of other Iranian films produced for both local and international markets. Domestically interest in this topic illustrates the degree to which the presence of millions of Afghan refugees in Iran's cities was to become a subject of national public debate in Iran in the mid-1990s. These refugees have not been limited to border camps and have largely integrated into the workforce and economy of Iran, yet they suffered myriad forms of social and legal discrimination, including difficulty in accessing the national educational and healthcare systems and generic forms of racial or ethnic discrimination directed at particular Afghan ethnicities, such as Tajiks. In addition, by being relegated to the lowest socioeconomic levels, Afghans have often been unprotected from abuse as unskilled or skilled laborers at construction sites, farms, factories, and other workplaces. Given this context, the Afghan balloon seller in *The White Balloon* profoundly relates to and identifies with the various forms of alienation and marginality experienced by other characters, whom the protagonist of the film meets in her adventures in the markets near her Tehran home. The film subversively draws parallels between the Afghan refugee and these other characters in order to raise questions about the identity of Iran as a nation.

Yet beyond using Afghan refugees to draw attention to Iran's complex social mosaic and the limitations of conventional Iranian nationalism in addressing this diversity, Iranian filmmakers often fixed upon the naked forms of injustice suffered by Afghan refugees in order to illustrate more endemic political and social injustices within Iranian society. For example, when Iranian students assembled in mass demonstrations against press restrictions in the summer of 1999, they commonly compared the Iranian government to the Taliban in slogans and speeches. This association was particularly troubling to the conservative clerical authorities, given the assiduous attempts made by these Iranian leaders to distance themselves from the perceived excesses of Taliban religious interpretations. Yet the accusation obtained due to the undeniable similarities between the agendas of the official postrevolutionary ideologies of the Iranian government and those of the Taliban. The effect of this uncanny presence on Iranian domestic politics was not insignificant; for example, in 1998 a proposal by conservative Iranian politicians to impose gender segregation on medical training and care was eventually scuttled, in some measure due to its perceived similarity to Taliban policy.[10] After the threat of war between

Iran and Afghanistan surfaced in the summer of 1998—arising out of a simmering tension between the countries and stoked into flames by the murder by the Taliban of a number of diplomatic staff at the Iranian consulate in the city of Mazar-i Sharif—Iranian reformists and dissidents found the comparison between the conservative wing of postrevolutionary Iranian politics and the Talib activists of Afghanistan useful and effective in attacking their political opponents.[11] Because of the Mazar-i Sharif killings and the mutual hatred between the Taliban and Iran's leaders that resulted from Iran's support for Afghan mujahideen factions opposed to the Taliban, Iran mobilized a military force of over 250,000 troops and carried out maneuvers along the border, leading to clashes before an eventual stand-down was negotiated. For several months, however, the Iranian leadership appeared to be preparing the ground for a large-scale conflict with the Taliban.[12] While Iranian leaders mobilized popular support for their confrontation with the Taliban, critical voices inside Iran seized upon perceived similarities between the fundamentalist right wing in Iran and the fundamentalist Taliban in Afghanistan to support the reformist movement inside Iran.

Iranian filmmakers were themselves effective in using Afghan contexts and subjects to raise questions that were perceived to be intimately critical of specifically Iranian social norms or political policies. In *Baran* (2001) the director Majid Majidi sets an Afghan girl as a cross-dressing laborer on a construction site as the object of desire for an Iranian boy working at the same site. The figure of a female laborer, able to work only disguised as a boy, highlights forms of gender-based discrimination and entrenched class distinctions in a society that appears more and more imperfect to the young Iranian protagonist.

While these films enjoyed success with international audiences, their critical reception showed that the social complexity of the Afghan refugee experience in Iran (and the use of Afghanistan as a political exemplar to attack the Iranian right wing) had been largely overlooked in favor of the perceived universal dimensions of the narratives. The specificity of Afghan social dynamics and the interplay between Iranian and Afghan social and political forces have rarely been the focus of critical engagements with these films. Yet it would be wrong to place this burden simply on the critical reception of these films in Europe and the U.S. Indeed some Iranian and Afghan filmmakers have been inclined to produce films for a global audience, situating their work as internationally marketable through an endeavor, however futile, to focus on universal themes in their work.

"A Time without Images":
Visualizing Afghanistan after September 11, 2001

> Again, there seems to be a time warp. Sometimes it feels as if we have been brought back not just to a time before modern entertainment but to a time before art—a time in which reality was just more real, a time without images and ideas and representations, only actual events.
>
> JOHN SIFTON, "Temporal Vertigo," *New York Times*, 30 September 2001

Commentators on the September 11, 2001, attacks have observed that these were acts of terrific violence with no obvious military or tactical purpose. Yet from the moment video images of the burning and collapsing towers in New York were transmitted across the world, the attacks, while causing significant material and human loss, conveyed an unprecedented power as spectacle. Slavoj Žižek and Jean Baudrillard have highlighted the "symbolic" challenge to American power conveyed by the images of the attacks: "We have not yet had any symbolic event of such magnitude that it is not only broadcast all over the world, but holds globalization itself in check—not one."[13] Though prescient, such comments were far from the minds of many, for example those New Yorkers who for months found themselves living with intimate reminders of the material consequences of the attacks, much less the families of those who perished. Yet outside the immediate circles of intimate grief, anger, and self-reflection that radiated from the locus of the attacks, the international recirculation of these images took on features of a global spectacle, implying that the attacks intended to match and better the forms of spectacular violence previously more often the purview of Western militarism.[14] This feature of warfare was manifest in post–cold war militarism practiced by the U.S. throughout the 1990s, whether in the first Gulf war, in Panama, or in the bombing campaigns in Kosovo and Serbia. The grainy black-and-white video segments released by the U.S. military to illustrate the bombing campaigns on Baghdad and Belgrade produced the effect of immediate visual identification with the field of action at the point of impact, replayed in heavy rotation on international news outlets, implying an omniscience and efficiency outpacing any form of resistance.

Finding the imperative of a military response to the September 11 attacks—which within days had been imprinted on the visual memories of a significant proportion of the population of the world, abstract as the image may have seemed to many—the television media and other cultural producers in the U.S. were confounded by one feature of the new campaign to come: the invasion of Afghanistan. Where a visual vocabulary for "the enemy" was often readily available in other recent military conflicts after years of war, Afghanistan was largely disregarded by Americans after the withdrawal of Soviet troops, and hence was seemingly a society bereft of visual images to draw upon. While al Qaeda's own media did embrace a level of sophisticated self-representation and loops of video from the organization's training films became part of the rotation of images on mass media outlets, the Taliban's rule was famously marked by a disdain for visual representation on grounds of their puritanical religious interpretations. The Taliban leader Mullah Omar was perhaps the first authoritarian of modern history to not only refuse the production of official portraits and press photographs, but also to largely escape the omniscopic eye of global media outlets. Frustrated news outlets were left with only a small selection of blurry video stills of an indistinct, bearded and turbaned man to illustrate this enemy leader. In an article published in the *Guardian* the humanitarian worker John Sifton wrote that Afghanistan under the Taliban appeared to be a land "without images and ideas and representations," setting the terms by which post-Taliban approaches to Afghanistan were to be measured.[15] After September 11 the need to produce not only images of but also representations for Afghanistan would be intimately related to the cause of reintegrating the nation into a globalized world, whether by military or humanitarian endeavor.

The U.S.-led campaign in Afghanistan marked a reemergence of Afghan society upon the stage of the global theater, or rather its screen. The paucity of visual referents for Afghanistan impacted American debates on the war. As the headline of one British article of August 2001 termed it, Afghanistan was "the land without a face." Opponents and critics bemoaned the invisibility of Afghans, the anonymity of the millions of Afghan refugees lost in camps or in marginalized urban shantytowns in Pakistan and Iran. Advocates of the war sought out images to illustrate a central claim of the war effort, that overthrowing the Taliban would liberate Afghans from years of terror and tyranny.[16] The suffering of Afghan women—after years of the barest lip service in American official circles— took center stage as a justification for the war effort, marked by the troubling, if colorful, portrait of the burqa-clad Afghan woman.[17]

Iranian Politics, Iranian Legitimacy: Afghanistan as Cause, Afghanistan as Metaphor

When I was shooting the film [*Journey to Kandahar*], I was wondering how I could say things for people who know nothing about Afghanistan. . . . I told myself: You have to give a lot of information. Forget about making a film.

MOHSEN MAKHMALBAF, quoted in Alan Riding, "A Suddenly Timely Afghan Journey: New Resonance for a Little-Noticed Iranian Film," *New York Times*, 5 November 2001

In response to the emergence of public debates on the question of war in Afghanistan in the weeks after September 11, enterprising American distributors at Avatar Film Distribution rushed to sign a national distribution contract with Mohsen Makhmalbaf for his film *Journey to Kandahar*. Makhmalbaf was already known in the U.S. and Europe as an astute and often complex filmmaker whose films had gained significant global audiences relative to those of other regional filmmakers, but *Journey to Kandahar* had gained little interest in the U.S. prior to September 11. Now, rushed to the market with a publicity campaign linking it directly to the tragic events of that day, the film even screened at the White House to a presidential audience in the days preceding the U.S.-led attack on the Taliban and al Qaeda forces in Afghanistan.[18] In France and Italy *Kandahar* was a hit and over the course of the year out-sold its other foreign-language competitor, the U.S. blockbuster *Moulin Rouge*.[19]

Makhmalbaf's interest in the subject of Afghan refugees in Iran long preceded his work on *Kandahar*. In *The Cyclist* (*Bicycle-ran*, 1988) an Afghan refugee in the border region of Baluchistan volunteers to attempt a spectacular feat: bicycling in a circle for a week in order to raise enough money to pay for his wife's medical care in a local hospital. Over the course of the 1990s Makhmalbaf often publicly involved himself in the Afghan refugee issue in Iran, advocating for greater support for the refugees and criticizing official neglect of their plight. His investment in the issue included providing financial support to an effort to establish free schools for Afghan children in Iran. His dismay at the relative silence surrounding the brutality of Taliban rule motivated his interest in producing a film inside Afghanistan—an interest that found practical application upon his meeting of an Afghan Canadian journalist, Niloufar Pazira. Inspired by her personal interest in traveling to Kandahar to locate an old friend, Makhmalbaf developed the script with Pazira playing herself.

In an interview with the *New York Times* upon the film's release in the U.S., Makhmalbaf articulated the missionary intentions he had in making the film, differentiating it from his previous work due to the urgency he felt the topic merited. Yet in the several months following its debut as part of the official selections of the Cannes film festival in May 2001, the film attracted no attention at all from American distributors, despite the fact that a number of Makhmalbaf's previous works had been quickly brought to American art house screens.[20] European reactions were mixed. The film generally merited less positive critical responses than some of his previous works; one British reviewer described it as "narratively awkward but dramatically powerful."[21] The commercial potential of the film was similarly deemed insignificant; a *Guardian* article reported that at the festival "[neither] critics nor buyers paid much attention to it."[22] Indeed at Cannes the film was nearly dismissed, recognized only with an obscure "ecumenical" award, despite the prior awards won by its filmmaker. Even the film's official screening time (on a Sunday at 8 A.M.) seemed determined to relegate it to the margins of the festival.

Part of this ambivalence may well have been due to the peculiarly pedantic elements that Makhmalbaf's script relies upon, elements seemingly at odds with his prior tendencies toward reflexive, autocritical filmmaking. To begin with, much of the central dialogue is delivered in English, including a first-person voiceover that frames the film. Part of the dramatic action occurs in scenes including Pazira and Tabib Sahib, an African American Muslim who initially went to Afghanistan to join the fight against Soviet occupation but eventually settled there and practices simple medicine among Afghan villagers.[23] Both Pazira and Tabib Sahib comment on the situation in ways that are clearly meant to appeal to a presumptive European or North American audience. Digressions within the dialogue aim to educate more than to advance the narrative or develop the characters; for instance, early on a teacher tells a classroom of refugee children, "One day other people in the world may become aware of your plight and will help you." Yet it would seem that Makhmalbaf's initial hope to make a film that would do just this were dashed on the rocks of a miscalculation about the appeal of these strategies for the presumptive global audience of the film. Then, only four months after the Cannes film festival, the attacks of September 11 played a central role in opening doors in the European and American markets for the distribution of *Kandahar*. Lacking many other visual referents, Afghanistan (the "land without a face") was to be observed by these audiences in a portrait provided by Mohsen Makhmalbaf.

But the film also may be read within the framework of Iranian domestic politics, a reading that has been overlooked by most critics. The scenes of *Kandahar* that work best dramatically focus on the absurdities and injustice of Taliban gender segregation in areas such as healthcare. It is instructive to recall, however, that the film was made during a time when debates about such segregation in the healthcare system were prevalent in Iran.[24] Thus the memorable scene in which Tabib Sahib is shown examining a female patient through a hole in a curtain works not only to illustrate the corruption of gender segregation as a principle but calls on a discourse of global human rights to raise international concerns for the plight of Afghans and intervenes in a very potent domestic political issue. In the context of ongoing contestation between so-called radicals, political reformists, and conservatives in Iran, the presentation of gender segregation as a central effect of Taliban policy would reflect poorly on the domestic agenda of the conservative wing of the Islamic Republic, despite the general branding of the Taliban ideology as antithetical to Iran's predominant revolutionary ideology. It is this nuance that a reading of *Kandahar* would miss or gloss over when examining only the film's impulses toward universal themes.

To a great extent the major legitimizing element in the success of *Kandahar* was the perception that its representation of Afghanistan under the Taliban was authentic. For European and American audiences—particularly urban cultural elites, who are the major consumers of international art house cinema—the picture of Afghanistan created by an Iranian filmmaker was refreshingly free of social complexities. Yet such a perspective tends to miss the very particular political context that frames Iranian conceptions of Afghanistan, a context no less fraught with differential power dynamics, historical and cultural prejudices, and nuanced conceptions of national and ethnic difference than that which mediates, for example, European and U.S. conceptions of the same society.

Few among the American audiences of *Kandahar* would be drawn to the inherent critique of Iranian authoritarianism that lies at the heart of the film, or to the critical view of Iran's refugee policies presented in the first scenes of the film. Yet the delicate regional dynamics that have character-ized international relations between Iran and Afghanistan, and the social relations between the citizens of these countries—to say nothing of the complex historical relations between the myriad social subgroups that exist within them—are often neglected in favor of a search for universal themes. For audiences that now may regard the Western eye of an American or European filmmaker with a modicum of distrust when it represents a distant and unfamiliar locale such as Afghanistan, the conflation of Iranian and Afghan positions tends to overlook the power differentials involved in the production of such films.

Also Iranian filmmakers have become increasingly conscious of the global market that may serve as the primary consumers of their films, as Makhmalbaf's public comments on his rationale for making *Kandahar* show. With such considerations, Iranian films on Afghanistan such as *Kan-dahar* appear as a peculiar appendage on the uniquely national cinema of postrevolutionary Iran. Yet this dynamic has also escaped a comprehensive analysis by critics of Europe and the U.S. A number of commentators found the preponderance of English dialogue in *Kandahar* disconcerting; a few saw it as evidence of a new relationship between Iranian filmmakers and their global cinema audiences.[25]

The New Afghan Cinema and Its Audience(s): *Osama*

Siddiq Barmak's *Osama*, a film that debuted at Cannes in 2003, received major prizes at international festivals and was celebrated as the reemer-gence of a domestic Afghan film industry. *Osama* was produced with financial and technical assistance from Mohsen Makhmalbaf and post-production funds from European sources. The production credits for the film are filled by technicians who have worked with Makhmalbaf for years, including the cinematographer and music composer. The film exceeded all expectations in gaining access to a global market. With a major studio distribution contract with MGM and United Artists in the U.S., *Osama* has managed a feat that sets it in an economic sphere very different from the vast majority of foreign films released in the U.S., most of which do so through independent distributors. The film was the recipient of the Golden Globe award for Best Foreign Film in 2003 and was screened in commercial multiplexes across the U.S.

Some of this success is no doubt due to the film's construction of its audience as global: the film text of *Osama* seems more closely to follow the transnational strategies adopted earlier by its Iranian producer than to show evidence of the development of an organic national Afghan cinema industry, what we might term a film industry by Afghans for Afghans. *Osama* seems largely to build upon the template of *Kandahar* in its attempt to appeal to a global audience. Makhmalbaf's *Kandahar* begins with an English-language monologue in the voice of Niloufar Pazira and with her journey by helicopter to Afghan refugee camps on the border of Iran. The Anglophonic introduction, matched visually by the camera's aerial descent into the camp area, provides a point of identification to audiences familiar with English. Barmak's *Osama* goes even further in framing a foreigner's point of view in the introduction to his film. The opening shot is a first-person perspective (apparently through a video camera viewfinder, although it is incongruously shot on film) of a Kabul street. A young street vendor enters into the frame and begins speaking to the camera (and thus the "camera person") in broken English, attempting to solicit business from a tourist. A hand from behind the camera offers the boy payment in U.S. dollars, and the boy goes on to offer an explanation of what is happening in the street. The point-of-view shot interpellates the audience into the position of a foreign traveler to Kabul, unfamiliar with the situation and requiring the services of a local native informant to be paid in U.S. currency. The exchange of money only codifies the camera's perspective as one of privilege and cultural unfamiliarity. The frame eventually presumes an omniscient position, now showing us the European man whose perspective we had initially shared. This opening scene may be read as a

2   A foreigner's point of view in Barmak's *Osama*.

metaphor for the film itself, with the cameraman as audience and the boy
as the film text itself.

Yet in a climactic scene near the end of the film, when the girl protagonist Osama is sentenced to death for the crime of publicly assuming the
role of a boy (it goes without saying that in this way *Osama* applies a theme
already explored in *Baran*), the only individuals shown to be executed by
the Taliban are the aforementioned cameraman and another European, a

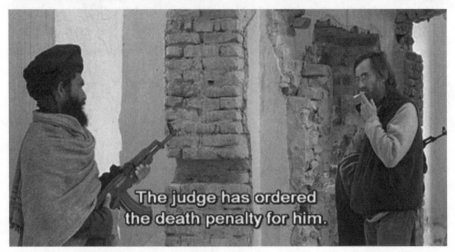

The judge has ordered the death penalty for him.

3 Lead-up to executions in *Osama*.

woman. Notwithstanding the factual inaccuracy of this narrative element (the Taliban imprisoned several Westerners over the course of their rule, but never executed any of them) the film presumes the tragedy of the death of the character with whom the audience is to initially identify as a central narrative moment. This universalizes the trauma of the Taliban era, but does so by fictionalizing the true and horrific brutality of the Taliban, which was directed much more at Afghans than at foreigners.

Barmak's *Osama* sets the stage for a global Afghan cinema, one that is modeled roughly on the strategies that have been utilized by other Iranian directors seeking global audiences. These strategies move away from presuming a national or regional audience as they have been conventionally conceived of within the international art house market. Instead they make claims of having universal dimensions through a set of aesthetic and narrative choices, such as limiting the use of dialogue, using English, and using foreign characters, presumably as a mechanism by which to interpellate nonlocal audiences.

While *Osama* received accolades by some critics and enjoyed a reasonable success in multiplex commercial cinemas in the U.S. and Europe, *Kandahar*'s use of similar strategies may in fact have detracted from its reception at first. However, both films succeeded by presenting comprehensible representations of Afghanistan under the Taliban to audiences after September 11 outside of Iran and Afghanistan, thus benefiting from the topicality of their issues especially among European and North American audiences.

Conclusion

These films illustrate a range of perspectives offered by Iranian filmmakers who have turned their attention to the recent historical experiences of Afghans, either as refugees or as victims of the Taliban's brutality. This framework has played an important role in the development of what may best be termed a global audience. Iranian directors have made use of cultural and historical ties between Iranian and Afghan societies not only to make films about Afghanistan for this global market, but also to participate in Afghan-made films. In a sense Iranians have become intermediaries for representing Afghanistan to a global audience, and these representations have played an important role in setting the terms for political and cultural debates around Afghanistan in the U.S. and Europe.

On the global stage, representations of Afghanistan's traumas in the period directly before and after the overthrow of the Taliban have been greatly conditioned by the activities of Iranian interlocutors, often in collaboration with European and American film industry networks. The success of Iranian cinema in general at European and American festivals and the success of some Iranian filmmakers in gaining access to global markets have played an important role in the channeling of representations of Afghanistan through this Iranian frame. However, the implications of this relationship have been less often subjected to a critical analysis, which illustrates the complex ways these representations have affected both regional and global political discourse on Afghanistan in recent years.

Notes

1 *Five in the Afternoon* debuted at the Cannes Film Festival in 2003 and was awarded the Special Jury Prize before going on to screen at over thirty-five other international festivals.

2 *The Kite Runner* itself makes use of Iranian film professionals in the casting of Homayoun Ershadi, a noted Iranian actor, in one of its key roles.

3 By *cinematic discourse* I mean a set of discursive motifs, tropes, and themes linked to cinematic aesthetics and form, what is often termed "the language of cinema." For more on this, see Metz, *Film Language*; Prince, "The Discourse of Pictures."

4 My use of the term *globalized cinema* focuses on two points: first, the market for and consumption of cinema works, and second, the presumptive audience for these works as may be discerned through aesthetic and formal strategies employed by filmmakers. While *globalized* is employed here in a highly problematic manner, my use of it seeks to highlight a critical approach to the concept of globalized cultures. The term *transnational cinema*, which I do not use in this setting, may be better thought of as relating to the field of production of cinematic works; undoubtedly some of the films discussed in this essay may also be understood as examples of transnational cinema. For a critical approach to cultural formations in a globalized context, see Tomlinson, *Globalization and Culture*. For an example of a critical approach to the question of art house "world" cinema and its relation to what I call *globalized cinema*, see Roberts, " 'Baraka.' "

5 For scholarship examining Iranian cinema as an example of globalized cinema, see Over, "Iranian Cinema."

6 *The White Balloon* was one of the first postrevolutionary films to obtain a North American distributor and to be commercially available for sale or rent on video in the major video rental outlets.

7 The total number of Afghan refugees who have lived in Iran is unclear. During the Taliban era the figure of 2 million was often cited; however, that estimate is certainly low given the fact that in 2003, after the fall of the Taliban and after an active repatriation program had begun in 2002, an Iranian government census counted 2.3 million Afghans living in Iran, of which about half, 1.1 million, were

registered as refugees with the United Nations High Commission for Refugees. See Strand, Suhrke, and Berg Harpviken, "Afghan Refugees in Iran."

8 Farahmand, "Perspectives on Recent (International Acclaim for) Iranian Cinema," 95.

9 Kenneth Turan, "Prize-Winner 'Balloon' a Satisfying Search for Fish," *Los Angeles Times*, 31 January 1996, Home ed., 2.

10 Iranian women were at the forefront of protesting these policies. See "Iran's Female Students Protest at Segregation: Medical School Sit-ins Reflect Growing Demands for Sexual Equality," *Zan*, 28 January 2000. The U.S. government has for years incorrectly claimed that gender segregation is enforced in Iranian health-care training and practice. See U.S. Department of State, "Report on Religious Freedom."

11 This must also be seen within a long history of conflict-ridden Iranian-Afghan relations dating back to the nineteenth century and earlier. Rodney J. Steward's essay in this book presents a partial overview of this history.

12 Goodson, *Afghanistan's Endless War*, 80.

13 Baudrillard, "L'Espirit du Terrorisme," 403. See Žižek, *Welcome to the Desert of the Real!*

14 See Imre Szeman's essay in this book.

15 John Sifton, "Temporal Vertigo." *New York Times*, 30 September 2001, sec. 6.

16 See the essay by Maliha Chishti and Cheshmak Farhoumand-Sims in this book.

17 See also Gwen Bergner's essay in this book.

18 Ali Jaafar, "Bombing Won't Stop 'Horse' Shoot," *Variety*, 18 May 2007, online (accessed 7 August 2007).

19 Liza Bear, "Journey to 'Kandahar': After Going to the End of the Earth for His New Film, Mohsen Makhmalbaf Landed in the Center of a War," *Boston Globe*, 6 January 2002, N8.

20 His film *Gabbeh* (1998) received wide European and North American art house distribution, and his films *A Moment of Innocence* (1997) and *Salaam Cinema* (1996) both received limited releases in the U.S. and wider releases across Europe.

21 Jonathan Romney, "What We Need Around Here Is a Good Turkey," *The Independent* (London), 20 May 2001, online (accessed 7 August 2007).

22 Geoffrey Macnab, "The Land without a Face," *Guardian* (London), 11 August 2001, online (accessed 21 May 2008).

23 The character Tabib Sahib was modeled roughly on the actor who performed the role, Hasan Tantai. Makhmalbaf met Tantai while researching *Journey to Kandahar*; he claims that it was only after the release of the film that he became aware of rumors that Tantai is in fact the American fugitive David Belfield, who fled the U.S. after assassinating Ali Akbar Tabatabai, a diplomat of the shah's government, in Maryland in 1980. Belfield apparently joined the Afghan mujahideen during the Soviet invasion. He remained in Afghanistan after the rise of the Taliban and acted as a doctor in impoverished areas. For more information on this, see

Fiachra Gibbons, "Actor or Assassin?," *Guardian* (London), 10 January 2002, online (accessed February 2008); Silverman, "An American Terrorist."

24 These debates were contentious enough to spark violence and threats of violence against doctors and others who spoke out against the proposed policy of gender segregation in healthcare in Iran. See the Human Rights Watch report "Speaker of Iranian Parliament Asked to Condemn Comments Endangering Woman Lawyers."

25 K. Jones, "Center of the World."

Conclusion

The Current Amazement

Afghanistan, Terror, and Theory

Imre Szeman

This society does not want to recognize itself in the mirror of terror; instead,
it becomes even smugger under the impression of horror. The more forcefully
it is shown its limits, the more vehemently it insists on its own power, and the
more stubbornly it cultivates its one-dimensionality.

ROBERT KURZ, "Totalitarian Economy and Paranoia of Terror,"
Folha de São Paulo, 30 September 2001

The aide said that guys like me were "in what we call the reality-based community," which he defined as people who "believe that solutions emerge from
your judicious study of discernible reality." I nodded and murmured something about enlightenment principles and empiricism. He cut me off. "That's
not the way the world really works anymore," he continued. "We're an empire
now, and when we act, we create our own reality. And while you're studying
that reality—judiciously, as you will—we'll act again, creating other new
realities, which you can study, too, and that's how things will sort out. We're
history's actors . . . and you, all of you, will be left to just study what we do."

RON SUSKIND, "Without a Doubt,"
New York Times Magazine, 17 October 2004

In the months and years since the first blow was struck in the war on terror,
the country that housed the Taliban and Osama bin Laden had until
recently taken a backseat to the war in Iraq in both media reports and the
public imagination. Reports on the first successful election in Afghanistan
—the usual, by now completely expected public step in the legitimization

of a precariously reinvented nation backed by foreign powers—made the papers, but not the headlines (unlike the more recent second and less successful election). The coincidence of the final confirmation of Hamid Karzai's victory on 3 November 2004 with the celebration of the election of George W. Bush to a second term in office may have had something to do with this, just as the intensity of the final months of the U.S. presidential campaign overshadowed the Afghan election itself, held on 9 October 2004. There were occasional reports about the eagerness of Afghans to vote (later repeated with the exact same insistence in Iraq), the large number of candidates running for president (including a woman), and, more hesitantly, the challenges being made against universal suffrage within Afghanistan's patriarchal culture and the likely limited control of any new government over much of the country beyond the capital, Kabul. But with democracy thus secured, Afghanistan faded for years into the media background, behind and below the geopolitical puzzle named Iraq.

In the wake of the drawn-out war in Iraq and the ceaseless (if ineffective) challenges to the legitimacy and competency of the Bush administration, Afghanistan became either a sign of the success of the war on terror or, because bin Laden remained at large, a sign of what had yet to be done. But even when it came to the latter, Afghanistan, the fate of bin Laden, and the larger war on terror were separated in media reports and public understanding, a fact brought home by the failure of Senator John Kerry to score points against Bush over his mishandling of the Afghanistan situation during the election campaign in 2004. Until the election of Barack Obama, whose attempts to redress the mire in which the U.S. finds itself in Iraq has meant an increased focus on Afghanistan, under Bush's last term Afghanistan settled into the semiobscurity of Grenada and Panama: one more name on the list of small states scarred by foreign intervention, drained even of the symbolic resonances that have accrued to names such as Vietnam and Cuba.

At that time one could see the massive attack on Afghanistan, which led to untold civilian deaths and the unjust imprisonment of scores of young Afghan men suspected to be al Qaeda members, as yet another example of the trigger-happy application of brute military force that has dominated U.S. foreign policy since the end of the nineteenth century.[1] It should be obvious by now that the actions of the U.S. government abroad were self-interested in direct proportion to its rhetoric of spreading freedom and democracy, which has been shouted out more loudly, intensely, and un-apologetically than ever during the current war on terror. The apparent successes of the campaign have been revealed as increasingly threadbare. With each passing year the justifications thrown up for the military inter-vention—geopolitical self-defense, the spread of democracy, the extension of human rights—have begun to give way to what is at the core of the West's interest in the Middle East and Central Asia: a cold economic calculus connected to the preservation of the smooth operation of global capital-ism, both in terms of access to resources and also with respect to the need to manage global crises for the benefit of capital.[2]

Much had been written about the hypocrisy and danger of the Bush administration in its dealings with the rest of the world.[3] To its credit—if that is the right way to put it—that administration and its ideologues (preeminently Robert Kagan and the slew of other conservative authors who have offered justifications for the U.S. military and political decisions made since 9/11) operated in a nearly postideological fashion, able to function with impunity even outside of the zone of media spin, while still also making use of the typical secrets and lies favored by past administra-tions. Commenting on the positions embodied in the now infamous "Proj-ect for the New American Century," Tariq Ali writes, "The language of this [Bush] coterie, compared with the euphemisms of the Clinton era, is commendably direct: to preserve U.S. hegemony, force will be used wherever and whenever necessary. European hand-wringing leaves it un-moved."[4] Thus while some of the details of *how* the U.S. government pursued its foreign policy may have been hidden, the *why* certainly was not. Though media coverage of the wars in Afghanistan and Iraq were managed by the military in the usual way—through the simultaneous control over the dissemination of knowledge about the war and the garnering of sympa-thetic media coverage by embedding reporters with troops on the ground —the process by which American economic interests were nakedly pur-sued through the introduction of faux freedom and democracy down the barrel of a gun received significant critical coverage in both alternative and mainstream media sources, including the *New York Times* and even *USA Today*.[5] Anyone who was interested could easily find out what was happen-ing in Iraq and Afghanistan, or at least could learn enough to grasp the outlines of the political lay of the land: the articles, essays, and op-ed pieces available both online and in print—from both Western sources and journalists from the region, like the journalists Altaf Ullah Khan discusses in this book—are now legion. In this context what was frustrating for the Left everywhere was how little effect the direct and naked use of power had on American attitudes toward the government that made these decisions in its name, even if poll numbers showed increasingly negative attitudes toward the Bush administration (which culminated in the political sea change of the election of Obama). In the case of Afghanistan and Iraq the truth has failed to win out—and not because it was not expressed repeatedly at every level, from the philosophical speculations of Judith Butler and Slavoj Žižek, to the editorial pages and articles in *Harper's* and *The New Yorker*. The failure lies not with the limits of expression, but with some deeper (and thus much more difficult to address) failure and trauma of the political at the present moment.

This collection presents views from various perspectives. Some of these authors have worked on the ground in Afghanistan (Altaf Ullah Khan, Cheshmak Farhoumand-Sims, and Maliha Chishti); some may have personal or cultural connections to the region but are generally operating from a distance and trying to understand Afghanistan's current place within global political, cultural, and economic networks (Nigel Gibson, Zubeda Jalalzai, David Jefferess, Rodney Steward, Gwen Bergner, and Kamran Rastegar). My own small contribution to the task of thinking about Afghanistan after 9/11 as a nonexpert in the region is to explore the contributions that members of the academy might be able to make to the production of alternative viewpoints on the exercise of American power. What can academics—at least those involved in literary and cultural studies—do to intervene into the Realpolitik that guides American power, and indeed Western power more generally? The vehement insistence on the West's power, which Kurz points to in the first of this essay's epigraphs, demands immediate attention, as does the all too confident assertions made in the second epigraph about the ability of the Bush administration to shape reality. Though administrations and tactics may have changed, the initial entry into Afghanistan during the world's current engagement there has set up dynamics that are still clearly at play and that call out for intellectuals (among many others) to take action; on Afghanistan, at least, Obama is more like Bush than his partisans might want to believe. But what form should and can this action and attention take?

There is an easy answer to this question, one that has been repeated often not only in response to political and social circumstances after 9/11, but more generally over the past quarter century, if not longer. What should academics do? Why, reach out to the public of course, making their viewpoints known more widely! In an issue of *Profession* published in 2004 Cathy Davidson and David Theo Goldberg claim, "The university remains one of the only places in the United States public sphere for informed, sustained, critical analysis. . . . We must face the challenge and assume the social responsibility of translating our specialized knowledge in ways that inform the public, contribute to policy discussions, and in the process show university administrators and state legislators the potential importance of the humanities."[6] Their essay is yet another in a long line of essays suggesting how politically motivated academics should conceive (or reconceive) of their social role. It is hard to question the intentions behind such calls to action to transform academic insight into socially responsible information; there is no question that Western public discourse could stand to have more figures like Edward Said and Noam Chomsky involved in ongoing debates. At the same time this kind of demand for academics to go public with their knowledge begs several questions. If academics had access to the public, through the media, for instance, would it make a difference?

First, it has to be pointed out that all kinds of academic experts already have access to the public and to policymakers. The editorial pages of major newspapers are littered with the thoughts of political scientists, sociologists, think-tank intellectuals, and writers affiliated with NGOs, and the filing cabinets of government agencies groan with reports either commissioned directly from scientists and social scientists or making reference to their work. What Davidson and Goldberg really point to is that *certain* academics do not have such access, whether due to their ideology or their area of study. They are complaining that the *humanities* lack access. Given the often disastrous policy outcomes produced as a result of the access that other segments of the university have to the public and to government, it is easy to see why one might hope that humanities professors would be able to contribute in some small way too. Yet as much as humanities professors might feel they have something to offer, it is important to see how such knowledge appears to the publics to which it is proffered. English professors may engage in increasingly political work in their departments, but given existing social divisions of knowledge and the legitimating character of disciplinary study, it is almost impossible to convince newspaper editors or other media outlets that English professors should be given an opportunity to speak to the public about (say) Afghanistan, as opposed to the grammatical implications of text messaging or the appearance of youth movies drawing on Shakespeare. Given the state of much of what passes for political reflection in the humanities, this resistance is probably not an entirely bad thing.

Second, the very idea that increasing public knowledge and awareness and getting the word out on issues of social and political substance can turn things around is not only contradicted by the amount of information generated by journalists, for instance, on the state of politics after 9/11 (as I suggested earlier), but betrays a fundamental misconception about the complex social process by which knowledge becomes effective—how it takes hold (or does not) and becomes ingrained in everything from institutional formations to daily habit. As habitués of media, politicized academics imagine that making their voices and ideas public will swing things around in a way that will make an immediate political difference. If only every professor spoke out, things would change! As well-intentioned as this thought might be, it seems to me dangerously naïve. Lurking behind these fantasies of public effect is a vision of the public sphere as a largely neutral arena in which ideas can be freely exchanged and a vision of politics that is fundamentally volunteeristic, driven by the will of individual subjects—in other words, a utopic liberal society of a kind that has never existed. (New information in, new action out: the Enlightenment dream in a nutshell.)

Missing in both cases is something to which academics are usually attuned: the impact of larger, objective social structures which contain, influence, and affect what is and can be said, what public interventions ultimately mean, and how these are (or are not) taken up. For instance, when it comes to making their knowledge public, academics seem to have in mind taking on temporarily the role of journalists. No doubt any op-ed will have a greater readership than even the most well-read academic essay. But it is also read in a specific way: first, through the lens of the presentation of expert knowledge, with the class overtones that the cult of expertise carries with it; second, through the formal structure of the media, a form which overdetermines content in every instance. In the temporal drift of contemporary media one idea gives way to another with alarming speed; today's great exposé of state power is replaced by another, and another, and another, and yet the overall legitimacy of the state form is left virtually untroubled. Indeed that is no doubt part of the very point, consequence, and effect of freedom of the press, which developed alongside and in conjunction with capitalist democracies and their hegemonic apparatuses, and not despite and against their growth and expansion.

Davidson and Goldberg are right, of course: the university is one of the few remaining spaces for critical thought in contemporary society, a point that critics such as Henry Giroux have made tirelessly over the past two decades. They are correct too that it is a space worth fighting for and that those engaged in research in the humanities need to pay attention to the neoliberal reorganization of higher education, which threatens such small critical spaces that still remain. While I do not think it wrong to insist that the knowledges produced in these spaces take more public forms, I want to insist on the fact that one of the most productive things that academics can do in relation to the contemporary political situation is what they have always done best: focus on long-term analyses and on an assessment of the limits (and possibilities) of existing social structures and institutions. What should academics do? They should do their work *as* academics, as workers in the institution of the university. They should furthermore struggle to make the university fulfill its promise as a site of knowledge production (as opposed to what it has mainly been: an institution of knowledge legitima-tion). One of the most effective things they can do as academics is not get caught up in the immediacy of events, but insist in their teaching and research on long-term continuities and discontinuities—on elaborating the shape and character of those large social structures that produce, among other things, the experience of liberal individuals which under-writes the self-understanding of most members of North American society, including academics.

Lest I be misunderstood, I am not saying that academics should hide in their ivory towers, avoiding contact with the public at all cost. But there are political costs to gearing one's activity entirely toward the public, not to mention the costs associated with the comforting self-loathing that has been produced in the many manifestoes that have berated academics for their lack of political activity. It is easy enough for academics to criticize themselves and their colleagues for not standing up to the powers that be; more difficult, but perhaps ultimately more revealing, is probing how and why humanities professors began to imagine this role for themselves in the first place.[7] The immediacy of vast human suffering in the world today demands of individuals living in safe, comfortable parts of the world some kind of reaction. As important as it is to speak out against the abusive use of power of the kind that has characterized U.S. foreign policy since the birth of the republic, it is equally important to engage in the difficult, patient work of unfolding how power came to assume this form, and to understand why it was so easy for the American public as well as the international community to forget for so long about Afghanistan, and then to remember it over the past year as involvement in Iraq was coming to a prospective end and the going in Central Asia was getting especially tough. This requires a different kind of work than the aspiration to journalism, which all too often passes for politics in the academy today.

In this context I want to make two small contributions by way of conclusion to this valuable book of sustained and informed analyses of the Afghan situation. First, I want to add a cautionary note to the laudatory demand that academics go public. I do this by offering an overview of Pierre Bourdieu's analysis of the limits of the media and its effects on the academic sphere in France. Going public can raise awareness of issues that are not part of public discourses; it can also reinforce cults of expertise and legitimate views that are simply opinion rather than the result of research. My points about the media and journalism will of course have different valences in other parts of the world; Khan's fascinating work on Pukhtoon journalists shows this very clearly. Second, and in a rather sketchy way, I want to add to the chorus of innovative work that has emerged on Afghanistan, Iraq, and 9/11 that has insisted on thinking about these events in relation to larger and longer term narratives of the West in relation to "the rest."[8] I aim to insist on the need for academics and researchers to continue to trace out the broader forces that shape and define the political, work which might not have a direct, immediate political impact in the way that many might hope for, but which is no less important as a result, since it is here that we can begin to grasp the multiple strands of the social that make up the political today—including, it should be added, the very ideas we have about the space of the public in relation to the university.

Journalism's Limit, or, Academics on Television

There has been no end to the criticisms of the media coverage of the Bush administration and of the policies and actions carried out in the wake of 9/11—not least by the media itself. In particular the mobilization of fear by the infamous color-coded terror alert system, broadcast in airport terminals throughout the United States and over the public airwaves, which helped support the administration's imposition of its draconian Homeland Security measures. This led many on the Left to decry vocally the lack of alternative viewpoints in the mainstream media. One solution to this media problem has been the creation of alternative media forums, such as Air America Radio and Democracy Now. The advent of the Internet and other new media has also meant that the mainstream has become less and less dominant as a space for the dissemination of news in any case, opening the way for nontraditional sites and spaces of information dissemination. The prime-time audience for Fox News, which barely reached one million viewers at the height of the presidential campaign in 2004, fell to fewer than half a million in April 2005 in the twenty-five to fifty-four age bracket; NBC *Nightly News*, the most watched supper-hour news program, pulls in an audience of just under eight million viewers—this in a country of almost 300 million people.[9] These numbers might lead one to wonder where people get their news, especially when what might be considered national dailies, the *New York Times* and the *Wall Street Journal*, barely count three million subscribers between them.[10]

The decline of viewers and readers of mainstream media and the opening up of alternative news sites have not mitigated the demand that scholars have imposed on themselves to go public. As laudable as this desire to communicate alternative viewpoints might be (I would be the last to say "Do not speak out!"), it is incumbent upon academics to first understand the character of the formal and social structures into which they are going by going public. As the general dissatisfaction with the contemporary media suggests—the very dissatisfaction that prompts one to wish to offer correctives to the limited perspectives on display—the limits of the media are widely known. But these limits are hardly restricted to content. The *form* of contemporary media overdetermines its content, but when it comes to academics participating in the media, this formal overdetermination has a deleterious impact on the normal functioning of the academy to which careful attention needs to be paid. Put differently: there are costs to going public that Davidson and Goldberg do not account for, which bear directly on the issue of how academics might approach the politics of a place like Afghanistan.

There has been a vast amount written on the formal limits of television news, web news sources, newspapers, film, and so on. (In this book Gwen Bergner discusses the interested nature of the media's coverage of Kabul's supposed liberation, and Kamran Rastegar draws attention to the formal, political limits of foreign art house cinema.) When it comes to assessing the connection between these limits and the impact on the academy of scholars being involved in the day-to-day activity of journalistic commentary, the most trenchant analysis has been offered by Pierre Bourdieu in *On Television*, which in many respects extends his assessment of the academic field he offered in different ways in *Homo Academicus* and *The Political Ontology of Martin Heidegger*.

Bourdieu's virulent criticism of journalism emerged only in the last decade of his life, a time in which he became a public figure and one of Europe's leading political voices on the Left. Self-consciously adopting a position he described as *gauche de la gauche*, "the Left of the Left," he was an outspoken and prominent critic of the neoliberal ethos that has managed over a few decades to replace collective and social initiatives with the strict, remorseless logic of the market. To some this public, political face of Bourdieu no doubt seemed out of step with his previous sociological work. For unlike many of his compatriots on the Left, Bourdieu's vision of social life has often been described as conservative and pessimistic, drained of just the kind of political activity in which he himself became increasingly engaged. His analysis of the interaction of symbolic and economic capital in contemporary societies—that is, forms of social power achieved through the acquisition of status and prestige, as opposed to the power produced by money—highlighted its tendency to perpetually reproduce existing structures and forms of power. In an intellectual era dominated by discourses stressing agency, resistance, activism, and revolution, whether in the streets or of the armchair variety favored by postmodern thinkers, Bourdieu's work suggested the opposite: that the process of social change was exceedingly difficult and likely to be protracted.

But describing the mechanisms by which society operates and claiming that how things *are* is how they *should* be are very different things. For Bourdieu sociology was a way of "uncovering some of the best-concealed limits of thought," of discovering the "truth" (as problematic as this notion has become) behind the complex games of culture, in order to bring about some "genuine freedom from one's determinations."[11] In other words, the aim of sociology, which combines theory and practice, philosophy and fieldwork, armchair reflections and marching in the street, was to identify the truth of society in order to allow us to bring about a world better than the one in which we collectively suffer. In his commitment to this goal Bourdieu tried to tell it like it is: the fact that the structure of society seemed to override individual agency was not a cause for pessimism so much as it was a demand for a greater and more concerted effort to bring about positive change. To recast Antonio Gramsci's well-known phrase, Bourdieu advocated an *optimism* of the intellect to go along with an optimism of the will, so long as neither interfered with an unflinching look at the character of contemporary societies.

In his decades-long research into the spaces and places where society reproduces itself, Bourdieu took on an examination of everything from the educational system to the practices of amateur photography. Yet there are few things that he was as critical of as journalism. Why single it out for special attention? His deep distrust of journalistic practice seems linked to the goals of his own work: the broader utopian goals of sociology. For the vast majority of us, journalism is our main lens on the social world. It is through the news that we come to understand social space and obtain information essential to navigating it. Is it a dangerous world, one in which we are likely to be attacked if we walk down the street after nightfall? Are certain groups to be avoided or feared? What are our neighbors up to, and what are they interested in? What are the threats to our way of life? What *is* our way of life, and who makes up the *our* in this phrase?

As social and civic spaces recede and our encounters with others outside of our immediate circle of friends and acquaintances diminish, these are questions that we turn to journalists to answer. For the most part journalism answers them badly. While journalists pride themselves on isolating the truth that hides behind the rhetoric of governments and the business elite, in the end they accomplish the exact opposite of what Bourdieu hoped sociology might achieve. Instead of exposing the way things work, journalism mystifies them further. And because it claims to be showing us the truth, it manages to transform many of *its* myths into social reality.

In *On Television,* his most sustained critique of journalism, Bourdieu's criticisms of the contemporary media run through a familiar range of complaints that critics have been voicing for decades. He suggests that under the guise of objectivity the daily news offers a limited, highly suspect view of the world, which results in social disengagement and cynicism toward politics. The news that most of us get amounts to little more than what he characterizes as a "variety show . . . a litany of events with no beginning and no real end, thrown together only because they happened on the same day."[12] Since the news focuses on breaking events and tries to capture audience interest by focusing on new stories and situations, journalism produces a form of cultural amnesia. Events seem to have no antecedents or consequences, no links to larger and more persistent histories and structures. Things happen, and they seem to happen out of the blue. Journalism operates in perpetual crisis mode, swinging its attention from one thing to another, from the legitimacy of the Bush election victory to 9/11, to the titillating troubles of Gary Condit, to the legal status of the al Qaeda prisoners in Guantánamo Bay. What gets lost in the onslaught of events and images is what we might call *history*. There is nothing more disturbing than watching old TV news footage, which is filled with fearless expert predictions and projections of the dire consequences that might unfold from breaking stories, stories that we now either cannot remember or cannot imagine as ever having been of much importance.

It is not surprising, then, that the world presented by journalism, especially the world outside of one's immediate national context, is a mysterious and dangerous place, defined mainly by political strife (demonstrations, coups, wars) and natural disasters (floods, earthquakes, hurricanes). These are the kind of events that are typically imagined as naturally inviting the journalistic gaze, while in reality their importance and central position in news coverage emerges out of journalism's own sense of the forces and actions that produce reality. By covering such events instead of those salacious scandals that have in fact come to dominate the news, from the saga of the Bobbits to that of O. J., from the death of Diana to the trial of Amy Gehring, journalists believe they provide an indispensable service to the public. (Who were the Bobbits? What did Gehring do? Already these have faded from memory.) But the coverage of scandals and the coverage of disasters are more similar than one might think. Lamenting the lowering of the news standards to that of the tabloids merely disguises the degree to which even supposedly serious news offers a parochial vision of the world. This vision informs not only the public's perception of the world, and of the events and issues that it is important to focus on (the crisis in welfare one day, the crisis of Medicare the next), but also guides the actions of those empowered to act on behalf of the public: those inveterate media junkies called politicians.

Probably none of this comes as much of a surprise. Even if they do not fully understand the degree to which their view of the world is shaped by the journalistic eye, most people seem to know that what journalism tells them might not be worth knowing. But rejecting journalism does not mean that one can avoid the world it has brought into existence. What makes Bourdieu's criticisms cut deeper and closer to the bone than those voiced by other media critics is that his analysis of the failures of journalism is linked to an elaboration of the structure of the journalistic field. *On Television* awakened the ire of journalists in France and elsewhere, who took Bourdieu's criticisms as a personal affront, as a challenge to their journalistic integrity. The first question voiced by P. R. Pires in his interview with Bourdieu for the Brazilian daily *O Globo* is indicative: "Do you think that the professionals and the public are really so blind to the mechanisms of the media in a world in which the media are so present?"[13] Yet as he hoped to do throughout his work, Bourdieu's real intention was to highlight the *structural* limits and imperatives of the journalistic profession which constrict the possibility of presenting a less "fragmented and fragmenting" vision of the world. Far from attacking individual journalists, Bourdieu wanted to give them the conceptual tools with which they could help to actualize the democratic possibilities of journalism, and in so doing tear down the artificial limits on what we imagine as socially and politically possible. Unlike Noam Chomsky, Robert McChesney, and other media critics, Bourdieu never imagined the link between journalistic practice and its effects on the public to be an intentional way of "deterring democracy." His interest was in exposing the accepted conventions and practices of journalism which have a way of turning what is a social invention (a certain idea of what counts as news, for instance) into a fact of nature: unassailable, unchanging, "the way things are."

The structural limits on journalism have been much discussed in recent years due to the megamergers that have taken place in media around the world. Follow the money trail, and you can understand why NBC is reluctant to criticize General Electric, or why a supposedly esteemed journalist like Bryant Gumbel can get rooked into hosting the concluding episode of *Survivor*. But for Bourdieu, more insidious than such "economic censorship" was what he described as "invisible censorship": precisely those structural limits of the journalistic profession that dictate how and why news events are covered. These limits appear to journalists to be common sense—the rules of reportage, plain and simple. The journalistic field, like all social fields, is "based on a set of shared assumptions and beliefs, which reach beyond differences of position and opinion."[14] Journalists imagine that they stand in for the public at large, when in truth they reflect what interests them. As just one example, Bourdieu points to the way journalists cover politics: as a game played by high-level competitors, each struggling to achieve and consolidate power in his or her profession. Since the journalists who cover Parliament or Congress have a degree of inside access to the players, it is not surprising that political coverage comes across as either a sport or a soap opera. All too frequently missing is the content or consequences of the games: cabinet shuffles garner more attention that the drab banalities of government reports, though it is really in the latter that true political action lies.

Another form of invisible censorship is produced by the inevitable limits of time and space involved in reporting. Time is perhaps the more crucial term for Bourdieu. Though I have been speaking about journalism in general, Bourdieu's true bête noire was television journalism. "With television," he writes, "we are dealing with an instrument that offers, theoretically, the possibility of reaching everyone."[15] Television has, or had, the potential to be a radically democratic medium. This potential has never been actualized, in large part due to its abuse of its most precious commodity: time. Every sensational story, every image of car crashes and burning houses that passes for news takes away from the time spent on more important matters. Of course the fact that television is a visual medium means that journalists are already attracted to the spectacular, sensational, and dramatic. Yet what looks good is not always what is essential, serious, or genuinely informative.

It is tempting to think that, by contrast, print journalism provides greater space for discussion and contextualization of important issues. The real danger of television, Bourdieu believed, was not just that it offers an especially limited view of the world, or that it is the medium through which most people receive the news, but that the logic of television was beginning to override and influence the form and character of print journalism. In his discussion of *On Television* with Pires, Bourdieu drew attention to the way *Le Monde*, the serious paper of record in France, has rapidly increased its coverage of celebrity scandals and the ephemera of popular culture in response to the commercial pressures of television, a shift in direction that the paper describes positively as a "way of adapting to modernity and 'enlarging its curiosity.'"

On Television was presented quite literally on television. Wary of the limits that television places on what can and cannot be said—again, structural limitations, limits of time and format—Bourdieu went on TV on his own terms: no time limits, no restrictions on topic or format. The effect of such a performance was twofold. First, beyond the actual contents of his lectures, the form in which he presented them already offered viewers a very different sense of what TV could do. Just as important, it highlighted one of the things that Bourdieu was most critical of in the years preceding his death, and the issue of most concern to us here: the deleterious impact of television on the activities of intellectuals.

At times the whole of Bourdieu's oeuvre seemed to constitute a persistent inquiry into the compromises and difficulties of intellectual and artistic production in the twentieth century. Intellectuals, whom he memorably described as the "dominated fraction of the dominant class" in *Distinction*, have an especially deep stake in the game of symbolic capital. Poorly paid and overworked, their rewards come through the accumulation of honorifics, prizes, and prestige, symbols that generally have little meaning to the rest of society. It might seem as if intellectuals could provide the context and historical specificity missing in most mainstream journalism. Indeed the airwaves are full of talking heads with doctoral degrees whose function seems to be just that. However, instead of improving the information we receive, for Bourdieu it was clear that adding intellectuals to television not only did little for TV, but inevitably corrupted academic life. For intellectuals the visibility of television offers a way to score quick points outside of the academy, points that would normally require years of patient labor and peer review to accumulate inside it. On television (and in journalism more generally) intellectuals are as constrained by time and form as anyone else, and so as much as they might want to say something of substance, they cannot. Slow, deliberate thought and reflection—what rightly or wrongly the academy is known for—is replaced on television by "fast thinking": the voicing of received ideas and commonplaces stands in for genuine insight; the adoption of one of two opposed positions on any topic (for or against, good or bad) constitutes democratic debate and discussion; and memorable sound bites and quick analyses replace detailed study and deliberation (one need only point to the performance of Bernard Henri-Lévy on CNN International in the wake of Nicholas Sarkozy's presidential election in 2007).

Slow thoughts, not fast thinking, was the core of Bourdieu's sense of what journalism needed to offer if it was to actualize its possibilities. At its very best, this is what the growing forms of independent and alternative media have bravely managed to produce, though inevitably they too end up taking their cue from the concerns of mainstream media. For instance, while independent coverage of the events following 9/11 were informative and incisive, often offering more in-depth and far less shrill analyses of the circumstances and causes of terrorism, there was still a tendency to frame the event in terms deriving from a position *opposed* to that offered by the mainstream media. In the alternative press the U.S. was the real aggressor, its involvement in Afghanistan would result in a second Vietnam, the fragile American coalition with Islamic countries would crack with horrific consequences, and so on. This too constitutes a form of "fast thinking," if from a different ideological position. In a different way this is also the problem with a magazine like *Adbusters*, which apocalyptically mirrors the fascination of the mainstream media with the advertising image, as opposed to questioning whether these images are truly definitive of our culture or have a real grip on us. Slow thoughts rather than fast thinking: if this is what Bourdieu wanted from journalism, it also happens to be an apt description of his own work, which, however prolific, never gave in to the temptations of intellectual fast thinking that has recently afflicted the historian Stephen Ambrose, the legal scholar Richard Posner, and so many others who think that television is the medium through which they can spread the word. Indeed what else is this but a description of the kind of old-fashioned scholarship that might well be able to tell us more about Afghanistan than all of the words spilled in the current amazement over the all too predictable foreign adventures of the United States?

Theory and Afghanistan

Given the dangers that the journalistic field poses for academic work— dangers that are not so great as not to be risked, but serious enough to make it clear that the demand that we go public is not without serious problems and limits—how might we orient our *political* thinking as schol- ars? How might those of us concerned with abuses of power, the seemingly unstoppable spread of neoliberalism, and the global decline of democracy, but who are not experts on Afghanistan or the Middle East, contribute meaningfully to an assessment of our current circumstances? It is essential that we focus our efforts on understanding the broader frame and the longer term: the context and history of contemporary social formations, which help to explain why we are where we are, and where we might go from here. Our astonishment at the endless political perversions and hy- pocrisies is somewhat misguided: the idea that the U.S. could even now engage in a militaristic adventure in Afghanistan betrays a strange fantasy about the point of the state to begin with (has it not always been nothing more than the agent of the capitalist class, as Marx suggested, even or especially at its most Keynesian moments?) and of history more generally. It is just this that Walter Benjamin draws to our attention in "Theses on the Philosophy of History": "The current amazement that the things that we are experiencing are 'still' possible in the twentieth century is *not* philo- sophical. This amazement is not the beginning of knowledge—unless it is the knowledge that the view of history which gives rise to it is untenable."[16]

In his exhaustive study of the work of the Frankfurt School, Rolf Wig- gerhaus suggests that this thesis acted as a guiding motto for Max Hork- heimer and Theodor Adorno when they were composing *The Dialectic of Enlightenment.*[17] It gets to the heart of their aims in the wild rhetoric of their book: to unnerve the dominant view of history, which acted as the base narrative around which all of the other events of the age were conceptualized and thus inserted into a longer history. The "amazement" of what is "still" possible that all three thinkers were addressing was fascism, the Holocaust, and anti-Semitism. How could such things happen in the twentieth century? How could it happen after the trauma of the First World War, and after centuries of enlightened discourse, modern progress, and democratic rule?

Why such questions *are not* properly philosophical is because they presuppose the very questions that need to be fully elaborated and addressed. Only by seeing the events of the twentieth century as aberrations, as incidental crisis points in an otherwise smooth upward unfolding of modernity, is it possible to be amazed that such events still occur. Whatever its merits or deficits, what *The Dialectic of Enlightenment* accomplished so brilliantly is a disruption of the conceptual smoothness of modernity by recasting the so-called aberrations as the very stuff of history. How different the century looks when one narrates it as a succession of crises: the First World War; totalitarianism; fascism; the Second World War; state socialism; military dictatorships in Africa, Southeast Asia, Latin and South America, Korea, Vietnam; the first Gulf war; the endless series of conflicts between Israel and its neighbors—and these just to name a few of the major events, to which one could add the endless series of political and economic scandals that make up the daily news of every country, which even in their ubiquity and ceaselessness are reported as if they occur against a ground in which capitalism and democracy are functioning soundly and smoothly. It is in fact our view of history, this untenable view that still permits the production of amazement (at the rise of the New Right in Europe, at the scandals of Enron and Worldcom, at the stripping away of social provisions by the state, at the *maquiladoras* and the labor conditions experienced in other free-trade zones, at the new public consensus on the values and efficiency of the market, at the discounting of the environmental future in favor of jobs in the present, at 9/11). This view of history is part of the reason we seem unable to recognize the *real* structures of the world that we have made for ourselves, and that prevents us from remaking it or unmaking it.

The view of the Enlightenment that Horkheimer and Adorno challenge —a view that has become a touchstone for arguments both for and against modernity—is the one articulated by Kant in his short essay "An Answer to the Question: What Is Enlightenment?" The essay offers an unambiguous answer to the question posed in the title right at the essay's outset: *"Enlight-enment is man's emergence from his self-imposed immaturity."* Enlightenment is the process of individual and social maturation, the development of human faculties through the free use of reason—or at least the free use of reason at certain moments and under certain conditions. The backdrop to Kant's essay is significant. Written only a few years after the French Revolu-tion it seems designed to drain the energy out of the revolutionary spirit by insisting on the need for Enlightenment to be a process rather than a break. Revolution, Kant suggests, quickly reproduces the original conditions of unfreedom that the revolutionaries hoped to get past, changing the people in power without altering the conditions within which they work. Genuine enlightenment was already possible, at least in certain states, such as the one in which he happened to be living: "On all sides I hear: *Do not argue!* The officer says, 'Do not argue, drill!' The taxman says, 'Do not argue, pay!' The pastor says, 'Do not argue, believe!' (Only one ruler in the world says, *'Argue* as much as you want and about what you want, *but obey*!')."[18]

Argue publicly, but obey—that is, keep the system going, do not chal-lenge your social role or responsibilities. This structure and order are for Kant the only guarantee of the free public use of reason; otherwise reason invites the tyranny of the terror that followed the French Revolution. However important free public use of reason has been—a fact that we can certainly appreciate, having experienced the crisis following September 11, when even this liberty was in jeopardy—the limits of the Enlightenment demand for obedience is evident: one can proceed here only if one can believe that political rule is itself Enlightened in a manner that is beyond further questioning.

Genuine enlightenment, the kind that seeps through the cracks of Horkheimer's and Adorno's interrogation of the violent ordering of his-tory, demands that we address ourselves to the *disorder* of thought rather than comfort ourselves with limits that we describe as freedom. These limits are reinforced when we comfort ourselves with the shock of the "current amazement that the things that we are experiencing are 'still' possible." Even in the case of Afghanistan the activity of theory remains essential to challenge the false continuities and discontinuities that the powerful bend into the seamless narrative of history. This is what separates the work of someone like Susan Buck-Morss, whose short book on 9/11 focuses on understanding the surprising links between the thought of

Sayeed Qutb, the intellectual inspiration of the Muslim Brotherhood, and the Frankfurt School from the vast majority of the published materials on the (generally expected) post-9/11 intransigencies of the state of the United States.[19]

Can this be right? Can I actually be demanding that we avoid going public and write texts about the current amazement for the survivors of this moment? Let me say one more time: it is not that the hope and ideal of communicating with the public should be abandoned, but that in our desire to do so we should not thereby give up on the other activities of scholarship. As frustrating as it might be in the wake of the context of the innumerable political obscenities generated by states and politicians on an almost daily basis, the continued importance of creating a broad and long-term map of the structures in and through which we live cannot be gain-said. Conscious of the growing suspicion of the activities of the Frankfurt School in the midst of the war against fascism in the summer of 1943, Max Horkheimer wrote a long letter to Friedrich Pollock explaining his commitment to philosophy even in that dark age:

> When we became aware [of] what a few of our American friends expected of an Institute of Social Sciences, that it engage in studies on pertinent social problems, fieldwork and other empirical investigations, we tried to satisfy these demands as well as we could, but our heart was set on individual studies in the sense of Geisteswissenschaften [the humanities] and the philosophical analysis of culture. . . . There may be many who don't share out philosophical standpoint and who contend that today is not the time for studies which seem to be so utterly aloof. (My personal opinion is that it is just this kind of intellectual work . . . this time needs more than anything else. This pragmatism and empiricism and the lack of genuine philosophy are some of the foremost reasons which are responsible for the crisis which civilization would have faced even if the war had not come.)[20]

This seems to me to be as true today as it was in 1943.

Notes

Thanks to Zubeda Jalalzai and David Jefferess for their comments and suggestions on this essay.
1 For an account of one facet of the effects of the Afghan war on civilians, see Dexter Filkins, "Flaws in U.S. Air War Left Hundreds of Civilians Dead," *New York*

Times, 20 July 2002, online (accessed 4 November 2004). Andrew Ross's and Kristin Ross's collection *Anti-Americanism* traces in great detail the history of direct and indirect intervention by the U.S. in virtually every part of the world, and the forms of anti-Americanism that have been created as a result.

2 See Arrighi, "Hegemony Unravelling"; Duménil and Lévy, *Capital Resurgent*.

3 As a sample of a vast literature, see Hersh, *Chain of Command*; Žižek, *Welcome to the Desert of the Real!*; Butler, *Precarious Life*.

4 Ali, "Re-Colonizing Iraq," 8.

5 The *New York Times* coverage has been noticeably more critical since they engaged in an unprecedented editorial *mea culpa* about the limits of their coverage of the Iraqi war. See "The Times and Iraq," *New York Times*, 26 May 2004, online (accessed 8 November 2004).

6 Davidson and Goldberg, "Engaging the Humanities," 60.

7 As just one example of such a narrative, see Perry Anderson's *Considerations on Western Marxism*. The switch from a Marxism focused on the pragmatic and logistical problems of mass movements and parties to the model of the Frankfurt School, in which social and cultural analysis comes to the fore, offers a potentially productive back story to the demand for public engagement in the Western academy.

8 The best accounts of the *longue durée* of U.S. imperialism are found in Harvey, *The New Imperialism*; Smith, *The Endgame of Globalization*.

9 For the Fox numbers, see the website of Newshounds. The viewer numbers for NBC are from an Associated Press story on Nielsen ratings, on the *L.A. Daily News* website (link no longer working) (both accessed 23 June 2005).

10 Numbers are from the *Washington Post* online (accessed 23 June 2005).

11 Bourdieu, *The Rules of Art*.

12 Bourdieu, *On Television*, 6.

13 "Bourdieu Contra a TV: Interview with P. R. Pires," *O Globo* (Rio de Janeiro), 4 October 1997, 1.

14 Bourdieu, *On Television*, 47.

15 Ibid., 14.

16 Benjamin, "Theses on the Philosophy of History," 257.

17 Wiggerhaus, *The Frankfurt School*, 327. The Frankfurt School (founded in 1923) was a group of neo-Marxist philosophers, including Max Horkheimer, Friedrich Pollock, Leo Lowenthal, Theodor Adorno, and Walter Benjamin.

18 Kant, "What Is Enlightenment?," 42.

19 Buck-Morss, *Thinking through Terror*.

20 Quoted in Wiggerhaus, *The Frankfurt School*, 344.

Bibliography

Adamec, Ludwig W. *Historical Dictionary of Afghanistan*. Lanham, Md.: Scarecrow, 1997.

Afghan Research and Education Unit. *A House Divided: Analysing the 2005 Afghan Elections*. Kabul: AREU, 2005.

Afghanistan Justice Project. "Amnesty Would Jeopardize National Reconciliation and Security." Afghanistan Justice Project website, 2004 (accessed May 2007).

Afghanistan Online. "Getting More Women into Politics." www.afghan-web.com (accessed April 2007).

——. "The Plight of the Afghan Woman." www.afghan-web.com (accessed May 2007).

"Afghanistan Peace Building." Chr. Michelsen Institute website (accessed May 2007).

Afshar, Haleh. "War and Peace: What Do Women Contribute?" *Development, Women, and War: Feminist Perspectives*, edited by Helah Afshar and Deborah Eade, 1–7. London: Oxfam, 2004.

Ahmed, Akbar S. *Millennium and Charisma among the Pathans*. London: Routledge and Kegan Paul, 1976.

Ahmed, Leila. *Women and Gender in Islam*. New Haven: Yale University Press, 1992.

Ahmed-Ghosh, Huma. "A History of Women in Afghanistan: Lessons Learnt for the Future." *Journal of International Women's Studies* 4, no. 3 (2003), 1–14.

Ali, Tariq. "Afghanistan: Mirage of a Good War." *New Left Review* 50 (March–April 2008). Online (accessed 1 July 2008).

——. *Masters of the Universe? NATO's Balkan Crisis*. New York: Verso, 2000.

———. "Re-Colonizing Iraq." *New Left Review* 21 (2003), 5–19.

Amin, Tahir. *Afghanistan Crisis: Implications and Options for the Muslim World, Iran, and Pakistan.* Islamabad: Institute of Policy Studies, 1982.

Anderson, Perry. *Considerations on Western Marxism.* London: Verso, 1976.

An-Na'im, Abdullahi Ahmed. *Human Rights in Cross Cultural Perspectives.* Philadelphia: University of Pennsylvania Press, 1992.

———. *Toward an Islamic Reformation: Civil Liberties, Human Rights, and International International Law.* Syracuse, N.Y.: Syracuse University Press, 1990.

Appiah, Kwame. *Cosmopolitanism: Ethics in a World of Strangers.* New York: W. W. Norton, 2006.

Ardizzoni, Michela. "Unveiling the Veil: Gendered Discourses and the (In)Visibility of the Female Body in France." *Women's Studies* 33 (2004), 629–49.

Arrighi, Giovanni. "Hegemony Unravelling." *New Left Review* 32 (2005), 23–80.

Asia Foundation. "Afghanistan in 2006: A Survey of the Afghan People." Online at http://www.asiafoundation.org (accessed February 2008).

Azarbaijani-Moghaddam, Sippi. "Afghan Women on the Margins of the Twenty-first Century." *Nation-Building Unraveled: Aid, Peace and Justice in Afghanistan,* edited by Antonio Donini, Karin Wermester, and Nora Niland, 95–116. Bloomfield, Conn.: Kumarian, 2004.

———. "On Living with Negative Peace and a Half-Built State: Gender and Human Rights." *International Peacekeeping* 14, no. 1 (2007), 127–42.

Bagley, Hubert E., Jr. "Afghanistan: Opium Cultivation and Its Impact on Reconstruction." U.S. Army War College. USAWC Strategy Research Project. 3 May 2004. Strategic Studies Institute website (accessed November 2005).

Baker, Mary A. "Winning the Peace? An Examination into Building an Afghan National Army (ANA) and New Iraqi Army (NIA)." U.S. Army War College. USAWC Strategy Research Project. 3 May 2004. Defense Technical Information Center website (accessed November 2005).

Baran. Directed by Majid Majidi. 2001.

Barber, Benjamin R., *Jihad vs. McWorld: Terrorism's Challenge to Democracy.* New York: Ballantine, 2001.

Barefoot to Herat. Directed by Majid Majidi. 2002.

Barfield, Thomas J. *The Central Asian Arabs of Afghanistan: Pastoral Nomadism in Transition.* Austin: University of Texas Press, 1981.

Baudrillard, Jean. "L'Espirit du Terrorisme," *South Atlantic Quarterly* 101, no. 2 (2002), 410–15.

BBC. "Afghanistan Women Stoned to Death." BBC News online, 23 April 2005 (accessed May 2007).

Beijing Declaration and Platform for Action, Fourth World Conference on Women, September 15, 1995. University of Minnesota website (accessed February 2008).

Benjamin, Walter. "Theses on the Philosophy of History." *Illuminations: Essays and Reflections.* New York: Schocken, 1968.

Berger, Anne-Emmanuelle. "The Newly Veiled Woman: Irigaray, Specularity, and the Islamic Veil." *Diacritics* 28, no. 1 (1998), 93–119.

Berlant, Lauren. *The Queen of America Goes to Washington City.* Durham: Duke University Press, 1997.

Bhabha, Homi. *The Location of Culture.* New York: Routledge, 1994.

Biswas, Soutik. "Women Under Siege in Afghanistan." BBC News online, 20 June 2007 (accessed 20 June 2007).

BNET. "Karzai for Holy War on Opium Trade." Online. 10 April 2004 (accessed 15 September 2009).

Bourdieu, Pierre. *Homo Academicus.* Translated by Peter Collier. Stanford: Stanford University Press, 1984.

——. *On Television.* Translated by Priscilla Parkhurst Ferguson. New York: New Press, 1996.

——. *The Political Ontology of Martin Heidegger.* Translated by Peter Collier. Stanford: Stanford University Press, 1991.

——. *The Rules of Art.* Stanford: Stanford University Press, 1996.

Braun, David. "How They Found *National Geographic*'s 'Afghan Girl.'" *National Geographic News*, 7 March 2003. Online at http://news.nationalgeographic.com/ news/ (accessed 7 April 2004).

Brunet, Ariane, and Isabelle Selon-Helal. "Seizing the Opportunity: Afghan Women and the Constitution Making Process." Rights and Democracy Mission Report, May–June 2003. United Nations website (accessed February 2008).

Buck-Morss, Susan. *Thinking through Terror.* New York: Verso, 2003.

Burnes, Alexander. *Cabool: Being a Personal Narrative of a Journey.* 1836. Graz, Austria: Akademische Druck U. Verlagsanstalt, 1973.

——. *Travels into Bokhara.* 1834. 3 vols. Karachi: Oxford University Press, 1973.

Butler, Judith. *Precarious Life: The Powers of Mourning and Violence.* London: Verso, 2004.

Canada, Government of. Protecting Canadians—Rebuilding Afghanistan. Online (accessed June 18, 2007).

Centre for Strategic and International Studies. *In the Balance: Measuring Progress in Afghanistan.* Washington: CSIS, 2005.

Chandler, David. *Empire in Denial: The Politics of State-Building.* London: Pluto, 2006.

Chishti, Maliha. "The International Women's Movement and the Politics of Participation for Muslim Women." *American Journal of Islamic Social Sciences.* 19, no. 4 (2002), 80–99.

Chomsky, Noam. *Hegemony or Global Survival: America's Quest for Global Dominance.* New York: Metropolitan, 2003.

CNN. "Kabul Liberated." 18 November 2001. CNN website (accessed 18 November 2001).

Cockburn, Alexander. "Green Lights for Torture." *The Nation* 278, no. 21 (2004), 9.

Coleman, Isobel. "Women, Islam, and the New Iraq." *Foreign Affairs*, January/February 2006. Online (accessed April 2007).

Collins, Joseph J. *The Soviet Invasion of Afghanistan: A Study in the Use of Force in Soviet Foreign Policy.* Lexington, Mass.: Lexington Books, 1986.

Cooley, John. *Unholy Wars: Afghanistan, America, and International Terrorism.* London: Pluto, 2002.

Crews, Robert D., and Amin Tarzi, eds. *The Taliban and the Crisis of Afghanistan.* Cambridge: Harvard University Press, 2008.

Curphey, Shauna. "Women in Afghanistan Fear New Taliban-Like Rule." *Women's E News,* 15 May 2003. Online (accessed April 2007).

Cyclist, The. Directed by Mohsen Makhmalbaf, 1987.

Davidson, Cathy N., and David Theo Goldberg. "Engaging the Humanities." *Profession,* no. 1 (2004), 42–62.

Davis, Anthony. "How the Taliban Became a Military Force." *Fundamentalism Reborn? Afghanistan and the Taliban,* edited by William Maley, 43–65. New York: New York University Press, 1998.

Delbaran. Directed by Abolfazl Jalili, 2002.

De Waal, Alex. *Famine Crimes: Politics and the Disaster Relief Industry in Africa.* Bloomington: Indiana University Press, 1997.

Djomeh. Directed by Hassan Yektapanah, 2000.

Donini, Antonio. "An Elusive Quest: Integration in the Response to the Afghan Crisis." *Ethics in International Affairs* 18, no. 2 (2004), 21–27.

———. "Principles, Politics, and Pragmatism in the International Response to the Afghan Crisis." *Nation Building Unraveled? Aid, Peace, and Justice in Afghanistan,* edited by Antonio Donini, Norah Niland, and Karin Wermester, 188–230. Bloomfield, Conn.: Kumarian, 2004.

Donini, Antonio, Norah Niland, and Karin Wermester, eds. *Nation Building Unraveled? Aid, Peace, and Justice in Afghanistan.* Bloomfield, Conn.: Kumarian, 2004.

Duffield, Mark R. *Global Governance and the New Wars: The Merging of Development and Security.* London: Zed Books, 2002.

Duménil, Gérard, and Dominique Lévy. *Capital Resurgent: Roots of the Neoliberal Revolution.* Cambridge: Harvard University Press, 2004.

Dupree, Louis. *Afghanistan.* Princeton: Princeton University Press, 1973.

Elliot, Jason. *An Unexpected Light: Travels in Afghanistan.* New York: Picador, 1999.

Ellis, Deborah. *Women of the Afghan War.* Westport, Conn.: Praeger, 2002.

Elphinstone, Mountstuart. *An Account of the Kingdom of Caubul.* 2 vols. Karachi: Oxford University Press, 1972 [1815].

Emadi, Hafizullah. *State, Revolution, and Superpowers in Afghanistan.* New York: Praeger, 1990.

"Failed States Index 2007, The." *Foreign Policy Magazine,* July/August 2007. Online (accessed 20 June 2007).

Fanon, Frantz. *A Dying Colonialism.* New York: Grove, 1965.

Farahmand, Azadeh. "Perspectives on Recent (International Acclaim for) Iranian Cinema." *The New Iranian Cinema: Politics, Representation, and Identity,* edited by Richard Tapper, 86–108. London: I. B. Tauris, 2004.

Farhoumand-Sims, Cheshmak. "Implementing CEDAW in Afghanistan: Barriers to Women's Rights in Afghanistan and Efforts to Overcome Them." Dissertation in progress, York University, Toronto.

———. "The Three Block War: Is it Working?" Paper presented at the 15th annual Violent Interventions Conference at York University's Centre for International and Security Studies, Toronto, 7–8 February 2008.

Finely, Laura L. *The Torture and Prisoner Abuse Debate*. Westport, Conn.: Greenwood, 2008.

Fitzgerald, Timothy. *Discourse on Civility and Barbarity*. New York: Oxford University Press, 2007.

Five in the Afternoon. Directed by Samira Makhmalbaf, 2003.

Foster, George. *A Journey from Bengal to England*. 2 vols. London: R. Faulder, 1798.

Freeman, Christopher. "Introduction: Security, Governance and Statebuilding in Afghanistan." *International Peacekeeping* 14, no. 1 (2007), 1–7.

Gabbeh. Directed by Mohsen Makhmalbaf, 1996.

Gohari, M. J. *The Taliban: Ascent to Power*. New York: Oxford University Press, 2000.

Goodhand, Jonathan. "Aiding Violence or Building Peace? The Role of International Aid in Afghanistan." *Third World Quarterly* 23, no. 5 (2002), 837–59.

———. "From Holy War to Opium War? A Case Study of the Opium Economy in North Eastern Afghanistan." *Central Asian Survey* 19, no. 2 (2000), 265–80.

Goodson, Larry P. *Afghanistan's Endless War: State Failure, Regional Politics, and the Rise of the Taliban*. Seattle: University of Washington Press, 2001.

Gramsci, Antonio. *Selections from the Prison Notebooks*, edited and translated by Quintin Horace and Geoffrey Nowell Smith. New York: International Publishers, 1972.

Gregorian, Vartan. *The Emergence of Modern Afghanistan: Politics of Reform and Modernization, 1880–1946*. Stanford: Stanford University Press, 1969.

Griffin, Michael. *Reaping the Whirlwind: The Taliban Movement in Afghanistan*. London: Pluto, 2001.

Griffiths, John C. *Afghanistan: Key to a Continent*. Boulder: Westview, 1981.

Grover, Verinder, ed. *Afghanistan: Government and Politics*. New Delhi: Deep and Deep, 2000.

Haqqani, Husain. "Think Again: A Forgotten War." Center for American Progress. 12 December 2003. Online (accessed 15 October 2004).

Harb, Mouafac. "Powell Sees Afghan Election as Illustration of Iraq's Potential." America.gov website, 12 October 2004 (accessed 15 October 2004).

Hardt, Michael, and Antonio Negri. *Empire*. Cambridge: Harvard University Press, 2000.

———. *Multitude: War and Democracy in the Age of Empire*. New York: Penguin, 2004.

Harris, Geoff. T. *Recovery from Armed Conflict in Developing Countries*. New York: Routledge, 1999.

Harvey, David. *The New Imperialism*. Oxford: Oxford University Press, 2003.

al-Hassan, Ahmad Y., and Donald Hill. *Islamic Technology: An Illustrated History*. Cambridge: Cambridge University Press, 1986.

Heath, Jennifer, ed. *The Veil: Women Writers on Its History, Lore, and Politics.* Berkeley: University of California Press, 2008.

Hersh, Seymour M. *Chain of Command: The Road from 9/11 to Abu Ghraib.* Toronto: Harper Collins, 2004.

——. "Torture at Abu Ghraib." *The New Yorker,* May 10, 2004. Online (accessed November 2004).

Human Rights Watch. "Afghanistan: Women Under Attack for Asserting Rights." Online (accessed 11 February 2005).

——. "Speaker of Iranian Parliament Asked to Condemn Comments Endangering Women Lawyers." 19 May 1998. Online (accessed 7 August 2007).

——. "Women and Elections in Afghanistan." Online (accessed 11 February 2005).

Ignatieff, Michael. *Empire Lite: Nation-Building in Bosnia, Kosovo, and Afghanistan.* Toronto: Penguin, 2003.

International Crisis Group. "Afghanistan: Women and Reconstruction." Online (accessed 8 February 2008).

IRIN Humanitarian. Integrated Regional Information Networks. UN Office for the Coordination of Humanitarian Affairs. Online (accessed May 2007).

Jaffer, Jameel, and Amrit Singh. *Administration of Torture: A Documentary Record from Washington to Abu Ghraib and Beyond.* New York: Columbia University Press, 2007.

Jalali, Ali A. "The Future of Afghanistan." *Parameters: U.S. Army War College Quarterly* 36. no. 1 (2006), 4–19.

Joint Electoral Management Body of the Islamic Republic of Afghanistan. Online (accessed May 2007).

Jones, Kent. "Center of the World." *Film Comment,* January/February 2002, 24–26.

Jones, Owen Bennett. *Pakistan: Eye of the Storm.* New Haven: Yale University Press, 2002.

Journey to Kandahar. Directed by Muhsin Makhmalbaf, 2001.

Joya, Malalia. "The U.S. Has Returned Fundamentalism to Afghanistan." Common Dreams website, 10 April 2007 (accessed May 2007).

Kakan, Hasan Kawun. *Government and Society in Afghanistan: The Reign of Amir Abd al-Rahman Khan.* Austin: University of Texas Press, 1979.

Kakar, M. Hassan. *A Political and Diplomatic History of Afghanistan, 1863–1901.* Leiden: Brill, 2006.

Kampark, Binoy. "The Trial of Saddam Hussein: Limits and Prospects." *Contemporary Review* 288 (summer 2006), 192–200.

Kandiyoti, Denize. *The Politics of Gender and Reconstruction in Afghanistan.* Geneva: UNRISD, 2005.

Kant, Immanuel. "What Is Enlightenment?" *Perpetual Peace and Other Essays.* Translated by Ted Humphrey. Indianapolis: Hackett, 1983.

Khalid, Adeeb. *The Politics of Muslim Cultural Reform: Jadidism in Central Asia.* Berkeley: University of California Press, 1998.

Khalidi, Rashid. *Resurrecting Empire: Western Footprints and America's Perilous Path in the Middle East*. Boston: Beacon, 2004.

Khan, Riaz M. *Untying the Afghan Knot: Negotiating Soviet Withdrawal*. Durham: Duke University Press, 1991.

Kite Runner, The. Directed by Marc Forster, 2007.

Klass, Rosanne, ed. *Afghanistan: The Great Game Revisited*. New York: Freedom House, 1987.

Koehler, Jan, and Christoph Zuercher. "Statebuilding, Conflict, and Narcotics in Afghanistan: The View from Below." *International Peacekeeping* 14, no. 1 (2007), 62–74.

Kramer, Jane. "Taking the Veil." *The New Yorker*, November 22, 2004, 59–71.

Lederman, Arline. "The *Zan* of Afghanistan: A 35-Year Perspective on Women in Afghanistan." *Women for Afghan Women: Shattering Myths and Claiming the Future*, edited by Sunita Mehta, 46–58. New York: Palgrave Macmillan, 2002.

Magnus, Ralph, and Eden Naby. *Afghanistan: Mullah, Marx, and Mujahid*. Boulder: Westview, 1998.

Maley, William, ed. *Fundamentalism Reborn? Afghanistan and the Taliban*. New York: New York University Press, 1998.

Maley, William, and Fazel Haq Saikel. *Political Order in Post-Communism Afghanistan*. Boulder: Reinner, 1992.

Maloney, Sean. "Soldiers Not Peacekeepers." *The Walrus*, March 2006. Online (accessed 18 June 2007).

Mamdani, Mahmood. *Citizen and Subject: Contemporary Africa and the Legacy of Late Colonialism*. Princeton: Princeton University Press, 1996.

——. *Good Muslim, Bad Muslim: America, the Cold War, and the Roots of Terror*. New York: Pantheon, 2004.

Mansoor, Weeda, "The Mission of RAWA: Freedom, Democracy, Human Rights." *Women for Afghan Women: Shattering Myths and Claiming the Future*, edited by Sunita Mehta, 68–83. New York: Palgrave Macmillan, 2002.

Marsden, Peter. *The Taliban: War, Religion, and the New Order in Afghanistan*. Karachi: Oxford University Press, 1998.

Masson, Charles. *Narrative of Various Journeys in Balochistan, Afghanistan, the Panjab, and Kalat*. 4 Vols. London: Richard Bentley, 1844.

Matinuddin, Kamal. *The Taliban Phenomenon: Afghanistan 1994–1997*. Karachi: Oxford University Press, 1999.

Mayer, Ann Elizabeth. *Islam and Human Rights: Tradition and Politics*. Boulder: Westview, 2007.

McClintock, Anne. " 'No Longer in a Future Heaven': Gender, Race, and Nationalism." *Dangerous Liaisons: Gender, Nation, and Postcolonial Perspectives*, edited by Ann McClintock, Aamir Mufti, and Ella Shohat, 89–112. Minneapolis: University of Minnesota Press, 1997.

McCoy, Alfred W. *The Politics of Heroin: CIA Complicity in the Global Drug Trade*—

Afghanistan, South East Asia, Central American, Colombia. Revised ed. Chicago: Lawrence Hill, 2003.

McGirk, Tim, "On the Trail of bin Laden." *National Geographic* 206, no. 4 (2004), 2–27.

McQuaig, Linda. *Holding the Bully's Coat: Canada and the U.S. Empire*. Toronto: Doubleday, 2007.

Medica Mondiale Basic German Women's Group. "Information about CEDAW and CEDAW in Afghanistan." Kabul, 2003. Stasek website, http://www.stasek.com (accessed 25 January 2008).

Mernissi, Fatima. *Beyond the Veil: Male-Female Dynamics in Modern Muslim Society*. Bloomington: Indiana University Press, 1987.

Metz, Christian. *Film Language: The Semiotics of Cinema*. Oxford: Oxford University Press, 1974.

Mohanty, Chandra Talpade, *Feminism without Borders: Decolonizing Theory, Practicing Solidarity*. Durham: Duke University Press, 2003.

——. "Under Western Eyes: Feminist Scholarship and Colonial Discourses." *Dangerous Liaisons: Gender, Nations, and Postcolonial Perspectives*, edited by Ann McClintock, Aamir Mufti, and Ella Shohat, 255–77. Minneapolis: University of Minnesota Press, 1997.

Moment of Innocence, A. Directed by Mohsen Makhmalbaf, 1996.

Montgomery, John D., and Dennis A. Rondinelli. *Beyond Reconstruction in Afghanistan: Lessons from Development Experience*. New York: Palgrave, 2004.

Mustafa, Nadia. "Afghanistan's Turf Wars." *Time*, 3 June 2002. Online (accessed 22 August 2007).

Nasr, S. V. R. "The Rise of Sunni Militancy in Pakistan: The Changing Role of Islamism and the Ulama in Society and Politics." *Modern Asian Studies* 34, no. 1 (2000), 139–80.

Nesiah, Vasuki. "The Ground beneath Her Feet: 'Third World' Feminisms." *Journal of International Women's Studies* 4, no. 3 (2003), 30–38.

Newell, Nancy Peabody, and Richard S. Newell. *The Struggle for Afghanistan*. Ithaca: Cornell University Press, 1981.

Newman, Cathy. "A Life Revealed." *National Geographic*, April 2002. Online (accessed 6 June 2008).

Nojumi, Neamatollah. *The Rise of the Taliban in Afghanistan: Mass Mobilization and the Future of the Region*. New York: Palgrave, 2002.

Oates, Lauryn. *National Report on Domestic Violence against Women: Afghanistan*. Washington: Global Rights, 2007.

Oates, Lauryn, and Isabelle Solon-Helal. *At the Cross-Roads of Conflict and Democracy: Women and Afghanistan's Constitutional Loya Jirga*. Montreal: Rights and Democracy, 2004. Rights in Practice website, http://www.wraf.ca (accessed 25 January 2008).

Obama, Barack. "Remarks by the President in Address to the Nation on the Way

Forward in Afghanistan and Pakistan." The White House, Office of the Press Secretary. 1 December 2009. Online (accessed 30 January 2010).

O'Brien, Susie, and Imre Szeman. "Introduction: The Globalization of Fiction/The Fiction of Globalization." *South Atlantic Quarterly* 100, no. 3 (2001), 603–26.

Osama. Directed by Siddiq Barmak, 2003.

Over, William. "Iranian Cinema: Life Spans and Social Movements." *Passages* 3, no. 2 (2001), 228–51.

Overby, Paul. *Holy Blood: An Inside View of the Afghan War*. Westport, Conn.: Praeger, 1993.

Parenti, Christian. "Afghan Wonderland," *Middle East Report*, summer 2006.

———. "Chaos and Fear Stalk Afghanistan on 9/11 Anniversary." *The Nation*, 25 September 2006.

———. "Taliban Rising," *The Nation*, 30 October 2006. Online (accessed 22 August 2007).

Peace Operations Working Group of the Canadian Peace Coordinating Committee. "NGO/Government Dialogue on Provincial Reconstruction Teams (PRTs) in Afghanistan and the Militarization of Humanitarian Assistance." 13 December 2003. Human Security Gateway website (accessed 25 January 2008).

Pieterse, Jan Nederveen. "Globalization as Hybridization." *The Globalization Reader*, edited by Frank J. Lechner and John Boli, 99–106. Malden, Mass.: Blackwell, 2000.

Piñeiro, Niurka. "Afghanistan Out of Country Election Turnout in Pakistan and Iran." International Organization for Migration. Press briefing notes. 12 October 2004. Online (accessed 30 November 2004).

Polanskaya, Ludmilla, and Alexei Malashenko. *Islam in Central Asia*. Reading, England: Garnet, 1994.

Pottinger, Henry. *Travels in Beloochistan and Sinde*. London: Longman, Hurst, Reese, Orme, and Brown, 1816.

Poullada, Leon B. *Reform and Rebellion in Afghanistan, 1919–1929: King Amanullah's Failure to Modernize a Tribal Society*. Ithaca: Cornell University Press, 1973.

Prince, Stephen. "The Discourse of Pictures: Iconicity and Film Studies." *Film Quarterly* 47, no. 1 (1993), 16–28.

Project for a New American Century. "Statement of Principles." 3 June 1997. Online (accessed 20 October 2004).

Rashid, Ahmed. "Afghanistan on the Brink." *New York Review of Books*, 22 June 2006, 25–27.

———. *Descent into Chaos: The United States and the Failure of Nation Building in Pakistan, Afghanistan, and Central Asia*. New York: Viking Penguin, 2008.

———. "New Afghan Cabinet Configuration Source of Discontent for Many Pashtuns." EURASIANET. 24 June 2004 (accessed 22 November 2004).

———. *Taliban: Militant Islam, Oil, and Fundamentalism in Central Asia*. New Haven: Yale Note Bene, 2001.

Ravishankar, Ra. "Afghanistan: The Liberation That Isn't." *Counterpunch*, 2 March 2004. Online (accessed 11 May 2004).

Revolutionary Association of the Women of Afghanistan website. Online (accessed 16 January 2007).

——. "U.S. Supporters Welcome RAWA at V-Day in New York City and Washington, D.C." Online (accessed 16 January 2007).

Roberts, Martin. "'Baraka': World Cinema and the Global Culture Industry." *Cinema Journal* 37, no. 3 (1998), 62–82.

Robson, Brian. *The Road to Kabul: The Second Afghan War, 1878–1881*. London: Arms and Armour, 1986.

Ross, Andrew, and Kristin Ross. *Anti-Americanism*. New York: New York University Press, 2004.

Rostam-Povey, Elaheh. "Women in Afghanistan: Passive Victims of the Borga or Active Social Participants?" *Development, Women, and War: Feminist Perspective*, edited by Haleh Afshar and Deborah Eade, 172–87. London: Oxfam, 2004.

Roy, Oliver. *Islam and Resistance in Afghanistan*. 2nd ed. Cambridge: Cambridge University Press, 1990.

Rubin, Barnett. "Constructing Sovereignty for Security." *Survival* 47, no. 4 (2005), 93–106.

——. *The Fragmentation of Afghanistan: State Formation and Collapse in the International System*. 2nd ed. New Haven: Yale University Press, 2002.

——. "Rebuilding Afghanistan: The Folly of Stateless Democracy." *Current History* 103, no. 672 (2004), 165–70.

Said, Edward W. *Representations of the Intellectual*. New York: Vintage, 1994.

Salaam Cinema. Directed by Mohsen Makhmalbaf, 1995.

Scott, Peter Dale. *Drugs, Oil, and War: The United States in Afghanistan, Colombia, and Indochina*. Lanham, Md.: Rowman and Littlefield, 2003.

Secretary-General to the UN Security Council. *Report on the Situation in Afghanistan and Its Implications for International Peace and Security*. United Nations Assistance Mission in Afghanistan. 7 March 2006. Online (accessed May 2007).

Segal, Aaron. "Why Does the Muslim World Lag in Science?" *Middle East Quarterly* 3, no. 2 (1996). Online (accessed 7 October 2009).

Senlis Council. "Afghanistan Five Years Later: The Return of the Taliban." News release. 2006. Online (accessed February 2008).

——. "Losing Hearts and Minds in Afghanistan: Canada's Leadership to Break the Cycle of Violence in Southern Afghanistan." 2006. Online (accessed February 2008).

——. "Prime Minister Harper Must Dramatically Overhaul Canada's Strategy Development, Aid and Counter Narcotics Policy in Afghanistan." 28 May 2007. Online (accessed 18 June 2007).

Sidahmed, Abdel Salam, and Anoushiravan Ehteshami, eds. *Islamic Fundamentalism*. Boulder: Westview, 1996.

Silence between Two Thoughts. Directed by Babak Payami, 2003.

Silverman, Ira. "An American Terrorist." *The New Yorker,* 5 August 2002, 26.

Simonsen, Sven Gunnar. "Ethnicizing Afghanistan? Inclusion and Exclusion in Post-Bonn Institution Building." *Third World Quarterly* 5, no. 4 (2004), 707–29.

Smith, Neil. *The Endgame of Globalization.* New York: Routledge, 2005.

Soil and Ashes. Directed by Atiq Rahimi, 2004.

Stabile, Carole, and Deepa Kumar. "Unveiling Imperialism: Media, Gender, and War on Afghanistan." *Media, Culture, and Society* 27, no. 5 (2005), 765–82.

Stewart, Rory. *The Places in Between.* London: Picador, 2004.

Strand, Arne, Astri Suhrke, and Kristian Berg Harpviken. "Afghan Refugees in Iran: From Refugee Emergency to Migration Management." Chr. Michelsen Institute. 16 June 2004. Online (accessed 25 July 2008).

Talbot, Ian. *Pakistan: A Modern History.* New York: St. Martin's, 1998.

Tocqueville, Alexis de. *Democracy in America and Two Essays on America.* New York: Penguin, 2003.

Tomlinson, John. *Globalization and Culture.* Chicago: University of Chicago Press, 1999.

Trinh T. Minh-ha. "Not You/Like You: Postcolonial Women and the Interlocking Questions of Identity and Difference." *Dangerous Liaisons: Gender, Nations, and Postcolonial Perspectives,* edited by Ann McClintock, Aamir Mufti, and Ella Shohat, 415–19. Minneapolis: University of Minnesota Press, 1997.

Truell, Peter, and Larry Gurwin. *False Profits: The Inside Story of the BCCI, the World's Most Corrupt Financial Empire.* Boston: Houghton Mifflin, 1992.

United Nations, "The Situation of Women and Children in Afghanistan." Report presented by the secretary-general at the forty-seventh session of the Commission on the Status of Women, 3–14 March 2003. CSW website at http://www.un.org/ womenwatch/daw/csw/.

United Nations Development Fund for Women. "Women in Afghanistan: Progress for Women Is Progress for All." Fact sheet. 2007. UNAMA website (accessed 6 June 2007).

United Nations Division for the Advancement of Women. Convention on the Elimination of All Forms of Discrimination Against Women. Full text of the convention in English on UN website at http://www.un.org/womenwatch/daw/cedaw/ (accessed 25 January 2008).

———. Human Rights of Women. Fact sheet no. 9. UN website (accessed February 2008).

United Nations Office for the Coordination of Humanitarian Affairs. "Afghanistan-Iran-Pakistan: Largest Refugee Election Participation in History." Integrated Regional Information Networks. 16 November 2004. PlusNews website (accessed 16 November 2004).

United Nations Security Council. "Women, Peace, Watch: Beijing Declaration and Security." Platform for Action, 1995. PeaceWomen website (accessed 5 May 2008).

United States. Department of Defense. "Bremer Says Transition to Iraqi Sovereignty Gaining Momentum." 23 February 2004. U.S. Embassy Italy website (accessed 15 October 2004).

United States. Department of State. Bureau of Democracy, Human Rights, and Labor. 2004. "Report on Religious Freedom." 2004. Online (accessed 21 May 2008).

——. "Report on the Taliban's War against Women." 17 November 2001. Online (accessed 17 January 2007).

United States. Government Accounting Office. Report to the Committee on International Relations, House of Representatives. *Afghanistan Security: Efforts to Establish Army and Police Have Made Progress, but Future Plans Need to Be Better Defined.* June 2005. Online (accessed 23 August 2007).

——. Report to Congressional Committees. *Afghanistan Drug Control: Despite Improved Efforts, Deteriorating Security Threatens Success of U.S. Goals.* November 2006. Online (accessed 23 August 2007).

Voll, John Obert. *Islam: Continuity and Change in the Modern World.* Boulder: Westview, 1982.

White Balloon, The. Directed by Abbas Kiarostami, 1995.

White House. Office of the Press Secretary. "Fact Sheet: The Way Forward in Afghanistan and Pakistan." 1 December 2009. Online (accessed 30 January 2010).

——. "President Bush Meets with President Karzai of Afghanistan." Press release. 15 June 2004. Online (accessed 15 October 2004).

——. "President Urges Readiness and Patience." Remarks by the President, Secretary of State Colin Powell, and Attorney General John Ashcroft. Press release. 15 September 2001. Online (accessed 20 October 2004).

——. "Radio Address by Laura Bush to the Nation." Press release. 17 November 2001. Online (accessed 8 October 2004).

Whitlock, Gillian. "The Skin of the *Burqa*: Recent Life Narratives from Afghanistan." *Biography* 28, no. 1 (2005), 54–76.

Wiggerhaus, Rolf. *The Frankfurt School: Its History, Theories, and Political Significance.* Translated by Michael Robertson. Cambridge: MIT Press, 1994.

Women Living under Muslim Laws website. Online at http://www.wluml.org/ (accessed February 2008).

Women's International League for Peace and Freedom. "CEDAW Chairperson Applauds New Afghan Constitution." Peace Women website (accessed 15 January 2008).

World Bank. "Afghanistan: National Reconstruction and Poverty Reduction—The Role of Women in Afghanistan's Future." 2005. Online (accessed 18 May 2007).

Yuval-Davis, Nira, and Floya Anthias, eds. *Women-Nation-State.* London: Macmillan, 1989.

Zine, Jasmine. "Between Orientalism and Fundamentalism: The Politics of Muslim Women's Feminist Engagement." *(En)Gendering the War on Terror: War Stories and Camouflaged Politics*, edited by Krista Hunt and Kim Rygiel, 27–50. Hampshire, England: Ashgate, 2006.

——. "Muslim Women and the Politics of Representation." *American Journal of Islamic Social Sciences*, special issue, "Islam and Women," 19, no. 4 (2002), 1–22.

Žižek, Slavoj. *Welcome to the Desert of the Real! Five Essays on September 11 and Related Dates*. New York: Verso, 2002.

Contributors

GWEN BERGNER is an associate professor of English at West Virginia University. She is the author of *Taboo Subjects: Race, Sex, and Psycho-analysis* (University of Minnesota Press, 2005) and articles on race and postcolonial theory in *American Quarterly*, PMLA, *The Psychoanalysis of Race*, and *Frantz Fanon: Critical Perspectives*. She is currently working on a book tentatively titled *Legal Tender: Tales of Law, Justice, and Civic Authority* about human rights, immigration, and U.S. nationalism.

MALIHA CHISHTI is currently a Ph.D. candidate at the University of Toronto. She is the former director of the Hague Appeal for Peace and a participant in the NGO working group that initiated the historic Security Council Resolution 1325 on Women, Peace, and Security. She has worked as a gender consultant in Afghanistan on the Arghandab-Irrigation Project in Kandahar and conceptualized and supervised a postconflict capacity-building training program for more than ninety women's organizations across Afghanistan.

CHESHMAK FARHOUMAND-SIMS is an assistant professor in the Con-flict Studies Program at Saint Paul University in Ottawa and a conflict resolution consultant. Her current work focuses on the consequences of international engagement and policies in Afghanistan, especially as they pertain to Afghan women. She traveled to Afghanistan in 2003 and 2008 and has served on the Afghan Women's Advocacy Committee of Canada. She is currently a member of the Afghan Reference Group.

NIGEL C. GIBSON is director of the Honors Program at Emerson College in Boston. He is the author of *Fanon: The Postcolonial Imagination* (Polity Press, 2003), the editor of *Rethinking Fanon: The Continuing Dialogue* (Humanity Books, 1999), and the coeditor of *Contested Terrains and Constructed Categories: Contemporary Africa in Context* (Westview, 2002), *Adorno: A Critical Reader* (Blackwell, 2002), and *Biko Lives* (Palgrave, 2008).

ZUBEDA JALALZAI is an associate professor of English at Rhode Island College in Providence, specializing in postcolonial theory and early American literature. She has written articles on early American, Native American, and Caribbean literatures as well as on representations of Afghanistan, transatlanticism, and postcolonial and feminist theories.

DAVID JEFFERESS is an assistant professor of English and cultural studies at the University of British Columbia, Okanagan. His first book, *Postcolonial Resistance: Culture, Liberation, and Transformation,* was published in 2008. He has also published numerous articles, including postcolonial critiques of discourses of development aid, human rights, and Canadian identity.

ALTAF ULLAH KHAN is an assistant professor of journalism and mass communication at the University of Peshawar in Pakistan. He is the author of *Indo Pak Press: An Unpopular View* (A. H. Publishers, 1998) and *News Media and Journalism in Pakistan and Germany* (Owais, 2003) and has translated the works of the American philosopher poet Khalil Gibran into Pashto. Khan has worked as a strategic communication consultant for the Federally Administered Tribal Area Capacity Building Project and is the project director of a training program for journalists in the tribal areas of Pakistan's North West Frontier Province, funded by the United States Institute of Peace. He was a Fulbright professor at the Center for International Studies at Ohio University (2008–9). His current research involves community radio in the NWFP.

KAMRAN RASTEGAR is an assistant professor of Arabic literature at Tufts University, where he teaches comparative cultural and literary histories of the modern Middle East. His recent publications include "Trauma and Maturation in Women's War Narratives: *The Eye of the Mirror* and *Cracking India*" in *Journal of Middle Eastern Women's Studies* and *Literary Modernity between Europe and the Middle East* (Routledge, 2007). His translation of Mahmoud Dowlatabadi's novel *Missing Soluch* was published by Melville House Press in 2007.

RODNEY J. STEWARD received a Ph.D. in history from Auburn University in 2007 and is assistant professor of history at the University of South Carolina, Salkehatchie. His fields of research (American, modern European, and Islamic) are pulled together by his focus on traditional societies in conflict with the onslaught of modernity.

IMRE SZEMAN is Canada Research Chair of Cultural Studies at the University of Alberta. He is the author of *Zones of Instability: Literature, Postcolonialism, and the Nation* (Johns Hopkins University Press, 2003), the coauthor of *Popular Culture: A User's Guide* (Nelson, 2004, 2nd ed. 2009), and the coeditor of *Pierre Bourdieu: Fieldwork in Culture* (Rowman and Littlefield, 2000), *The Johns Hopkins Guide to Literary Theory and Criticism* (Johns Hopkins University Press, 2005), and *Canadian Cultural Studies: A Reader* (Duke University Press, 2009).

Index

ZUBEDA JALALZAI is an associate professor of English at Rhode Island College.

DAVID JEFFERESS is an assistant professor of English at the University of British Columbia. He is the author of *Postcolonial Resistance: Culture, Liberation, and Transformation* (2008).

Library of Congress Cataloging-in-Publication Data

Globalizing Afghanistan : terrorism, war, and the rhetoric of nation building /
edited by Zubeda Jalalzai and David Jefferess.
p. cm. — (American encounters/global interactions)
Includes bibliographical references and index.
ISBN 978-0-8223-5001-9 (cloth : alk. paper)
ISBN 978-0-8223-5014-9 (pbk. : alk. paper)
1. Afghanistan—History—2001–
2. Afghan War, 2001–
3. Women—Afghanistan—Social conditions.
4. Afghanistan—Foreign relations—United States.
5. United States—Foreign relations—Afghanistan.
I. Jalalzai, Zubeda II. Jefferess, David III.
Series: American encounters/global interactions.
DS371.4.G563 2011   658.104'7—dc22   2010049718